Henry S Brown

The Bible of the Religion of Science

Henry S Brown

The Bible of the Religion of Science

ISBN/EAN: 9783337100193

Printed in Europe, USA, Canada, Australia, Japan

Cover: Foto ©Lupo / pixelio.de

More available books at **www.hansebooks.com**

Yours for the True Religion
H. S. Brown M. D,
Milwaukee Wisconsin

—OF THE—

RELIGION OF SCIENCE

—BY—

H. S. BROWN M D.

AUTHOR OF

"A Permanent Republic Cannot be Established by Despotic Family Laws," "Scientific Spiritualism is the Basis of a Scientific Religion and Government,"
and other Works.

The law god is the true natural god that agrees with the natural man, and all of the spiritual and material sciences.

The god of revelations or words is an enemy of the natural god and the natural man, and all the natural, spiritual, moral and social sciences.

MILWAUKEE, WISCONSIN.
PUBLISHED BY THE AUTHOR.
AUGUST 1st, 1882.

This volume is most respectfully dedicated to those persons who will cordially unite with others to establish the religion of truth and a just government, by the scientific methods of reason, experience, experiments and observations. For this is the way to wisdom, and to the material, mental, moral, social, and spiritual sciences, that make peace on earth and good will among men.

BY THE AUTHOR

Entered according to Act of Congress in the year 1882, by H. S. BROWN, M. D., in the Office of the Librarian of Congress, at Washington, D. C.

GODFREY & CRANDALL, PRINTERS, 114 MICHIGAN ST., MILWAUKEE.

PREFACE

When the last writer in the christian's holy bible was inspired to use the following language near its end, it gives all people a fair chance to judge what the real characters of the Gods, spirits and men were that inspired the whole book, and the kind of religions and governments they would establish on earth. "If any man shall add unto these things, God shall add unto him the plagues that are written in this book. And if any man shall take away from the words of the book of this prophecy, God shall take away his part out of the book of life, and out of the holy city and from the things which are written in this book." This shows that the writer of the sentences, and the spirits back of him were so self satisfied, and self conceited that they thought they had stated all things right, and made no mistakes in words or prophecies in the book. Yet from Genesis to Revelations, their words concerning the making of the heavens and earth are acknowledged to convey falsehoods to the minds of ordinary readers; the word day means an immense period of time, or it is false in fact. And the words of the revelator, in the last book in the bible, convey equally false ideas regarding the punishing of the wicked in the bottomless pit, and the rewarding of the just in heaven, and are the fabrications of persons who had the lowest idea of the God of heaven and his angels that ever entered the minds of wicked deceivers; and all through the books of the bible are stories and dogmatisms that would disgrace any man to tell as facts, or assert as just, in this age; yet these falsehoods were allowed to be believed by the people as true, until the scientists demonstrated them to be false.

The Astronomers first exposed some of these falsehoods, then came other scientists, and last of all came the scientific spiritualists. Then the Jewish and Christian priests discovered that the words of their bible were right, but their interpretations of them were wrong; and so the nations had been deceived for thousands of years. The writers who thought themselves such adepts in the use of words as to do this or who intended to deceive mankind, need no preface or introduction to the readers of their works; that task could well be left to priestly interpreters and translators. But all ordinary men and spirit writers, require or like to say a word to their readers about the reasons for the publications; some writers have not only put in a preface to their book, but left a blank leaf in it for the readers to have one page at least that would suit them if they could write such a page and wanted to have it in the book; modern writers outside the divinity schools, are anxious to be fairly understood; they want their words, sentences, and paragraphs to convey to the reader the same ideas that the writer has when he pens them. He does not want to use language to hide ideas, but to clearly express them, so that any intelligent reader will know distinctly what the writer means by what he says.

This is especially the wish of the writer of this book; he wants the critical and criticising readers to so understand it; and if they find passages, that are false in fact or unjust in principle, he wishes them pointed out, that they may be corrected in some subsequent edition or publication. And as he apprehends that the greatest curse that any religious book has ever inflicted on humanity has been done by claiming for it two meanings, one earthly that was plain to all and one or more spiritual meanings that was hidden from the minds of the great mass of readers, who never would have thought of it if the spiritual preacher had not come along and explained it. My object is to write a religious book that will be so plain that every reader of it will understand its spiritual, earthly, and all other meanings, without the aid of a spiritual preacher. And yet be so full of undamental religious truths as to attract the attention of every person who wishes to establish the religion of truth and humanity among the people of the earth.

Let all the pure in heart and mind, who are willing and determined to do their duty in the hard work of life, according to their ability, and acquire all the knowledge they can of their responsibilities in life, and live in accord with the best principles that are known and can be put in practice, join together as one person, on the scientific plan, which has been the greatest blessing to mankind that is known to man ; to establish the social, moral and religious sciences ; and after many hardships, trials and afflictions, the same that the material and spiritual scientists have suffered, they will succeed, because the God of the sciences is the true God, and the plan of the scientists the true plan, and the works of the scientists the just works that will harmonize the people to each other and to the true God. Hoping to see all the true and faithful people of the earth, with the purest spirits of heaven joined in love and harmony, to do this great work, and establish peace among the people of earth, I respectfully present this book to them and the public generally, for them to judge of its true value in directing the people how to live the most noble and useful lives. THE AUTHOR.

BOOK FIRST.

The Religious Teachings of Inspirations.

	PAGE.
CHAPTER I	1
Preparing to Make Time Out of Eternity.	
CHAPTER II	14
Making the Sun.	
CHAPTER III	22
The Making of the Planets.	
CHAPTER IV	32
The Earth and Its Productions Until Man Appears.	
CHAPTER V	40
Time from the Beginning of the Sun Until Man Appears on Earth.	
CHAPTER VI	59
Theology or God-making.	
CHAPTER VII	74
The Difference in the Time it Took to Make the Heavens and Earth as Estimated by Jews and Christians and by Scientists.	

BOOK SECOND. 86

The Religious Teachings of the Material Sciences.

CHAPTER VIII	86
Astronomy and the Religion It Teaches.	
CHAPTER IX	95
The Religious Teachings of the Science of Geology.	
CHAPTER X	101
The Religious Teachings of the Science of Chemistry.	
Fire, Caloric or Heat	108
Light	109
Electricity	113
Attraction of Gravitation	115
CHAPTER XI	118
The Religion Taught by the Science of Botany.	

CHAPTER XII 126
   Zoology—The Religious Teachings of the Science of the
   Origin and Growth of Animals.

BOOK THIRD. 135

The Religious Teachings of the Mental and Spiritual Sciences.

CHAPTER XIII 135
   The Religious Teachings of the Sciences of Reason, Mathematics and Phrenology.

CHAPTER XIV 145
   The Religious Teachings of the Science of Magnetism, Psychology, Psychometry or Mesmerism.

CHAPTER XV 153
   The Religious Teachings of the Science of Spiritualism as Proved Through Mediums in Their Varied Manifestations. Does a Little Spirit and Matter Know More Than the Whole? 163
   Phases of Spirit Manifestations.
      The Raps 175
      The Writing 176
      Laying Hands on the Sick 176
      Slate Writing 180
      Spirit Photographs 185
      The Levitation of Persons . . . 185
      Fire Test 185
      Spirit Materialization 186
      Clairvoyance 188
      Spirits Control a Hand or Arm . . 189
      Flower Mediums 190
      Articles Disappear from a Close Room and Reappear . 191

BOOK FOURTH. 198

The Religious Teachings of Some of the Sciences and Part Sciences.

CHAPTER XVI 198
   The Religious Teachings of Music, of Phonography, of Photography, Telegraphing and Inventions.
   The Echo 205

CHAPTER XVII 210
   The Religious Teachings of Agriculture.

CHAPTER XVIII 217
   The Religious Teachings of the Science, and Theory and Practice of Medicine Physiology . . . 228
   Pathology 231

CHAPTER XIX - - - - - - 236
　　The Religious Teachings of the Science of Law-making.

CHAPTER XX - - - - - 251
　　The Religious Teachings of Prophecy.

BOOK FIFTH. 259

　　The Sciences to be Formed and Adopted to Enable the People to Establish Just Governments, Systematized Knowledge, and a Scientific Religion.

CHAPTER XXI - - - - - 259
　　The Science of Morals.

CHAPTER XXII - - - - - 277
　　The Social Science.

CHAPTER XXIII - - - - - 295
　　The Science of Government.
　　　　Who Shall be Voters - - - - - 302
　　　　Who Shall be Voted for - - - - - 304
　　　　Salaries of Officers - - - - - 314
　　　　Money and Currency - - - - - 319
　　　　Taxes - - - - - - 341
　　　　Common Schools - - - - - 346
　　　　Criminals and Insane - - - - - 347
　　　　The Removal of the Capitol from Washington, D. C. - 354
　　　　Railroads and Their Management - - 361
　　　　Telegraph Companies - - - - 366
　　　　Miners and Manufacturers - - - - 366

CHAPTER XXIV - - - - - 372
　　The Religious Teachings of all the Sciences and Part Sciences.

CHAPTER XXV. - - - - 396
　　Conclusion.
　　　　Scientific Worship Requiring Just Judgment - - 402

THE BIBLE.

OF THE

RELIGION OF SCIENCE.

BOOK FIRST.

THE RELIGIOUS TEACHINGS OF INSPIRATIONS.

CHAPTER I.

PREPARING TO MAKE TIME OUT OF ETERNITY.

The law of nature is God—The shape of God is not known to science—space is filled with matter. Law is a natural intelligent power—Life powers in man wear out. Things made in eternity are made in no time—If God made the world in a day He can destroy it in a day. The writers of the Bible did not show as much knowledge as was known when they wrote—crash of worlds and wreck of matter. Time began with the sun—Earth's time began with the earth—The first man on earth—We begin time by years now, we go back to ages, and back of them to periods of time—matter can not exist without space—suns may contend for matter on the middle space between them. The law God does not need rest.—The world is not destroyed because the word God got tired.

BEFORE the beginning of time, was eternity. All space was filled with matter, spirit, force and perhaps motion. But eternity has the stillness of death, a cold motionless condition. or a little of order and a little of disorder, an irregular orderless motion to experiment with, like a man who is inventing a machine and builds it up a little, and tears it down again, and then builds and tears down until he gets a correct model in his mind; then he goes to work and completes the machine. Now the law God of eternity knew all things, all that was needed to prepare for time, and all the irregular motions that were necessary to prepare matter, spirit, force and motion to obey the laws of order and progress that would exactly measure time, and prepared these materials to come to time always. So the time measurement could be estimated without error. Or He was like man, and made experiments to learn by experience as man learns, and then set the works of time in motion so that it could be easily estimated by man as it now is, or the materials or immaterials of eternity were all ready to obey orders and establish time when called to the work, and needed no preparation or movement until they were called upon to make time. The God that science points out, is the law of nature; composed of all the natural essences and powers of the heavens and earth.

Wherever this matter and power exists, there is the natural ruling law God of the universalem or of all space where matter exists; and wherever space is, there is matter, so far as science can demonstrate its saying, space despises a vacuum. A scientist may imagine and put forth his idea of the shape of this God, and he may say because man is the most intelligent being he ever saw, that nature's God is shaped like him; or if they have any other shape, that they think is superior to man's, they may say their God is of that shape. But science does not give shape to its deity; it has not seen the form, and does not guess what it is; or what it should be. But it estimates its power by its work or by its manifestations. Science sees nothing back of the laws of nature to enforce them, so it makes these natural laws God, and it has determined that each law is an intelligent force that knows its duty and does it always and on time. The laws of attraction and repulsion may be the fingers of a personal God who has all the laws in His head and sends them out to do their work on time in all materialized space; and so of other laws; but as we do not know of any such personal head, it is better to hold that all nature is God, and each law is its own energizing power, not dependent on any other power to assist it; and yet are worked so harmoniously that there is never a break or mistake in the working of any law of nature. The life powers of every person are given to a certain extent to enable the person to live a certain length of life, if he lives in accord with the out-side laws of nature that give him health, that assures him the longest life that it is possible for him to live; and if he does not live in harmony with the life powers that give him good health, they will give out sooner than they would if he complied with these laws.

In time all beings and things and powers are under the natural law; and when man or any animal will not or does not obey the law that acts for its best good, it will sooner perish than if it did. And it may be that matter and spirit is being constantly thrown off of this world that is not wanted for its use now, and that other matter and spirit is coming to the world that is needed. When these views of earthly and timely matters are taken into consideration, the question naturally arises, what was the condition of things in the eternity that preceded time? The most reasonable idea is that it was a state of preparation for the incoming of the suns and worlds that were necessary to inaugurate time in some parts of the space occupied by eternity. The general impression got from the religious world is that it was chaos,—matterless and motionless in short—a vacuum where their God resides, who is without body or parts; that is, He is nothing, which the scientists say natural law despises and will not allow to exist; who can have any belief in the idea that the God of words spoke all these worlds into existence, and made them from nothing on the spur of the moment? The idea is so ridiculous that even the children of this age know better. When the statement was made to a boy that God could do every thing, he says no; God cannot make a three year old colt in three minutes. But when God makes a colt in eternity it is made in no time. Yet the account of the ancient religionists was that the earth and all its colts and cattle, with the sun, moon and all the stars, were made in six days, which was a much greater work than making a single colt three years old in one second of time. God spoke and this world was created. God spoke and the sun, moon and stars were created. God spoke the word and all kinds of cattle were made; and lastly He spoke and

a man was created; then He spoke again to make
women; but there are two accounts; one is that a man
and woman were created at one time. There is a little
conflict in the inspiration of the writers of the Jewish
bible, and people can take that which suits them. In
this way time was commenced, according to the inspirations of the Jewish and christian bible, and this God
is going to distroy time and the heavens and earth and
all things therein by his word, as He made them. The
inspirations of the bible, taken from Genesis to revelations inclusive, show that in their judgment a word has
made all things in time; and a word will unmake them
and bring on another eternity; and the last of these
writings were made by christian accounts nearly a
hundred years after the reign of Augustus Cæsar,
when all the learning of the Greeks and Romans was
known to the learned of that period. It seems the
religious writers and people of that age were the most
ignorant or malicious.of persons, and remained so for
hundreds of years, until the bible was finished, adopted
and declared God's sacred word of truth. In all this
time they seem to think that God made time and the
heavens and earth, the same as great kings make
nobles, earls and lords of the kingdom by His breath
or word; and the ignorant and superstitious often think
their king is God, and so worship him; and the whole
religious world have been making Gods by their words
in the same way. So the principle prevails of making
Gods that have no power only what the people give
them, and rejecting the law God of nature who rules

by His natural laws. But the scientific God, or the God of science, works by the laws of order, progress, and the regular succession of events, to establish time.

But when we go back of time, science becomes silent; calculations are made, and speculations entered into, and inspirations considered; and all are made the most, that the mind of man can make; it cuts loose from the facts of time, and goes candidly but ignorantly into the confines of eternity to try and find out what was going on there.

When the Christians say nothing existed except the God who was made of nothing, and all the other denominations of religious people have about the same idea. One expression in Shakespeare may be considered as giving the best and most poetical description of the doings in eternity according to scientific principles.

There was a "crash of worlds and wreck of matter." It was an orderless motion. It was the eternity when the laws of nature were getting their grip on spirit, matter, force and motion. There would be eternities when the law would not have power to make the powers that opposed the laws, obey, and then a crash would take place or a miracle would be wrought. One law might get control for a little eternity, and things would go well in that department; but entirely irregular in other departments; so that no time could be calculated. Then that law would cease to rule, and others be in command.

For instance, suppose the law of attraction to have power to enforce its commands, and repulsion to have no control, then all would go well for a little eternity; but soon there would be a crash of worlds; and suppose the law of repulsion to be in full force, and attraction had lost its power of control, then things would go well for a little season, but soon there would be a wreck of matter. These speculations might be indulged in for a long time. But they are outside of all great, vigorous and healthy organizations except of religion, and would be of that if it did not include every thing.

And now is the time to consider when eternity ended for the last time, when time began for the first time. Time first commenced in this solar system when the life-giving principles or laws that the sun had become sufficiently strong to command all spirit, matter, force and motion, needed to begin its work in regular order. There is the first beginning of time that we knew anything about. And this we only know by the inspiration of knowledge. After a vast amount of research the conclusion was reached that the sun was first formed, then planets, and then satelites. These commenced their formation in the substance of the sun, or outside of it but within its magnetic circle, so near to it that it could hold them in their orbit by its attractive and repulsive forces. But the sun was alone for millions of earth years before the first planet was thrown off; then the others were thrown into their orbits, until the earth appeared; each of the planets began its time out of eternity or out of the sun's time.

When we take into account the earth's time, we begin on the scientific plan, when it first rolled into its orbit; that was millions of earth years ago; or we take the old Jewish, Christian or Pagan religious ideas that time began but a little time before man appeared on the earth; and they thought and taught, and their followers now teach, that the earth was first made by the word of God; and the first time that it got separated from eternity was by His word made the beginning of earth time. That is, God spake the earth into existence; made it out of nothing, and at once time commenced by days on earth. This is a very definite separation, marked by the distinct formation. It was eternity a moment before the earth was made, it was time a moment after; and in a few days there was a man made, male and female, to mark the time, to converse with the God who performed the wonderful deed, and to be instructed in his duties on this new and productive earth.

If these inspirations could be proved true, there would be no difficulty in establishing exactly when the time of earth began, and the eternity of nothing ended. But here is the great question to be settled and although they have a geneology and a chronology that is continuous and unbroken for nearly three thousand years, and is continued in broken but generally continuous dates for another thousand. The first two thousand years of earth's time and the time man was made there is not the least error in the record of the genealogy, or it is continuous, so that if it actually took place as recorded, it is a marvel for any age.

But the nearer one comes to the historical age, the more difficult it becomes to calculate the time, and finally it ceases, about the time the Jews returned from their captivity in Babylon. This shows that the first inhabitants of the earth kept remarkably correct records, or they were made by some intelligent witness since, regardless of the truth, but determined to have them read well.

But notwithstanding all these inspirational statements of the works of their God, and men and their records, their truth is very much questioned, and proved false by the works and the fossil remains of vegetable and animal life. Time on earth did not begin in that way, and the first man on earth was not sufficiently intelligent to report any conversation with man or God. If we go to the Pagan nations, (and although they may have a different date for the beginning of time, they have the same general plan,) time commenced with their God making the earth; and they have monuments, relics and records to prove that the earth is a great deal older than the Jews make it; but the question regarding these is, is the true date of their being erected or made given? and their Gods have manifested no more power than the Christian God has, and He or they are not natural or historical Gods only in their religious history. And the scientists have to fall right back on the God of nature, the law God of the universalem, to determine as well as they can when time commenced and eternity ended.

If he starts now and goes back on the line of time as recorded by man, before he gets back three thousand years all dates are apochryphal, and then comes the time to be reckoned by ages of hyeroglyphics; for one character shows the last of that age, another shows the first; then back of that comes the age of copper, then back of that the stone, and back of this the wood age, which has left no vestige of its existence; and all the vestiges of man's work are ended in the rot and wear that has come upon them since that distant period of time. Then the scientist looks into the last leaf that the God of nature—the Law God—laid upon the earth, that is the soil that lays on the surface of the earth, over the rocks; here he finds productions of animal and vegetable life that speak of a space in time so long that he drops years and ages and adopts periods; and yet these are the ages of more generations of animals than we know how to estimate.

Then the scientist takes the top layer of the rocks and finds an immensely long period of time; and so he goes on until he comes to the bottom rock, and then calculates the time since the earth rolled into its orbit, and it dwarfs into insignificance, the longest time ever thought of by the most startling records of the length of time claimed by any religious people on earth; even the Chinese records are giving only an instant of time compared with the lapse of years, ages and periods of time that science points out as the beginning of earth time.

Then the scientist goes back of earth time to the sun's time, or to the sun's eternity; for if time commenced with the earth, here was an orderly eternity marked by many periods that man can make calculating guesses about their length, as well as he can of the earth periods of time; and when he has calculated the sun's time or eternity, then he goes back of our sun to the time when the great central sun existed, before our sun began to be made. That is, if it did exist. The proof that such a sun exists now, is derived principally from inspiration and spirit communications. It belongs to the theoretical or guessing part of astronomy. But supposing it does exist, and is as much older than our sun, as our sun is older than the oldest man on earth, and we have what may truly be called an eternity of time; that does away with the idea entirely that there is, or ever was an eternity without time, any more than that there was an eternity without matter. It is just as impossible to have space without matter, as it is to have matter without space.

From this it is plainly seen that the scientific principles of what made up the eternity of the past are just as different from the Christians' and Jews', as is their word God from the scientific law God. Then the way they went to work to separate earth time from eternity shows that their's was not the same God in principles, powers and duties, or in their plans of educating and governing mankind.

It is just as well to say that time commenced with earth time as any other way, because man can estimate the time by days as the earth rolls over every day, and circles in its orbit around the sun every year. It makes it a very easy way for man to estimate time in his short life on earth. But when man goes to his spirit home, where he lives for long periods of time in one sphere, he does not want to reckon by records with all the other multiples of time until he comes to years; and I have little idea how short a time they would want to divide up the long period of spirit life in one sphere; it may be that a hundred of our years would not seem in that life longer than one hour does in this; so that what we call a little eternity here would to us there be but a short time. But the only place where it seems possible for miracles and special providences, and where a crash of worlds and wreck of matter can occur upon scientific principles, is on the outskirts of the influence of the suns upon matter that they want to accumulate for their own use; and although they are twenty billions of miles apart, yet the lines of the attraction and repulsion of each may not be well defined, and the laws of each of the suns may perform prodigies of valor in collecting materials to make the largest and best sun; and in this conflict a chaos would be created that would allow every miracle to be performed that the most zealous worshipers of a word-god could think of or desire; only one thing they could not do; when they once got in the reach, and under the influence of the law of time, they would have to come to time, to order and to the demands of time, and miracles would cease to be produced, and special providences could not be made.

One thing is worthy of special notice : The natural law God never was known to get tired and require rest ; when he has promised to do some work, people find it done on time. There might be a suspicion that the word God would be so fatigued that He would be unable to do as He agreed to, because He might be so tired that He could not. This may have been the reason why the world has not been destroyed before, as so many of His prophets have prophesied it would be; and that may be the reason why time continues, and the earth and all the people have not been sent into the new eternity. When people find out that there is a second of variation in the law God's time in a day, they may truly prophesy that great changes, if not great catastrophes, will occur to the world and to man.

CHAPTER II.

THE MAKING OF THE SUN.

Earth time began with the earth, sun; time began with the sun, and tha and eternity is about the same to man. Science makes a religion of knowledge. The sun made to give light to prepare worlds to make man. The first sun began the first time. Distance from sun to sun. The genesis description of the making of the sun should not be taught to children. The sun collected what it wanted and rejected what it did not want. If people adopt any other God but nature they become murderers, whether Christ or Mohammed or Joe Smith. Nature's God takes care of himself. The worship of nature's God consists of good deeds and not of good words.

WE have seen in the previous chapter how difficul it is to determine by inspiration (and we have no other means) when time commenced. That is, what epoch man shall select to say when time commenced; was it when the great central sun was created, if we have such a sun, or when our sun was formed, or when the earth was formed and took its place among the planets in its orbit? or was it when man was made on the earth; or shall we say it commenced when the people of the earth became as intelligent as the Adam of the Jews was, and could calculate the coming seasons of each year, and could divide the time into seconds, minutes, hours, days, weeks, months and years? The object in asking these questions is to determine whether the beginning of the making of the sun was the beginning of time? or was the sun began and finished in eternity?

This question is important only when we talk of the making or forming of the sun upon scientific principles. There may be some doubt whether it should be called eternity, or time; but this we know, it is now working on time. Regarding this matter; this question will be treated as unsettled, and the expression of time and eternity will be applied to the space of time or eternity from the beginning of the forming of the sun until the earth rolls into its orbit. One name is as appropriate as the other. It would have no significance, only all the old religions treat the beginning of time as something that commenced with the formation of the earth; and but a few years ago, compared with the scientific religious ideas that are now working in the human mind. Science has unsettled all these notions of whatever interest they had attached to them, by declaring that the sun was made before the earth, and many stars also; and the natural law God worked to make all the heavenly bodies and the earth on such a different plan than that of the word Gods, that when the scientific principles harden into the scientific religion, it will be the religion of knowledge; such a one as the people of the earth never saw or heard of before.

This is the reason why it should be carefully considered at this time.

When the Law God had fixed upon the plan of establishing time in the space that is occupied by our solar system, the first great object to be attained was to have light; so the first business of law was to make a sun or suns to give light, and prepare for the making of other worlds, and finally to prepare a world or worlds where man could appear and live, and learn the ways of God to man, and understand the laws of nature; and finally to be able to be the companion of the God of the laws of nature if His existence admits of companionship. It will be seen that if our sun was the first sun that was started, it was the beginning of time in the first degree in the universe of space. If many suns were begun at the same time, then time commenced in many places at the same time. But they have determined that the beginning of time in our solar system was the beginning of the making of our sun; when the life center of our sun made its first movement to work out its destiny it marked the first movement of time in our solar system.

But how many thousands of centuries ago this happened, they have not determined. But one thing is certain, they allow that the sun had an immense amount of work to do; and an immense amount of power to do it; and time that is numbered by millions on millions of years to accomplish its work in.

The first work it had to do was to build itself up with the elements that were required to make all the planets and all satelites with all the vegetable and animal life that was to be made on them. And if our sun was the first sun started, it had all space to draw its spirit, matter, force and motion from, to build itself up with, and all the power of the law of nature to work with, until other suns of other systems were started. But if other suns of other systems were started at the same time our sun was, then each would be likely to draw their needed supplies from half the distance from sun to sun, and our sun would draw from space half the distance to the nearest suns in all directions. Now it must be considered that all space is filled with matter and spirit, and that the law of nature, God, had power to work this great amount of material into suns and worlds, planets, satelites, meteors, comets and systems of suns and their planets, or as much of this material as was needed for these purposes.

Then the heart of the sun commenced its movements with power to attract all the material it wanted, and repel all the substances that it did not need; in this way it grew from a mere speck of light in space until it obtained a body of nearly six thousand millions of miles in diameter, and became a great light in the system of suns then existing. This great body was collected with the greatest care under the laws of attraction and repulsion; not one particle of matter or spirit that was not needed was suffered to remain in it, and any particles that were needed and used at one time, if not needed in a subsequent time, were thrown off; and all the substances in the sun were worked over until the body of the sun was completed and ready for its next work. The space from which all this matter was taken, must also be prepared with its ether to hold this sun and all its coming children, the planets, in their places in their orbits. The rejected spirit and matter and force and motion was in the ether between the suns, to make it so strong that not a sun, or a child of a sun, could break through it only when required by the law of nature; and the distances between the suns was calculated so there would be no jar or conflict among them. The distance from our sun to the nearest sun in the heavens is estimated to be twenty billions of miles in round numbers; that is, in

Numerals, 20,000,000,000,000 of miles.
Sun's diameter, . 6,000,000,000 "
_____

Difference, 19,994,000,000,000 "

This will give the reader an indea of the great difference in the distance between the sun's center and circumference, and to the other sun, and if the other sun was equally as large, there would be no danger of their outer circumferences touching each other and rubbing together so as to spoil the work that had been done by so much labor and care. It will be seen I have taken the whole diameter of the sun, when but half of it is towards the other sun's side at any time, and the half of the other sun is towards our sun so the figures give just about the distance between the two suns when they were at their largest size. But now these suns are much smaller, and have been ever since man came on the earth. All were mere specks in space, little stars, except the sun and moon, when the ancient inspired writers said their "God made two great lights, the greater light to rule the day and the lesser light to rule the night; He made the stars also, and set them in the firmament of the heaven to give light upon the earth."

What would the people think if the God of science should make such statements in these days? Would they be inclined to say that the inspirations were very wise or true, and insist on their being put into the hands of children to be read, as true? Not one single true idea is conveyed to the child's mind by such language.

There is not one particle of scientific truth in the idea that the sun, moon and stars were made to light the earth. The sun and most of the stars that we see were made before the earth, and it would be much better to say the earth was made to serve the sun than to say as the ancients did; but the truth is, each has its duties to perform and does them well under the laws of nature; and man must learn to do his duties as well. This can not be done by theory or theology, but by observations, experience and reason, and be guided by knowledge gained in this way.

But we are now treating of the sun when it was finished to its largest size and contained all the elements that were needed to make the planets and all other bodies in our solar system, and to continue their existence until its time shall end. It lights in the most brilliant manner all the heavens of our space, including half the distance to the nearest sun, and appears like a star of the first magnitude to the inhabitants of the nearest planets of other suns to our solar system. It glows and sparkles and illuminates all this space with an inconceivable glory, and sends its rays beyond to the utmost distance where time exists, to let them know that our sun has risen, and our time has arrived when a great change in our sun's work is to commence, and all the outer space that was then occupied by the sun will be given to the use of the planets which will fly from it or be thrown from it to take their places in their orbits. All the matter accumulated in the sun for the purpose of making planets and their satelites will be sent off, and our beautiful planetary system will be established in the space the sun has occupied and prepared for it and them; and these children will be held as it were in the bosom of their parent to be warmed and fructified while their time of life continues as separate life-giving worlds.

It is a beautiful thought that this sun, this father of all his children, the planets, and their satelites, and all other little bodies like meteors and aerolites, with their vegetable and animal productions, were thrown into space that had been warmed and prepared by the father of all, the sun of glory of the heavens, who is always sending his light and heat to his children, and all the life giving powers that he has gathered with so much care in the whole time or eternity of his past existence, and thrown outside of them the powers and matter that will keep them in their places while they are ranging through their allotted space in peace and harmony, with all their productions, each one bearing its inhabitants so quietly that they do not know they are moving at all. But suppose they are on a fixed, stationary, still earth, except it is shook by an earthquake or made to tremble slightly by some great animal or by the thunder's roar or the lightning's crash, or by the falling of an avalanche of earth, rock, ice and snow, that sweeps down the mountain side with all the besom of destruction, roaring like thunder, and make the earth quiver as though its destruction was at hand. Then the inhabitants of earth look to the heavens where all seems so still and peaceful, and wish they were there where none can molest or make afraid. But it should be remembered that every star has its movement, and every planet has its racket, its thunders, and its own special disturbances, and the sun has inside heat and surface turbulence and troubles as well as the son of righteousness is said to have had in his life.

And when any people make a God out of anything but the laws of nature that made the heavens and earth, the sun, moon and stars, and establish a priesthood to appear for their God and proclaim his laws and commands, they institute a religion that makes priestly murderers for God's sake. The Jews made such a God and went to murdering people because they would not worship Him. The christians adopted the Jewish God and made a man God in addition; and as soon as they got power went to murdering people because they would not worship their one, two, three, one God. The Mohammedans adopted their one God and Mohammed as his prophet, and went to murdering people because they would not follow their God and his prophet. The Mormons adopted their one god after the Jewish fashion and Joseph Smith as his prophet, and went to murdering people who would not follow him.

Here is a little history of people who made Gods like men and said they had power to make the sun and did make it by a word; and because people would not take their words as truth, they tortured and murdered them. The adoption of such Gods make the people murderers by the commands of the priests. The reason is, their God has no power but words to make anything, or cause people to obey; and these words must be uttered by a priest under his inspiration. So the priests have to use their physical power to enforce his commands, and where people can not be made to obey, they must be murdered, or their God and religion will be a failure. But when persons adopt the natural law as God, or the laws of nature without calling them God, they have a power that can take care of itself, and not only that, but will take care of itself; and there is no power in heaven or on earth that can interfere in their special work. And the sun was made by the power of this law or these laws and was set in the heavens, and the persons who adopt these laws as their God, and then want to know their God so as to worship Him in an acceptable manner, will study the laws, instead of murdering their neighbors because they do not believe in him. They know that the natural laws punish and reward themselves and their enemies and friends, by immutable laws. If they live in accord with the laws that give them comforts and good health, they will have them; and if they live in violation of such laws, whether they know it or not, they have discomfort and ill health.

This makes their worship to consist of good works instead of good words. They see the great and glowing sun was built up by the royal laws of nature, and their own bodies and minds were made by the same kind of laws; and if they would be most happy and useful in their lives, they must do as the sun has done before them, obey strictly the laws of their being: and in this way they do all their religious duties, and will become the center of their peaceful little families and circles as the sun is the center of its great family and circles.

CHAPTER III.

THE MAKING OF THE PLANETS.

The life power of the sun—Whether the planets are made inside or outside of the sun is a question—Each sun may make a comet—1st, Neptune; 2d, Uranus; 3d, Saturn; 4th, Jupiter; 5th, the Asteroids; 6th, Mars; 7th, the Earth. The ancient religions taught that the earth was made before any other sun, moon or stars.—8th, Venus; 9th, Mercury. Ten periods passed—The planets the material mothers and the sun the material father of all production—The influence of moon and stars not fully known—The moon's rays poison fish—Comets have electrical effect on the earth—The ancients did not know a meteor from a planet—The natural God made man, and man made the word God—Thomas Paine, Bruno—Was there ever any truth in these priestly dogmas?—The truthful shall be leaders in heaven.

WHEN we take into consideration the immense power of the sun to pick out from space just the articles it wanted, and to prepare them by heat and cold to fill their places in the sun or to be thrown into space to do their work there either as planet or nebula, or in the spaces between these globular bodies of matter, we cannot comprehend the immense life power it possessed to do this work. Besides constantly sending off the light, heat, electricity, and magnetic attraction and repulsion, which were made by the life-power of the sun acting on the matter and spirit contained in it. Besides it was preparing hundreds, if not thousands, of the life center powers to make planets and their satelites and all the other bodies that traverse our planetary solar system. These were prepared either in the body of the sun when it had its greatest dimensions or within reach of its life-giving powers, where it could send its magnetic heat and life. Whether the planets were formed inside or outside of the body of the sun may be a speculative astronomical question; but that it has the mind, the body and the spirit to form them there can be no question, any more than there is that it gives life and vigor to the planets, and makes them produce animal and vegetable life as we see them on the earth at this time. There is a question whether any great bodies of matter are permitted to come into the midst of our solar planetary system that are not made by our sun.

If there are any such bodies, well known to astronomers, they are the comets. Where these are made is not known, and it may be that each sun has made a comet and has sent it to traverse the billions of miles from sun to sun, to give or leave with them the life powers that they want, and take away with them the obnoxious matter and spirit that each planetary system does not want; or it may be that these comets are made by a great central sun and sent out from it to correct every wrong condition in all the planetary systems that are in space, and return to the central sun to give off its objectional matter, and receive its life-giving powers and spirit, and the substances that are needed, and then it starts on its mission; however that may be, we find that the sun is finished to its greatest size, and one great long epoch in time is passed, and one of the first fruits of the sun that has ripened upon his surface is about to drop off, or be cast off. And it commenced, so far as is well known by astronomical calculations on this subject, by rolling Neptune from its outer surface into its orbit, and Neptune was ripe to be thrown off and take the responsibility of its life, and it went whirling into its orbit and commenced its diurnal motion around its own axis, and its annual motion in its orbit around the sun. It is estimated to be 2,745 millions of miles from the sun at this time, and its diameter is estimated to be thirty-seven thousand miles.

There may have been other planets thrown from the sun before this, but they are not well known to astronomers. But it is because astronomers have thought they have seen such planets outside of Neptune, that I have calculated that the sun was three thousand millions of miles from its center to its circumference, or was six thousand millions of miles in diameter, when it was largest.

2d—Uranus was sent from the sun and took to its orbit and quietly assumed its place, its motions and its duties as a planet. It is estimated to be 1753 millions of miles from the sun, and thirty-three thousand miles in diameter.

3d—Saturn was the the third planet that was sent from the sun. She, with her satelites, were ripened and sent off and assumed their motions and orbit. This planet is remarkable for its beautiful rings. It is estimated to be 872 millions of miles from the sun, and seventy thousand miles in diameter.

4th—Jupiter the fourth planet next ripened and took its leave of the sun and rolled into its orbit, and was soon attended by its satelites. This is the largest planet that has been found in our planetary system, and unquestionably it will accomplish the greatest work. Its distance from the sun is estimated to be 475 millions of miles, and its diameter eighty-five thousand miles.

5th—The Asteroids were the next set of planets that were thrown from the sun and took their places in their orbits. There is said to be more than one hundred and forty of them, and they are from 200 to 315 millions of miles from the sun. It may be they were a single planet when they left the sun, but it is more reasonable to suppose that each of these little planets had its life center formed in the sun, and was thrown from it separately, and had from the beginning separate orbits, the same as other and larger planets had; because natural law has order and system, and no special providences or special catastrophes, but delights in contrast; and here we have Jupiter, the largest of the planets, and the Asteroids, the smallest, side by side. And besides, the power of law is limited by order, and cannot go beyond its bounds; and when they had done the great work of making Jupiter, it would be natural for the small work to follow. But whatever the reason may be, the fact is that the greatest planet is followed by the smallest.

6th—Mars was the next planet that left the sun, ready for the life of a planet under the laws and order of time. It rolled into its orbit 139 millions of miles from the sun, and is 4,400 miles in diameter.

7th—The Earth was the next planet that took its place in its orbit, ninety-one millions of miles from the sun, and its diameter is 7912 miles. We know more of the life powers and productions of this planet than we do of any other, and many people are of the opinion that this is the only planet that can sustain the life of intelligent beings.

The religions of the past have taught that the earth was first formed, and the sun, moon and stars were made afterwards to give it light by day and night; and they wish to continue that kind of instruction notwithstanding they know it is not true.

If we are to be guided by the calculations of some of the most intelligent of modern scientists, and by the inspired words of some of the best modern mediums for spirit communications, we shall decide that there are many planets that are better prepared to support intelligent human beings than the earth is; and they are inhabited by a more intelligent people than are on earth.

But while there is so large a class of people on earth who will believe and teach according to the ancient religious traditions, and refuse to teach well known truth, it is of the greatest importance for a class of people to rise up and teach religious truth and nothing else; that is, when they cannot prove a position to be true they drop advocating it; not do as the christian priests do; keep on asserting bible stories as true when they know them to be false, and know they have been proved so; we want religious teachers that follow the examples of the true scientists: let inspirations go as questionable, and proved truth stand as the guide of people; and if we can not have an inspiration that can be proved true, let us have a religion of facts without inspiration, only as a speculation.

8th—The next planet that rolled into its orbit from the sun was Venus, which is estimated to be 66 millions of miles from the sun, and is seven thousand five hundred and ten miles in diameter. It is a bright and beautiful star that attracts much of the attention of people in the summer evenings.

9th—Mercury, the last of the well known planets that came from the sun and went to its orbit, 35 millions of miles from the sun, as estimated, and is three thousand and sixty miles in diameter.

The general opinion among Astronomers is that there are more planets in our system, some that were thrown off before Neptune, others since Mercury took its place in its orbit. John F. W. Herschel says he thinks there are about a dozen planets more in our solar system, in a work published in 1871. Supposing this to be true, these planets can not be taken into account in estimating the time or eternity of the making of our solar planetary system.

Here are at least ten immensely long periods of time marked by great and special formations in our solar system; and the heavens and earth were made and situated nearly as they now appear to us; and the earth and all the heavenly bodies were globular in form. And the heavens were resplendent with the glow and glitter of moon and stars by night, and with the still brighter sun by day, whose light dims or makes invisible the moon and stars. Then the laws made the planets, the material mothers of all the productions of life that were or were to be on them. And they made the sun to be the material father by its rays of light and heat and its magnetic and invigorating power over animals and plants. And these laws made the satelites or moons to be company for the planets in their orbit, and have an influence on their productions, which is not fully understood.

But their power to make the ocean tides is well understood; and it is well known that the moon's rays falling directly upon recently caught fish will cause them to change and decay and become unfit for food very much sooner than they will when it does not shine on them, and will even make them poisonous to man. And there is very much to learn by experiments and observations; and when the social and moral sciences are allowed to be established, so people will be in a condition to think and act on common sense principles, then the agricultural population will have, time and opportunity to closely observe the moon's influence on the growth of vegetable and animal productions. And each of the planets with their moons had and has its alloted time to roll in its orbit around the sun, and make their winter and summer North and South of the equator in their alloted year; and each was to turn on its axis in its appointed time and give their inhabitants day and night. But the sun was and is shining on some one-half of each of the planets all the time, and thus becomes the life of all its productions and the father of all its children, and gives them a day for activity and work, and a night for sleep and rest. And comets are made to flash through space and carry an electrical and magnetic influence that is not well understood.

They are said to excite the people to wars, and portend great excitement and trouble among nations. But the probability is that it will make good people do greater deeds of goodness and evil people do greater deeds of evil. That is, it gives greater energy and capacity to do any work they undertake. And then there is another office that they are said to fill; they bring supplies to the planets and their satelites, or within easy reach of their influence, so that meteors are said to fall to the earth in greater numbers when in its orbit it comes the nearest to the track of the comet; and besides they may take from the orbits of the planets the effete matter that has been left them, and so render the air of them purer because they leave a purer ether for the planet to .go through. Their duties may be to unite the planets of our solar system, by carrying from one to another what each needs, and taking away from each one what it does not need and depositing this with another that requires it for use. So the perfect balance is maintained in our solar planetary system; and besides this work they may be the agents to keep one solar system in harmony with another, carry the effete, useless matter from each system, and bring to it the useful that is needed; and there may be more of magnetism, electricity, and the powers of attraction and repulsion, than of any known material substances.

They may be constituted by law to do this, and much more, which man will find out when he leaves off worshiping the God of words and worships the God of law. Besides this, the little meteors flash through our atmosphere, and the writers of the ancient bibles took them to be the same as the suns and planets of other solar planetary systems; and the last writer of the Christian Bible it seems did not know any more about this matter than the first Jewish writer. It was entirely beyond the knowledge of any of these religious writers ; and a person reading the Bible would never suspect that there was any difference. But let anyone read astronomy a short time and the differences would be clearly in his mind. And this is the difference between Bible astronomy and scientific astronomy. And there is no advantage to be gained by attempting to reconcile them as made by the same God, or that they are relatives in any sense, only that the natural astronomical spirit and material god made man, and man made the talking, loving and hating god after his own image; and this man-made god has not as much power as man has on earth, nor so much wisdom, knowledge, discretion, justice or truth; and when a man gets under the influence of this man-made bible god he becomes insane or demented, and goes about the streets making prophecies of the wrath of God, that will be poured out upon the wicked, or that the earth will be destroyed, or he falls so low in his intellect as to call himself this god, and threatens to drown the wicked or burn up the world and the sinners that do not repent and follow him.

It was when the people of the Roman Empire became so ignorant and demented as to follow the priests of this god that the dark ages of Christendom were commenced; and they continued as long as the people implicitly obeyed the priest of their god, or the gods that the priests declared themselves to be; and the popes and bishops wrecked individuals and nations until the people began to study the laws and works of the natural god; then they assumed true manhood. They worshiped a god that priests could not imitate nor change by prayer in the least. Then the priests cried out it was blasphemy to worship such a god, and the people who did so must be tortured and murdered. And the mills of these gods were scattered over the land, and the cries of their tortured victims went heavenward, and the spirits of the murdered ones went to heaven and their blood flowed in rivulets on the earth, and filled the air with its terrible stench.

But the worship of the natural god by the natural man went on, and it was found that killing men for heresy did not prove the heresy false. And the inquiry went on until it was discovered that the knowledge gained, showed the inspired that ten immensely long periods of time or eternity had been passed, and no note made of it by the word God or any of his most inspired Bible writers; and then it dawned upon the searchers after truth what all these tortures and murders were committed for.

It was to prevent the people from learning the truth. As long as the people could be kept in ignorance, they would worship the priests or their tool the god of words. It should be remembered that these priests tortured and murdered people as long as the people would let them in this country, and are continuing these murders yet, where the people will let them. They dread with a perfect horror the inspirations which knowledge gives. For knowledge makes people think and reflect, and reflection causes them to reason ; and the priests condemn reason as dangerous, and curse the reasoner even in this country and at the present time. Just consider Thomas Paine's Age of Reason ; but they say all manner of falsehoods about the man. This they do to turn the truths which he utters into oblivion, by drawing attention to his character, which they make worse than it was, so people will not read his profound and truthful thoughts. This is their plan of action, where they cannot stop the thoughtful from uttering thoughts by cruelty. When Giordano Bruno uttered his astronomical truths and his theoretical conclusions, he was pronounced a heretic and the leader of heretics ; but was too moral and irreligious to live, because he had said that there were other worlds besides this. In this way they first blackened his character and then burnt his body ; and now they are blackening the character of Col. R. G. Ingersoll, and hunting up some old law that was made in the middle ages, and has not been repealed, to punish him because he is reasoning to stop the religious abuses that have arisen under the influence of the most pestilent and outrageous commands and laws of the God of Moses, and there is a general expression of approval of these sentiments among the religious papers ; not because he does not teach the truth, but because he is upsetting the minds of the people in their religious faith ; and it is not fully settled that such a governor as that of Delaware, at the head of a set of fanatical priests and their superstitious followers may get their merciless clutches on him and torture him into silence and prove beyond a doubt that the religionists of to-day are endowed with all the inhumanity of the Mosaic Dispensation, and all the cruelty and blood thirsty principles of the Middle Ages.

The theories put forth in these chapters may be erroneous, but those put forth by the writer of the books of Moses have been proven false. To err is human, but to torture people for stating theoretical truth or error is the diabolism of religious people. The hatred of the Christian priests to astronomers in the sixteenth century can only be estimated now by their cruelty to them. They were the first scientists to prove the falsehood of their astronomy from Genesis to Revelations. They hated them for telling the truth about the heavens and earth, especially the movements of the stars of heaven, and the earth. Now is the time for people to associate, to learn whether there is any truth in any of the priests' assertions; they have taken dogmatism for truth, and tortures and murder to prove it.

The idea now is to take astronomical truth as religious truth, and prove it by facts and figures, and reason from these premises, and show to the world that modern astronomy when put into modern religion, makes a reasonable humane religion that proclaims the peace and order of heaven to the people of earth, which says the discoverer of truth who proclaims and practices it on earth, shall be a leader of heavenly hosts and a peace-maker on earth.

CHAPTER IV.

THE EARTH AND ITS PRODUCTIONS UNTIL MAN APPEARS.

The Earth was the seventh planet and moves in its orbit and on its axis.—The Bible teaches that the earth stands still, and sun, moon and stars go around it.—The more ancient believed it rested on an elephant.—God can do all things and their word is God.—The first day and year of earth.—At first the earth was molten lava.—The earth prepared for vegetables and animals, and finally man, by being cool on the surface.—The first men were beastly and have been improving every since.—The Glacial period.—There is a fossil horse and may be a fossil man.—Man learns by experience only.—There is a royal road to knowledge.—The Bible says man was made of dust.—Such inspirations are from legends.—Their first man was very intelligent.—First man was made of dust and water.—Modern Inspirations say he was evolved from lower animals.—God's image is man.—The first man and woman stood upright; they were to fill the earth with loveliness and the heavens with joy.—The inspiration of every age is based on the knowledge of the age.—Modern inspiration agrees with modern science.

FROM what has been said it is seen that our earth was the 7th planet that rolled from the sun into its orbit, where it has moved at the rate of one million, five hundred thousand miles, more or less, in every day of twenty-four hours, besides turning on its axis at the equator twenty-four thousand miles each day, and more. These estimates are only approaches to the true distances the earth rolls along each day, and will give any reader an idea of the speed of the earth on which he or she lives and looks upon as still. But the Christians' holy bible will not give any reader the least inkling of such a movement, but will rather impress them with the idea that the earth is still, and the sun, moon and stars move around it, and prepare their minds to believe in the ancient religious notions that the earth rests on an elephant, and the elephant on a tortoise, and these on other beasts, until they exhaust their knowledge of strong beasts; and then they make a snake to reach the rest of the way to the bottom of the bottomless space. The Jews do not go so deep into this matter, but they give a description that is no more intelligent or true than the most ignorant religious people of the time; and they excel all others in their ignorant dogmatical inspirations and in their brutalizing falsehoods, and then establish a more fanciful god power, that can do all things; then go to proving it by words, and when they have done it, they call the word, God.

When the earth first rolled from the sun into its orbit, the first day of the year was the first time it turned on its axis in its orbit completely over, so that all its surface was turned to the sun and received its light, heat, and energising power. And the first year of the earth was the first time it made a complete circuit around the sun in its orbit. By turning on its axis the earth established a day of twenty-four hours for its inhabitants, and half of this day is called night, because it is dark, and the other half is called the real day because it is light; and the rays of the sun make the light, and the shadow of the earth from the sun's light makes the darkness. And the first three hundred and sixty-five of these days and a little more made the first year of the earth; in this time the earth went in its orbit round the sun for the first time, and made the first winter, spring, summer and fall of the earth. And this was the beginning of earth time, which has continued with unvarying exactness ever since.

When the earth first came from the sun it was molten lava at a white heat, surrounded by air, ether, steam and water, in the shape of rain; for when this rain fell upon the incandescent lava it was immediately converted into steam or vapor, and the atmosphere was filled with smoke and steam, and the lava was rolling in billows or was thrown up by the force of heat under its surface in billowy volcanic eruptions. And all was swaying, surging and moving in the greatest apparent confusion, and the most unintelligent commotion; but the law of order and progression began its work in this way to prepare the spirit and matter of the earth for its great work and progress in refinement, until man could have an earth and air that was suited to his needs and capacity, so he could grow in knowledge until he could learn the laws of nature that he was bound to obey, to have health, peace and security in his earth life. But at this time there was neither vegetable nor animal life on the earth, and no safe, solid place for them. All was fluid, vapor, air or ether. But the surface began to harden and become so cool in places that water would remain on its surface, and finally it became so hard that the rolling lava could not break it; and it continued to harden until the primary granite rock was formed and so thick that nothing but the strong power of volcanic eruptions could break through its crust, that covered the whole surface of the earth, and the surging, heated mass under this crust would beat against it and cause volcanoes and earthquakes.

During the immense period of time that was required for the formation of these rocks, there was very little if any vegetable or animal life and growth. But on the top of them, the secondary rocks were gradually formed, and the most crude and simple forms of vegetable and animal life are shown in the rocks by impression or petrifaction. From this time the rocks and earth show that there has been a constant improvement, until the present time, in the forms of vegetable and animal life, and new and distinct species appear, and old forms have died out and disappeared from among the living of this age. Many species seem to have perished during what is called the Glacial period, when ice of great thickness covered vast tracts of the earth, if not much more than half of it.

There is some evidence of man's existence before this time, and very likely some of the crudest forms of a primal mankind existed. But it does not seem that the earth was prepared for a well developed manhood until its surface had been cooled by ice and its soils mixed by the glacial movements in its northern hemisphere, where the most intelligent of mankind appear first. And its air purified by great changes in its temperature.

It is well known that some animals, almost like the animals at present, existed before the present species now on earth were fully formed and came upon the earth: the fossil horse is one marked spicimen, and there may have been such a man; and we may find the fossil man yet. And it is possible that it is found but not yet recognized. But after this period man appears on earth, and to all appearances they belonged to some of the present species of mankind, most of them developed so high in intellect as to enable them to make their Gods. But they were not endowed with the minds that Gods ought to possess. But the men that made them had the body of beasts and the minds of infants, not much better than the beasts of the fields; but capable of improvement that beasts have not equaled. He was surrounded by the animals and fruits of the earth for food for his body, and forced by hunger and pain to exercise his mind to supply his bodily and mental needs, under the laws of nature. His little infantile mind placed in a great coarse body gave little promise that it would be developed into a refined body and the master mind of the earth. But slowly under the influence of the laws of order and progression he is placed at the head of all the animals of the earth by his great mental capacity to acquire knowledge, and a wise way to use it. At first he had every opportunity to make great and important experiments, but he had not his mind sufficiently elevated to make them. His knowledge must come from the experiences that were forced upon him by his wants. He learned just as animals learned that were about him, and the only difference was and is, that man can learn more than animals, and can communicate their information better to their children than animals can to their young.

But they all commenced to get knowledge alike, and by the only plan that nature points out as the true way to get knowledge. Whenever man attempts to attain it in any other way he fails and grows ignorant until his mind is very little above the animals, and he becomes cruel and beastly in his habits.

To be sure there is a royal road to knowledge obtained by animal magnetism and spiritualism, but it is so apt to make the possessor of it to declare himself more than human, or a God or the son of God or the intimate counsellor of God, that the nations who put themselves under their direction are destroyed, because when these pretenders to all power are put to the test they can do but very little of what they pretend they can, and their sayings are not as important as they think or pretend to think they are. And worse than that, they are mostly false, taking the Jewish bible as a specimen.

The first man was made out of the dust of the earth directly by their God of words and oaths. Here was an inspiration made by the legendary stories of the Jews and Arabs, and has no more relation to the facts of the creation of man on earth, than has the Arabian nights entertainments to the facts of the lives of the Arabs in the desert of Sahara. Then they make the first man on this globe to be more intelligent than any man was for thousands of years after the first man was made, when we take the truest history that the inspiration that all the knowledge of the present age is derived from, the searchings, experiences and observations of the most intelligent people, combined with all inspirations that the magnetism of the earth and the spirits of heaven can give. The immediate relatives of the first man, according to Jewish inspirations and testimony, are mud puddles with a God of words to speak them into intelligent men and breathe them into spirit life; when he wants them he has only to say the word and they stand before him ready to do his bidding; or contend against his power and make him sorry that he made man in his own image or in the image of anything else; and he repented because of the actions of his one mud man and his progeny. And anyone must think it was time, when they see this word-God was cheated out of most of the world if not all of it by an inspired snake and this mud man and his help mate. This is a little inkling of the Jewish Arabian story of the origin of mankind.

But the scientific story made by the inspirations of knowledge, is that man was evolved from the earth by a long series of successions of animal life; slowly by the God of law and order, and not a word was said, no fault found; the god was pleased with the work of orderly law, and when man was created his immediate relatives were the animals around him that the law of God did not permit to stand upright; they were the monkey, the ourang-outang and the chimpanzee, or animals that stood a little more upright than they did. And when the God of law saw man standing upright, with all the possibilities in store in him to do great good, he was pleased and at once made a better earth and heavens for him; and the song of joy went booming through the earth and flashing through the heavens. The silence was broken; the man of promise was born. The man was to be filled with knowledge. The woman, his mate by his side, was to be filled with wisdom, and they equally together were to fill the earth with loveliness and the heavens with joy. Then again did the welkin ring with the sounds of joy and praise that were sent up from earth to heaven and back from heaven to earth, because the laws of order and progress had accomplished so great a work; and then the greatest confidence and joy was manifested, because these natural laws of spirit and matter had finally, after periods of millions of years of ceaseless action and toil, shown that they would accomplish all that love, hope, joy, truth, justice and mercy can wish for, if the principles are personified by the angels of heaven and the best people of the earth.

The question will naturally arise, who were the persons that made the welkin ring at the birth of the first man? it was the mother and father and their relatives and friends on earth, and their spirit relatives and friends in heaven; and it may be that there were joined with them spirit friends in heaven that were born of the spirits of heaven, and were never born in the flesh in this world; such are the reasonable conclusions of science, when the great object of all the work of making the sun, moon and planets, especially the earth, was so far accomplished, man was the object to be made; and man was made upon the earth. But oh, how lovely were the rejoicings over his birth, more like the rejoicing of birds over their young; and their songs more like the songs of birds over their young nestlings than it was like the artificial rejoicings of people in this age; it was the bubbling up of earth natures to join with the simple rejoicing of the pure heavenly natures that always dwell in the spheres of pure spirits.

Just compare this rejoicing with that of the legendery man of the Bible. When he was made, he had not a relative in the earth or heaven, except dirt and water, to rejoice at his birth; nor a friend, unless it was his god-father, who took so little interest in him that he went to the devil in a short time. He gave a little farm or garden to him and his help-mate to cultivate. But he was an Isrealitish Arab, and if there is anything in the world they hate it is the drudgery of farming; so he left it to his wife to do it, and she got to talking with a snake and he told her what to do to get clear of the drudgery, and she did it; and then she found her man, and told him what to do, and he did it. It should be remembered this was to eat an apple.

If it had been to go to work to raise it, I do not think there would have been a fall of that man. But he eat it and fell. And it is pretty well understood that any Israelitish Arab of the desert of Arabia would do the same thing in this day; and it establishes one fact, that dirt and water when turned into flesh and blood directly, without the interposition of animal and vegetable life, become hateful to the good spirit, even if it is his spirit father that made the man in that way. On the whole, the legend describes a bad son to a changeable father that make a very bad example to be taught to ignorant fathers and mothers and innocent children. The foundation of all inspirations in every age is the information of the age; because the people interpret the sayings by what they know. The principal part of the information of the people at the time when the Genesis of the Bible was promulgated among the Jews was fable, tradition, and legends. And the point not to be overlooked is, that there was no knowledge on the subject of the first man being made only inspirational at the time when Genesis was written or when anything was written.

There was not a person competent to write the facts at the time. There is no other pretense put forth that they knew anything about the facts except by inspiration. But in this age we have a vast amount of information on the subject of the formation of the earth and its productions; and when we reason from what we know about the making of the first man, our conclusions do not agree at all with the inspired statements of the Bible.

But when we get the modern inspirations, they agree with modern science and reason. These show that the design of the law God to finally make man as the crowning glory of his long work, beginning with the movements to make a sun, was done long before the Jewish Adam had an existence; and the glory of this discovery belongs to the intelligent people of this age.

CHAPTER V.

TIME.

Time estimated by years from the beginning of the sun until man appears on earth. Scientists calculate: do not jump to conclusions. It takes ten billions of years from the time the sun begins until man appears. Matter and spirit must be subjected to law, and heat and cold. Matter and spirit contain all the knowledge that man can get; matter goes through vegetable bodies before it is capable of producing the most intellectual people. A more special account of the time required to make the sun, the planets, and man. The natural laws are the fathers of the planets, the sun the mother. The earth's time divided into periods. The second proof of the immense time that elapsed before man appeared on earth. The lava was turned into rocks and became strong enough to hold high mountains. The tops were granite; on the sides and at the bottom were the secondary rocks. The rain and melted snows run down the mountain sides and formed springs and rivers. Names of different rocks. It is estimated that the rock crust of the earth is twenty miles in thickness. Jewish and Christian chronology opposed geological. Word God and law God do not agree about the time it took to prepare for man on the earth. Suppose the sun drew its nourishment out of so miles a year. The time it would require to prepare for man on earth. Infallible inspirations a declaration of man. The inspiration of coming events or prophecy; scientific prophecy and unscientific prophecy. How long will the sun and earth continue to exist? Religious prophets the flatest failures. Ancient and modern prophecies—their value.

HAVING given a very short account of the generic creations or formations from the beginning of time to man's appearance on the earth as the grand object and aim of all the creations, and marked a few incidents that show the lapse of time; now the question naturally arises, how we can estimate the length of time in years from the beginning of our solar system or sun until man appeared first on earth, in such a way that the minds of the readers will not be confused?

When astronomers are trying to find the distance to a star, situated so far away that they can not detect the least motion of it by their best instruments and utmost skill in handling them, they do not at once go to guessing the distance, but begin a series of observations on its reflected light, and in some other way that gives them a basis for calculating the distance; and by these means they obtain results which are of great value to mankind; and besides their plan will always keep the people who follow them in a reasoning or calculating state of mind. They may not find the right distance to the star, but they will give to the world their plan of proceeding to find it, which may finally result in a plan being adopted that will give the true distance. So with the geologist who wishes to know how long this earth has existed as a globe. He does not begin by guessing, but first begins to dig in its crust of rocks, observes the marks of time on them, and goes on calculating until he estimates the time this earth has been in existence as a separate body; and if he is not right, he sets people to thinking, and does great good.

All people who follow the scientific methods of investigating into the facts of all subjects that come before them for consideration, become the most intelligent and reasonable people of the earth; and wherever you find religious people who will not adopt the scientific method, they are or will become an inferior people, who will try to make people believe their doctrines by talk or persuasion; and when they fail they will resort to persecutions; and if they have power, to torture. There is no half way station that lasts long. People must reason or fight.

In introducing a scientific religion, only scientific methods must be adopted, and we must find out the time that has passed since our sun began its movements as best we can, and leave it for others to do better.

The reader has seen that the distance to the nearest

fixed star or sun of another solar system was estimated at twenty billions of miles, (20,000,000,000,) and the sun would naturally draw its spirit matter and force from half the distance, ten billions of miles; (10,000,000,000) at least that distance; for other suns in other directions were and are at immeasurable distances from our sun. From these premises it is easy to calculate that it would take a year of time to a mile of distance from the beginning of the sun's first motion to the time that the first man stood upright as man now stands, and walked and talked as man now does; or had the organs of speech well developed to do it when he had other men to talk to. By this plan of calculation it would require ten billions of years from the beginning of our time until man appeared on the earth. And this is no very small eternity for persons to think of.

And suppose any one should say it did not take more than half as long, still the time is immense, and there need be no hard words about it, as this plan of calculations may be superceded when a better one is devised.

But let us see what reasons we have to think it would take so long a time to build up the sun, and finish the earth, and refine them so that man could live on this earth. In the first place there are ten distinct periods of time marked by the making of the sun, and each of the planets. Then the time Mercury was thrown from the sun, which makes eleven distinct periods of time when our planetary system was perfected. This was the suns time, and the planets' time and the time since until man appeared. But let no one suppos that these eleven periods or epochs of time were of equal length.

It unquestionably took the sun longer to build itself up and prepare to send off the first planet, than it did to prepare to send off any of the other planets; and then it is reasonable to suppose that it took longer to prepare the large planets to be sent off than it did the smaller ones. And it would seem probable that it took longer to prepare and send off the more than one hundred and forty Asteroids which are recorded as one epoch than it did to send off the greatest planet. But there are other considerations of great importance to be taken into account. The sun must have just the articles, and no others, and just the amount it wants, and no more gathered into its substance; to make it balance in space in its place, and to furnish all the materials and power required for its great work. And it must be endowed with a delicacy of touch, and of a judgment that was unerring to draw to it what was wanting, and to reject what it did not want.

Then the spirit, matter, force and motion must be subjected to the greatest trials to make those that remain in the sun perfectly docile to the law of their uses, and also to have those out of the sun but within its sphere of influence perfectly adapted to their uses there. Then all that the law required must be subject to the great heat of the sun and the intense cold that is created by its absence, or the absence of its rays of light and heat; and to the sun's and the planet's greatest motion and their most perfect rest and quiet within their bodies; while the whole mass was flying at a speed that is almost inconceivable by man, although it can be calculated by him to a certainty. And also be empowered to make the greatest noises, and learned to be entirely silent. And to make discord, and the harmony of the most enchanting strains of music that ravishes the ear of the lover of its harmonious sounds. And then it must be educated to remember every incident of its history since time commenced with it.

This point is proved by psychometry when a small portion of this matter is put into the hands of a sensitive adapted to understanding its impressions or theme, or its language. Without this intelligence in matter and its surrounding elements, the animals and man could not be endowed with their mental capacity of memory and judgment which they display in earth life. And we may be well satisfied that there can not be an intellect on earth that will be endowed to know more than the spirit and matter knows of which it is composed; for here is where it gets its power to know.

The sun selected it first, and then the earth took it from the sun, and finally the earth gave it to animals and man, and it may be said to vegetables, and made it to know how to form its beautiful crystals, with all the colors of the rainbow; and its rainbow with all the colors of the crystals.

It is said that water will not rise higher than its fountain, and it is just as certain that man's intelligence will not be greater than its source on earth, or from the sun; for all are under the direction of the laws of nature and spirit, and had to comply with their orderly progression and the regularly successive events that they had planned. The end to be attained was to produce beings that were capable of knowing all that could be known; and such beings could not be created unless they were made of intelligent matter; and such matter had to be used in other vegetable or animal life before it could give man the great mental powers which he possesses to-day. And we find not only that matter is intelligent, but that for millions of years after the earth was cooled to allow vegetables and animals to live on it, they did live and die and left their bodies to turn into dust before man appeared. Here was all this preparation to be made before man could come upon the earth to stay.

I put this time required to make these preparations at ten billions of years. Will any man show us that it could be done in less time? Now let us take a more special view of those periods of time. In the first place we may suppose that it took onehalf the time from the beginning of the making of the sun until man appeared on earth, to make the sun; that is, it took five billions of years to make the sun and get it all ready to begin to make the planet Neptune; then it took a half of a billion of years to make it and send it off into its orbit. Before the sun commenced this, all its powers were used to form and grow to a maturity that would prepare it to send off its children, the planets.

If we refer to mankind, we find it takes about ten times as many years for the persons to grow so they are sufficiently matured to bear children as it does for them to build a child and born it into the world after they are matured and prepared for the work. So we will take this general law among human beings as the basis for calculating the time that it took the sun to get ready to produce the children of this solar planetary system, and have the ability to keep them in their places.

Here the question may arise, if the sun is the mother of these children, who is the father? The answer is, the law or laws of nature. We have not been able to get behind them to see any body or thing or being manipulating them. And consequently we say it is law, intelligent law, which is the law God.

Then we proceed a half billion years to the next child, which is called the planet Uranus. Then to the next the same time, and Saturn is born. Then another period of the same time, or near it, and the 4th child is born, called Jupiter. The 5th was the Asteroids. The 6th, Mars. The 7th, Earth. The 8th, Venus. The 9th, Mercury.

Then in a half billion of years comes man upon the earth, the great object, end and aim of all the previous great and long continued work, which was more persistent than human nature can comprehend, and that will redound to the greatest glory of its authors to the fartherest edge of eternity.

In this little sketch we have divided up the time from the beginning of the making of the sun until man appears on the earth. But during the last billion and a half of years, more or less, there has been another element upon which to estimate time. The earth thus rolled into its orbit and commenced its daily and annual motions. If there was prepared some machine to keep the count of the number of annual revolutions that the earth took in its orbit around the sun, and we could find the marks the machine had made, we could tell the number of years the earth has been moving in that way; but man has not discovered such marks and dots that he knows of, so the plan must be pursued of dividing the earth's time into periods as we have the sun's, and then calculate the number of years as well as we can.

We go back those three periods to the time when the earth was formed and thrown from the sun and took its place in its orbit. We have seen how the earth was formed into its present globular shape by its rolling motion, when in a soft liquid state, when sent on its mission in its orbit around the sun, and that it was molten lava, steam, smoke, air and ether, and that it gradually cooled and hardened on its surface until it became fit for the production and habitation of the most simple and crude of vegetable and animal life. It has been estimated that the time required to make this change was five hundred millions of years after it was launched from the sun.

The history of the earth in these millions of years is very simple. The lava hardened and became the foundation of the primary or fundamental granite rocks. These rocks are the lowest or basic rocks of the crust of the earth; and the highest on the tops of our highest mountains, thrown up there from the lowest rock formation by volcanic eruptions. But most, if not all the mountains, now exisiting were thrown up after the secondary and tertiary rocks were formed; and many of them seem by the shells found on their sides to have been hoisted from the bottom of the oceans, and long after the first period in the earth's history was passed.

The beginning of the secondary rocks is the beginning of the second period in the earth's history. I will not pretend at this point to estimate the time it was necessary to make that rock and all the species of vegetables and animals that lived and died in that time, but will say it was an immense number of species that are not found afterwards, and a very great length of time. Then the tertiary period set in with its great numbers of new species of vegetables and animals, very much improved upon the first formations. Then the quarternary period commenced, with a much improved vegetable and animal creation, and mountains were thrown up to so great a height that their summits were covered with perpetual snow, and rain fell in valley and on the mountain side, and snow that melted and the water run down the mountain sides, some on the top of all the rocky formations and much of it under the secondary rocks and all rocks above them, and some of this water burst through the rocks and formed cooling springs that was and was to be refreshing to thirsty animals and finally man, and make the beautiful, fruitful valleys, and the waters of the springs and rivulets run together; and rivers joined to rivers and rolled on to the ocean, and the mists went up into the air, and water formed there and came to the earth in snow, ice or rain; and in this way the waters of the earth were continually fresh, and the waters of the ocean were continually salt, because the salt could not rise with the vapor; and all this had to be done to prepare for man's advent upon the earth.

And yet not one half of the changes required to make him a good home have been touched upon. One was that the waters under the secondary and other rocks above them that could not burst out made many channels there that are unknown to man, and made their way to the oceans. These subterranean rivers will finally be found in desert places, and their waters will be utilized by artisean wells and will be made to irrigate the great sandy deserts and make them blossom and produce fruits that will support and nourish thousands upon thousands of people that can not be supported on earth by any other means known to mankind. But the question will be very naturally asked, how the water got in between the primary and secondary rocks and others that were formed on these rocks.

The answer is, that when the mountains rose up, the bottom granite rocks broke through all the rocks, that lay above them, and left them low down on the sides of the mountains or below the tops and when the water came on the mountain and run down its sides, it fell into the crevices between these layers of rocks and thus was kept from the fires below the granite rocks by this rock, and was prevented from rising to the surface of the earth by the secondary and other rocks because they were unbroken and the water could not break through them. So they have had to make their way to the oceans by channels unknown to man, under the rocks and earth.

The first rocks formed after the original granite, is called the Eozoic, meaning the first appearance or the dawn of life. It is hardly thought to be a secondary rock, because it was a long time after geologists commenced their observations before it was discovered that life existed in the time of this formation.

The secondary and other rock and earth formations are laid on these primary rocks and are divided into the following classes by geologists: 1st The primary fossiliferous rocks; 2d secondary fossiliferous rocks; 3d Tertiary fossiliferous rocks and earth, called Paleozois or Ancient, meozoic or middle and cenozoic or recent life periods. I give these general geological divisions and names, to enable persons who consult geologies to at once get at these periods by the names that geologists use. When they find these divisions subdivided to give the various formations from the first to the last of each general division. I do not touch upon them in this work only in a general way.

It is estimated that the earth's crust of rock and soil is twenty miles in thickness. This is not evenly so all around the earth; some parts are more, others less; but the average is about that thickness. Any one can see what an immense space of time was required to form this rocky covering to the burning lava that is supposed to occupy the whole of the center of the earth, and then they can see there is little danger that the deepest mining shafts or artisean wells will ever reach the fluid seething molten mass which surges so far beneath our feet.

The fundamental granite has been estimated to be twenty thousand feet in thickness, or a little less than four miles. This leaves for the superincumbent rocks and soil a thickness of about sixteen miles, where all the layers are complete in their order of formation; but in many places all the formations of rocky layers are not found, and in many others they are broken; and the estimates are calculated from premises that will admit of a greater or less estimate of the thickness of the rocky crust of the earth. And the same is true regarding the age of the earth.

The estimates are made from the best data known at the time. But there is one curious circumstance about these calculations; the more they are studied the longer seems to be the time required to accomplish this gigantic work; and so of each period. In the first place biblical chronology interfered; christians and Jews, opposed their records to the geological calculations and discoveries, and commenced to call their days periods of time. But with all their lengthening of the time of their days they still opposed the great length of time that the most common sense calculations of geologists required. So the geologists made the time as short as they could to accommodate the biblical and religious priestly scholars, and these scholars stretched their biblical time out as long as they could to meet the geologists.

These concessions confused all parties, and were of no use in settling the time of the earth's existence in its orbit. It must be remembered that these descriptions arise from two sources that are entirely different. The biblical descriptions are by a god that man made, and each word is a god. But the geologist's descriptions are based on the works of the law God that made man, and the descriptions cannot be reconciled with each other.

The first word of the biblical description of the earth is false, so far as our earth is concerned: "And the earth was without form and void." The geologist's earth had a globular form from its beginning as an earth; and the Bible says further, "and darkness was upon the face of the deep." The geologist's deep had no more darkness upon it than it had light; the sun was shining upon it all the time as it is now; some of the time the oceans were in the shade of the earth, and at some other times clouds prevented the sun from shining upon the sea of lava, or water; but all the time it was shining upon the earthly substances in the air or on the hard or soft earth. It has been calculated that the earth was void of vegetable and animal life five hundred millions of years.

But what can be the use of trying to reconcile the two descriptions when one makes every change that takes place depend upon a word spoken by their God? and the idea is constantly carried to the mind of the Bible reader that the change was made instantly on the word being uttered; and this was the understanding as proclaimed by priests and understood by the people, until the geologists showed its utter falsehood. And that there was a law of progression, and all changes were made slowly and orderly under this law.

Then the priests began to teach that the law power was God; but did not say so. The word power was still their God, when they did not have scientific men and facts to meet. And there they are to-day, praying and supplicating their word God to perform miracles and bless them and curse their enemies, nearly as they used to before geologists came. And then preaching as though all things were ruled by the God of natural law. Thus they are falling between two stools, crying by turns good word God, or good law God, save us. And it is time that the geologists stopped trying to save their priestly dignity, but tell them to choose the God they wish to serve and stand by him in sermon and prayer, or fall into infamy between the two. And say to the people, if you want to hear scientific truth and worship the God of the law by which the sciences were established, and wish a religion based on these truths, say to preacher and all others, we want this religion and must have the moral and social sciences established; to know what all our duties are to be in accord with this religion.

We have seen that the earth's crust was considered to be twenty miles in thickness, and that the little less than four miles in thickness of the primary granite rocks were estimated to be made in about five hundred millions of years; and then that more than sixteen miles of rock and earth has been formed on the primary rock; if we conclude it would take as long to each mile of thickness of rock, it would require two thousand five hundred millions of years to form it. That is, five times five hundred millions of years is the sum total of the estimate of the age of the world when man appeared on it.

Now we will drop these estimates that have been made by calculating the age of the world by its rocky covering, and go back to the estimate of the earth's age by calculating the whole age of the sun to the time man came on the earth. It is seen, by calculating, that it took the sun ten billions of years to get itself ready and make the earth and get that ready for man. This is done by calculating that in every year the sun would only clear a mile of space around it, and by that kind of speed in the work it would take the billions on billions of years.

Now we will calculate the time it would take if the sun did the work of five hundred miles in space in a year. This would require five hundred times less time for the sun and earth to do the work and prepare for man than the other basis of estimating the time required. Now we have ten billions of miles of space to be worked over by the sun, and the spirit, matter, force and motion taken from it that the sun required at the above rate we will make the same division of the time as we did before, and give the sun half the time to build and prepare itself for its great work. The distance to the nearest sun being settled in round numbers to be twenty billions of miles. The sun would naturally draw its nourishment from half the distance, that is, 10,000,000,000,000 of miles. Then calculate that it would draw out the nourishment it wanted of five hundred miles a year. This leaves twenty thousand millions of years that it took the sun and earth to be prepared for the advent of man on earth.

Now one-half of that time we will give to the sun to form itself before making any preparation for the making of a planet.

$$2 \overline{)20,000,000,000}$$
$$10,000,000,000$$

Here we have ten thousand million years for the sun's time alone, and subtract that from the whole and we have the sum, (10,000,000,000) ten thousand million years for the planets' time to form themselves, and this gives to each (1,000,000,000) one thousand million years ; and to the time after the planets were all in their orbits to the time the earth was prepared for man, (1,000,000,000) one thousand millions of years.

This finished the sun's time from the beginning until man appears.

Now we turn to the earth's time which is included in the above, but it is very important that it should be separated, because it was the mark of the natural laws upon the earth that first were used to prove the utter falsity of the ancient inspirations. To do this we go back to the birth of the earth, three periods, or three thousand million years (3,000,000,000.) On these three periods, whatever their length may be, when the people throw aside all the chronology that superstition and bigotry have fastened on the minds of the people by torture and murder, this subject will be thoroughly and scientifically considered and settled, not by murder, but by reason. And if any one is disposed to say that the inspiration given by this book according to present knowledge, give results vastly different about the ages of the sun and world, one calculation makes billions of years old and the other millions.

This is put before the reader to show that the inspirations according to science are not infallible, and vary according to the basis of the scientific calculations. But it is put in more particularly to inculcate the doctrine that there is to be no tortures or inquisitions put in practice because there is a difference of opinion made by the different inspirations from the rocks of the earth or works of the sun, or from any of the man-made gods; whenever and wherever you find persons declaring that their inspiration is from any source that is infallible, those persons are making a declaration of war on the rest of mankind. To know that we have an infallible inspiration, requires the person to be infallible who proclaims it; and those who follow the one who proclaims, must be made infallible by the first proclaimer or by some other means. Thus the words of infallible inspirations by the gods, prophets, christs, saviors, and messiahs, of the Jews and christians, made the believers of the infallibility of the Bible infallible. And upon this basis the infallible hosts went forth to war against Jews and Christians of another sort, as well as pagans and infidels; and the parties that were successful had the war proof that they and their god were truly infallible; and if they were defeated, it was because the people did not believe what they pretended to, and it was their sins against their God that caused him to allow them to be defeated. Their God was infallible, but they were not. And now these defeated fallible people must get in harmony with their God, and then they can whip their enemies as easily as a mother can spank her little infant.

The only proof of the truthful inspirations of the prophets and Gods of any of the religions of the past has been the gauge of battle; and where the victory was declared, there was the true God with his true inspiration, supported by the true people. The scientists wish to change this mode of arriving at an infallible inspiration. It would be just as logical for the lion to claim that his god was infallible because he killed a goat, and goat's god was fallible because he allowed him to be killed, as these claims of religious people. And the great object to be attained at this time is to establish the rule that any information obtained by inspiration shall be subject to proof by the principles of science and reason. And any person or persons who declare they have an infallible inspiration from an infallible god, should be pointed at as an enemy of the peace of mankind, and of truth and justice.

The history of the religious people who have made these pretentions, justify such a course. It must be remembered that all the information we have on this subject of past time is what we infer from facts. And if any one thinks that inspiration gives any other and better information, let them look at the ancient religious inspirations. There are none of them that give any better information than was current among ordinary people of the age when the uttered inspired information was given.

Having given the inspirational time past from the beginning of the formation of the sun, until man appeared on earth, and from the beginning of the earth until man came on it, it is now proper to give the time that the heavens and earth will continue in existence. We are now to consider the inspiration of prophecy. Here again we are under the law of inference. We infer from the past what the future will be, as we inferred from the present what the past has been. Science has pointed to some infallible signs by which some coming events can be told to a certainty. When a person takes up an almanac, looks for the time of the rising and setting of the sun and moon, or the eclipses and conjunctions, they are so certain that they are true that they hardly consider them prophecy; but when they look at the prophecy of the weather, they have no hesitation in calling it prophecy, and very uncertain prophecy at that. And when we begin to prophesy about how long the sun will continue in existence, and how long the earth will continue in existence, or when it will wear out, rust out, or be blown to infinitesmal atoms, is a prophetic question that has been discussed, considered and reconsidered for many centuries; and yet the prophecies have not proved more reliable than the prophecies about the weather.

So far the weather prophets have the advantage, for at certain seasons it is hot, at others cold, and there is a general mixture between these seasons that give them a chance to be right half the time; but the prophets that have prophesied the distruction of the earth, have never hit in the vicinity of right yet, that we know of. Religious prophets about the destruction of the world have been the flattest failures of any prophets that are well known.

The question naturally arises, how are scientists to prophesy about how long time will last on the earth and in the solar system? The sun existed twenty thousand million years before man was made to stay on earth, is the lowest estimate I have made for it to bring about that great result; the beginning of the end and aim of its existence. If it follows the rule of animal life and this was the beginning of its maturity, and the maturity is to last as long as its growth, then the sun will have a mature life of twenty thousand million of years, and then comes the gradual decay of old age and the same great length of time. This would give to the life of the sun sixty thousand millions of years, or more than thirty nine thousand millions of years yet to be passed; for man has not been upon the earth but a few hundred thousand years, if he has one hundred thousand.

When we come to estimate the earth's time of existence, we find up to the time man appeared on it may be estimated at three thousand millions of years old. Then it was sufficiently matured to produce the first fruits of its existence; and if its maturity continued as long as its growth, it will last three thousand million years; and then if its decay is of the same length, it will be more than five thousand millions of years before the end of the world will be reached; how much more we are not to say here, because we are not now estimating how long mankind have been on earth.

From any consideration which we can take of time on earth and in the solar system, on the scientific plan, there can be no idea formed that the earth will become barren or be destroyed for millions on millions of years. All the movements are directed by the law of nature.

There can not be a catastrophe, special providence or miracle out of the control of these laws. But what changes of sun and earth, these laws have in store for mankind, has not been well ascertained; and there are no well known data by which people can judge when great changes like the glacial period will occur; or that they are to occur at all. There has been some talk that the polarity of the earth is changing, and may change suddenly by the effects of attraction and repulsion under law; but there are no special data yet obtained that will give certain information on this subject. Then there may be the sinking of Islands and continents, and the raising of others, as there have been.

Many such things may be in store in time under the laws, to take place. Man has not yet got behind the curtains of the law power, so they can prophesy certainly of what is to come; and as it is said a counting machine will count many thousands consecutively correctly, and then will miss one, and the reason why there is this change in the count at that number is not well known.

So there may be things to occur under the laws, that man does not apprehend and can not account for when they occur, but still be perfectly under the laws of nature, order and progress. But the greatest amount of religious prophesy about the distruction of the world has been that it would be destroyed by fire sent down from heaven by an angry God because of the wickedness of the people. This prophesy has been the standing christian prophecy for eighteen hundred years, and was the Jewish one for a thousand years before that.

Whenever the religious priests wanted an extra scare to get converts; they would search out some prophesy in their bible and declare that the end of the world was at hand, and all the people who did not repent and follow Christ would be burnt up with it, and those who did follow Christ would be wafted to heaven in robes of white, unsinged. These biblical prophecies have failed so often that they attract but lttle attention at this time.

But with all the hellish machinery of Jews and christians to burn unrepentant spirits eternally, they fail to frighten people into their folds and make them pay the priests bribe money to influence God to save them from hell torments. If a person will look over the prophecies of the ancients, they will see that they had less knowledge to make a true prophecy upon than we have at this time; and their prophecies are just as much more worthless than the present prophecies are, as they were more ignorant. And as people become more enlightened and get more knowledge, their inspirations regarding the past history of the sun and its planets and of the earth will become better, and their prophecies of the future of this world and of time will be truer and more useful to the people; and the best preparation we can make for ourselves and the coming generations of mankind is to keep our own minds open to receive knowledge at all times and places where we can get it, especially on the theme of how long time has existed and how long it will exist, and who made it, and how time was made.

CHAPTER VI.

THEOLOGY OR GOD-MAKING.

The great work of religious people is God-making. This is the worst kind of business except worshiping them. The Ass spoke for God . The Christ God called the people devils. His God forsook him. He came to fulfill the law. But his followers did the murdering part. The heart of the Jewish God is shown by the life of David. The Southern and Northern sections of the Christ God's church. Man made Gods serve any people. We must reason or fight. The priests of the dumb-Gods do the talking. The God who rules by natural laws does not talk. Warriors and priests are one in fighting. Christ is pitiless on the erring when on His throne in heaven. Priests do on earth as many cruelties as Christ does in heaven. All Gods should be made in rhyme. The christian God. They say men can not be saved by good works. The Chinese Josh. confucius The Gods of Judea and Egypt. The Greeks, and Romans. The God of science in Rhyme. Persons can hardly know themselves: and much less God. God in the constitution. The best Gods are of wood and stone except the God of nature. When spiritualist and other law God religionists get ignorant enough, they will punish and kill people for unbelief. When religious people call for war to support their God's religion, they have no good reason to support it.

THE great work of all religious people has been to make Gods. This is wholly the work of inspirations, as the God that moves the heavens and earth on time, in order, has not been seen by man. But many people have declared they have seen Him and had long conversations with Him, and He has told them what to do, and when and how to do it. The difficulty about believing these people arises from the fact that His promises are not fulfilled, and that some of His orders have been too cruel and monstrous for any but insane people and the most debased of mankind to obey.

God-making would seem to be a very innocent emplyoment, and the making of Gods is really so. But when a man or a nation has made one and then commenced killing the people who would not fall down and worship him, the diabolism of the business begins to appear; and all the religions of the world of any great note have produced such a people with such results. It is time to consider if the conduct of the people who pretend they have the true God and it is blasphemy in persons to ridicule and speak against Him, and that the persons should be fined, imprisoned, tortured and murdered for doing so, the innocence of the business is questioned, and the idea gets into the minds of the people at once. Is not God-making the lowest and worst business that there is on earth? And the answer is; that there is but one lower, as shown by the light of history, and that is the God worshipers of these man-made Gods. At first they are as innocent and helpless as infants in their mother's arms, persecuted as the child is by the mother when it kicks out of order; and next they are a banditti of outlaws, robbers and murderers; and then they become a nation of torturers, with all the sins that belong to pirates and robbers.

Every person who does not worship their God should be deprived of their property, and if that does not cause them to turn from their ways and experience religion and worship the God adopted by the religious bandits of the nation, they must be murdered. This is the short history of all kinds of religious worshipers of the world. These people may worship the Jackass that spoke of the ancient Israelites to its priest rider; in Hebrew or the Chaldaeck or some other language, and told him to look before going ahead, or they may worship the angel that made him speak, or they may worship the God back of the angel that caused him to make the angel to make the ass speak. All this is innocent enough, but when these religionists began to murder those who would not worship the jack, or the angel, or the God that talked in this way to the ancient rider, then it becomes a serious matter. And when the infant Jesus Christ came upon the earth He was as innocent as other infants; and when He grew up and called the people that opposed Him the children of the Devil, and they told Him He was a devil. This brought Him on a level with the people that surrounded Him; and when He said people would be damned if they did not believe, He put Himself on a level with priestly bigots.

Then He denounced the priests and rulers as their history shows that they should be; and they murdered Him for it; as a devil, a disturber, that blasphemed their God. Before breathing His last He said, "my God, my God, why hast thou forsaken me?" now who or what His God was that had forsaken Him, He has not said, and it is not known; He had very evidently not adopted a God that was omnicient and every where present, because He could not have forsaken Him then and there if He was the one that is always, at all times present. The only evidence is that something which He called His God, had forsaken Him.

This could not be the law God which or who has charge of the life and death of the body: for He was right there doing His work with the greatest kindness, and soon after seperated His spirit from His mangled body. He always said His God was was a love God, a loving father, who would never forsake those He loved; so it would appear that this was not the God He worshiped at last, when in the agonies of death. It is evident His God was the Jewish God of words and miracles; and besides other bad reputations, has a most hateful and revengeful character. This God is one that holds out great pretentions of the good He has power to do, and will do, to His followers and worshipers. He is a great being, but

He leaves His followers in distress just as Jesus says He had left Him. When this question is asked by others in their more direful distress, no answer comes; He is as dumb as a barnacle on a good ship's bottom, that causes a painful delay in the ship's arrival in the harbor of peace and safety. He says He came not to destroy, but to fulfill the laws of this God.

It is very uncertain about His fulfilling any of these laws, but His worshipers and followers have murdered babes, mothers, and men with all the barbarism that the Mosiac God commanded when they destroyed the Waldenses and made the massacre of St Bartholmew, and established their inquisition throughout the world where they had power. This was done by the christians almost as thoroughly as the Jews did it in Judea when they conquered the various tribes of that now desolate land. And he was just the man that a few priests wanted to set up as the God man of christianity. He was murdered by the priests of the Jewish God and represented all the evils of that God's words, but very little of the evils of the priests of that God; and He appears in the role of reformer because he disputed with the priests and approved of the God they worshiped, and proclaimed him as his father in heaven. He was the God of Abraham. Isaac, and Jacob, and his heart is shown by the life of David.

When all these things are taken into account, that the last priesthood has proved more cruel, more bloody and more despotic than the first, is apparent.

> And if you oppose this God
> And the priest's Almighty nod,
> Your doom is under the sod.

And that is not all; if you do not follow their interpretation of what God says, they will strive to kill you just the same; no more savage wars were ever made than those headed by the priests of the different christian denominations of the God Christ, or even the different sections of the same denominations. Like the Northern and Southern sections of Christ's church in the United States, in the war of the rebellion, many of the leading generals on each side were intensely loyal to Christ. And if you would listen to their diatribes on each other, you might hear them say in substance as their master said before them, "you are the children of the Devil, and our Christ owned all the world and He would not give a foot of it to the devil or his imps of children;" and each one had the same God fighting by their sides and each had the imps of the same devil to fight against them.

Finally the Gods of the North prevailed against the devil of the South, and the spoils of the Southern devils came under the power of the people and God of the North. This is the Northern sentiment. The Southern interpretation of the result of the conflict is that the Northern imps have succeeded, driving back their God and His people, and their cause is lost only for a time until their God has time to spit on his hands and get the people ready to renew the fight; and during the lull that has prevailed since the war, these friends of the Southern God and enemies of the Northern devils have killed thousands of persons who were in agreement with the sentiments of the Northern people and of the God they worship.

In this way the strife is continued, and will be as long as there are people who make a Southern Christ God, and a Northern one to match him. This is the religious view on that subject; man-made Gods, no matter how inspired they are, can be made to serve any cause that fanatical priests can make poor, ignorant people fight for. So the Christ of one side is the devil of the other, and vica versa. The conflicts in Christendom about whose Christ and God shall rule, is like conflicts of other religious people in all the world where people seek to rule by means of their spiritual and mental forces, and who refuse to settle the differences in their beliefs or opinions by reason.

> People must reason or fight;
> There is no half way measure;
> They must adopt the law of right,
> Or in ghastly war take pleasure.

Whenever and wherever the priests put in a God where justice should be, that is a declaration of war on the people who ask for justice. The spirit God, man God or ghost God of the Jews and christians are no better than the Bull God, the fire God or stone God of Egyptians, Fire Worshipers and Pagans.

All these man-made gods either can not or will not reason to settle all disputed questions. They command their followers, and threaten those that will not follow them, or they are dummies like the gods of wood and stone; and the priests can only reason from the principles conveyed in the command or threats, as it is written, or the priests of the dumb gods speak for them, and do the commanding and threatening to suit their state of mind. But when they attempt to reason with a scientist, they find there is a god of works and laws always acting, always on time, and never changing these works and laws to suit any person. The persons must comply with these laws, because the laws will not yield to them. These laws give to persons all the power they have to make gods or to proclaim them. All priests must reason from what they know; and if this does not give them the command, and they are determined to have it, they must fight the rest of the way or give up the job as one not worth gaining, in that it costs too much blood and too much military falsehood and religious lying to pay them; and after all they may not succeed.

But some priests have been at the head or next to the warrior head of nations for many centuries. Warriors and priests mingle and commingle together as brothers engaged in the same cause, one fighting with material weapons to kill the body of the enemy, the other fighting by his mental and spiritual power to dampen and kill the spirits of opponents, and raise

that of their friends to the highest degree of enthu-
iasm. They are friends fighting the battles of the
lord, and when victorious, becoming lords of the mannor of society and of nations. When David was successful, his heart leaped with joy, and he danced like
a professional in short cloths; and when he was hard
pressed by his enemies, his heart sank within him,
and he cried piteously for help and the destruction of
his enemies; and when he had committed the most
diabolical of crimes, he called upon his god to slay his
wicked enemies, and proclaimed that they oppressed
him for no fault of his.

He acknowledged his sins and faults sometimes, and
asked his god to pardon him, but he told god not to
pardon other wicked persons, especially his enemies,
but to condemn them to everlasting infamy and pain.
He begged most piteously of god and man for success
in his undertakings, whether they were good or bad.
A more heartless, pittiless, souless person against
enemies is not found in history; and the heart of the
Jewish god is like him, and the Christians' first god is
the same and the second is like him in having no
mercy for the wicked, but only eternal torment, when
he sits on his throne at the right hand of his god father.
A more merciless god was never made or imagined
by man than the one who said he would say to
those on his left hand go ye into everlasting punishment prepared for the devil and his angels. Because
they had not fed the hungry and done other benevolent deeds that he thought they ought to have done.

What was the heart of the man or god or the man
god who could stand before a crowd and utter such
threats of what he would do when he got on the
throne of his glory? This son of man as he calls himself and this son-god and man-god of the Christians,
is pronounced the most lovely and loving of beings by
his followers, shows by his threats upon these erring
people that he was demented or that he has not a particle of humane feeling in his heart. If he had, he

would in theory, at least, when talking of what he would do when he got power, say to the wicked and erring, you shall have a fair chance to reform, instead of sending them to everlasting torture.

The most moderate of the humanitarian people say, give every person a fair chance to reform; never send them to the devil to gnash their teeth in hopeless anger and agony. And it may be truly said none but the most devilish beings will do it. And instead of the Jewish god and the Christians' man-god and ghost-god sitting on thrones of glory to do such deeds and give such judgments their theories are made infamous by their cruelty, upon the helpless.

I wish people to understand that these promises to his followers of thrones to some and glory to the rest, and terrible threats to those who did not follow him, were made by a man in the lower walks of life; who was supported, housed and feasted by his friends; and there was no occasion for him to deceive his friends and denounce his enemies in such a heartless manner; only disappointed ambition; and by so doing he caused a priesthood to be raised up which has been the most barbarous people in christendom which did on earth the most cruel deeds ever done by any learned people, what he said he would do in heaven, or what his father would do, the priests made the hell upon earth which he would make if he had the power on the outskirts of heaven. But this is not the worst part of this matter; he knew if he had any knowledge on the subject that our father in heaven, the law God, would not provide him or his followers any throne of power to judge the people; he was ignorant and wholly deceived in this matter, or he was a rank deceiver; which ever it was, his principles caused the priests to get control of the people and caused the devil of ignorance and cruelty to reign for a thousand years. And now at the end of fifteen hundred he is still rampant in many parts of christendom. See the Southern states and all Catholic countries.

But all these ancient Gods, and their qualities have been described without rhyme or reason. They have been the most prosy and false beings that ever cast a slur on any people. The time has now arrived when the Gods should be made in Rhyme, and any person who is unable or unwilling to make a God or describe one, or portray his qualities in Rhymes, should be cast out of the God-making and worshiping fraternity. Let us begin with the Jewish christian God.

> God is a spirit whose center fills all space;
> For His circumference there is no place.
> God is a man, a ghost is His mate;
> Words are their children that declare man's fate.

> A word is God, and spirit His friend,
> Man is an agent his cause to defend,
> And ghost flits about as best he can,
> To save or damn every woman or man;
> So you see the rule must be,
> That three make one, and one makes three.

> Judge not lest you be judged, if you do,
> Men, devils and bad women will judge you,
> You must do as I do, for I judge well;
> If you do so I will send you to hell.

> Thus mixed in His ways
> Like Rymester in his lays,
> Is the God who says
> Give all to the poor,
> If God you would please;
> Give all to the rich
> Or God will give you no ease.

It will be remembered that the talents were taken from the poor man and given to the rich man. Then comes the God-like aphorism, "For unto every one that hath shall be given; and he shall have an abundance; but from him that hath not shall be taken away even that which he hath." This Christ God christians consider the best that ever was made, and there can be no doubt but that he was as good as any of them or all of them, including the three ply God of the christians. Suppose you go to the Chinese Gods; they have a variable character; it is a little uncertain whether Confusius taught anything about the character of his God; he was a moral teacher, and his religion was more moral than spiritual. It may be a rather strong statement to say that he taught that good morals would save a person, without adding some principle like that of christians, which say that men can not be good enough to save them unless they take in Christ.

The Chinese have their God Josh, and the people of India and Egypt all have Gods, of a similar kind. The infantile minds of the ancients had but very little variety in the character of their Gods, but many names; and their idols had many shapes, and many animals were considered Gods as well as men; and all of them had the same kind of proof that their God was the true one; that is, they had gained victories in his name. The Greeks and Romans had many Gods that led them on to victory, and many evil spirits or devils that caused their defeat; and this has been the case with all religious people, only some had but one God and one devil, but most of them divided the honors and abominations as the work of a number of each kind. But all of them had and have human or beastly characters.

Now to get out of this line of making Gods like men or beasts, with all the loves and hates and changeable plans that characterize mankind, let us see what kind of a God science puts in the place of man Gods, beast gods, stone gods, wood gods, sun gods, or fire gods or any god or gods that man has ever made or adopted. Science teaches that

> God is spirit, matter, force and motion;
> Under laws which command our devotion,
> They teach small matter to find its true place,
> And keep great worlds in their orbits in space.

Omnicient, omnipresent, great and small
One and all must obey their mighty call.

    Not a song is heard
    From marvelous bird,
    Not a tinkling rill
    From a high capt hill,
    Not a thought's expressed,
    Whether worst or best,
    Not a man is blessed,
    Or cursed by a test
    On earth; or in hell
    Or heaven to dwell,
    Not a gem of thought
    By inspired man caught,
    Not a reptile crawls,
    Nor a snow flake falls,
    Not a motion is made
    In sunshine or shade;
    Whatever is done
    In earnest or fun.

But the great law and its God does the deed,
For the great God and His law must succeed.

    If it should occur to any thoughtful person that this law god is a little incomprehensible to the ordinary man, this idea will be most reluctantly acknowledged, and then the question will be asked of the thoughtful to point out a god that is comprehensible or comprehended by man? It was said to man, long ago, "Know thyself," as though it was a difficult task to learn. But to know the God that made thyself is a still more difficult matter, not fully accomplished yet.

    All the Gods of the Pagans had the same general character of those of the Jews and christians, their anger was appeased generally only by bloody sacrificial offerings. From some cause that is difficult to understand, the blood of man or animals was necessary to make God save people from bodily or spiritual torments. And the priests of all these gods have the same general character.

They have been, and are the most malignant, bloodthirsty and cruel of any learned body of people that the world has ever seen. And the question is, can there be a god thought of, that will be a humane god in the hands of any priests such as any history gives us any account of? The priest's history is a terrible story; merciless and bloody. They are now striving to put one or three of the gods in the constitution. The question is, what can this be for? Every person can worship god as he pleases; there is no hindrance; but the laws will not allow them to torture and murder people to make them worship god as the priests desire people to worship Him. There is no other object plainly visible. And as they are more noted for pious frauds and deceptions than any other people, the plain reason should be taken for the true one when opposing its adoption. But if we are to have any man-made gods in the constitution, it will be best to have a stone one—a primary granite one, because that is the oldest; then we wish for the psychometer, for it to tell the history of the world and the power of the law god that worked at the building from the time the rock was first formed, until it was shaped by man and pronounced god.

> The best Gods ever made under the sun
> By man were made of oldest wood and stone,
> Until by a good genius, science sublime
> Made one with all the witchery of rhyme.
> We get our inspiration from above
> Of a God of law and a God of love;
> Let us reason together of His will,
> And learn why He is so shy and so still.

People in this world can see matter, but not the god of matter. The spirits of heaven can see spirits, but not the god of spirits. Can any one tell why He is so shy about showing Himself in heaven or on earth, if He exists? Then we hear the whispers of angels as well as men, and the rattle of leaves on the trees as well as the thunder's roar; but we hear nothing from Him personally.

From every view of this matter, none but a god-maker would jump to the conclusion that there is a personal god. The scientist says, we know there is a law that governs, but we do not know that there is a personal god that rules the law, and we do not believe it is a good plan to lie about it and punish people who do not believe there is such a personal god.

When spiritualists, infidels, free thinkers and scientists get as low down in ignorance, superstition, bigotry, frauds and despotism, as the god-making or god adopting religionists that reject nature's law god, they will act as the pious god-making religionists have, and murder persons, because they have a belief of their own. And no persons ever do that until they have adopted the most degrading moral and religious principles such as will force people to profess to believe what is not known to be true, and will employ their time in calculating the influence of forms and ceremonies, tone of voice, mannerisms, catch words and phrases, solemnity, and cheerfulness, and all the arts of deception that belong to the pious charletan and mountebank.

The pretense for teaching the young in such ways is to impress religious truth on their minds, but it is not proved truth, and much of it is proved to be falsehood. And they may say as one of old did, we thought it true and we wanted to be all things to all men to make them believe it was true; and in that way and by such means and by the addition of war they have succeeded in a great measure in forcing people to adopt their religion.

The scientists take a very different course; they prove, first that their assertions are true; their god's truth is proved truth; then they use all their eloquence and powers of mind to convince people, that the truth is much better than falsehood to be the guide of people in religion as well as in all the other affairs of life. Will any one but a paid priest, and his superstitious, ignorant, or paid tools, who get their living by asserting as true unproved dogmas, pretend that the scientific method is not the best? The answer is, none.

The priests and others who make a religion of falsehood profitable to them in a worldly sense, care no more for humanity, justice and truth, than does the despot, the slave holder, or the rum seller. The greatest criminals expect Christ or the blood of the lamb or some other god or blood will save them in the next world if they can have a good easy time in this world. These are the people that scientists have to contend against by facts and reason as long as the superstitious religionists will reason; and when they cease to reason and begin the fight, as the rebel slaveholders did, and the word-god religious people always have when it has come to the last pinch, the scientists will be far ahead of all competitors except the Protestants, who are scientists in all material things, and will adopt scientific methods in war, and consequently will be hard to beat; and before the end of a long bloody war, will become scientific religionists, and will cease to fight against scientists and scientific principles. For they find that war is a despotism that pronounces death upon friend or foe who disobeys orders, and like every other despotism it does not wait to prove accusation true before it kills the mistaken or innocent offender.

There is no public jury trial there to sift all the evidence; but it is a trial where the judges are selected because they are educated in all the inhumanities of war, and the life or liberty of the soldier is disposed of by the despotic laws of war. If any one will look at some of the punishments, inflicted by Jeff. Davis when he had a command in our army before the rebellion, they will see what cruel tortures a rebel commander can inflict on a loyal soldier for disobedience or failure to obey the orders of a heartless rebel officer; and yet the worst god religionists have always preferred war to reason to arrive at the religious truth to be the guide of the people, while the worshipers of nature's law god say to all people, come, let us demonstrate by experiment, experience, observation, and reason, what is true in religion; and when we have found the truth abide by it, and have no more war about gods or prophets or forms of faith.

CHAPTER VII.

THE DIFFERENCE IN THE TIME IT TOOK TO MAKE THE HEAVENS AND EARTH AS ESTIMATED BY JEWS AND CHRISTIANS AND BY SCIENTISTS.

The only sources of information on these subjects are the reasonable deductions from the facts of science and information gained from inspiration. The Moses inspiration probably written by Ezra. All ancient inspirations, make the earth flat and stand still. And all their writings show that they make the heaven and earth in a short time, while scientists make it millions of years. The God of words or revelations is not like the God of nature; their works on different days, or periods, were different. Here are noted the works done by each in the same day or period. Professor Wm. Denton's periods and ages of the earth. The pretense of having of an infallible inspiration is as dangerous a pretense as was ever uttered.

THE only means that mankind have had or have now to come to a just conclusion regarding the way the heavens and earth were made, and the time it required to make them, are the reasonable conclusions from well established facts, and the impressions obtained from inspirations. Having got at the basic principles upon which calculations have to be made to arrive at the most reasonable conclusions about the making of the heavens and earth, and the time it required, the question naturally arises, which is the most valuable as a guide to obtaining the truth on these matters?

The slow method of getting facts upon which to reason, or the quick plan of getting up an inspiration to learn in that way what the impressions are that may be a guide for reasonable people. I include in the meaning of the word inspiration, the spirit communications, and all information that can be obtained by psychology and psychometry, or can be obtained by what is termed the royal road to knowledge. The enlightened condition that enables a person to know the past by an inspiration as ordinary people know the present by seeing and hearing what is being done. The modern inspirations agree with the modern knowledge as is declared by the modern sciences. And the ancient inspirations agree with the ancient mythical ideas of that time.

The old biblical Mosaic account of the creation has not the true sanction of an inspiration by Moses, or any body else; it has only the pretended sanction of some more recent writers that it was the inspiration of their God through Moses. But recent investigation into the history of this inspiration of Moses, shows very fairly that it did not emanate from him, but was concocted hundreds of years after his time by some priests, Ezra being the principal. There is some probability that there was some legend for it, but there is no proof that the copy is at all like the original. This account however is put in the christian's bible as the truth of their God to all the people of the earth; transmitted by that holy people the Jews to them as the truth of their God also. It is hardly necessary to go back of these inspirational writings to previous inspirations, which should not however be entirely overlooked, because they give inspiration that more clearly shows how the world is held in its place. They all get a flat earth and have the sun, moon and stars go over and under it; but the religious writers of other religious nations make their inspirations say it rests on an elephant, snake and tortoise or other strong animals; but Jewish record makes it rest upon the word of their God or his will, or it stands upon nothing and God keeps it there. But the Jews and all other religious people of ancient times have a God made heaven and earth that is made quickly, and man is put upon the earth a very superior being.

None of these inspired ancients had the idea that man was preceded by thousands upon thousands of generations of animals that progressed in intelligence from the least intelligent to man, the most intelligent, under the law of progression; none of the ancient religionists seem to have any idea of this law. Therefore it is not important that any other inspirations about the making of heaven and earth be referred to, of ancient times, only the Jewish christian, which is forced upon the people of christian countries by public opinion or by war.

This inspiration gives six days as the time their God required to make the heavens and earth with the sun, moon and all the hosts of stars; and man was the finishing stroke of work that was done before He took His rest on the seventh day. Now the first thing to be noticed, is that their God acted as a man does who has done a few very hard days' work; he needs rest and must take it, or he becomes enfeebled; can not go on with his tasks on earth.

They do not say their God was tired as man is; but He acted as man does when he is tired, and needs rest. This shows the great difference between the artificial God of the christians, and the natural law-God of the scientists. The very first step made by the scientist with his nature's God is that he has made the heavens and earth, all that is in them, including the first man, and has been millions of years in doing it; and, never has been caught napping: He has not had a day's rest. He is different from man and from the christian God in that particular.

Then again the Jewish christian God spoke things into existence at once; in this way the earth was made, and light on the first day. On the second day He spoke and divided the waters, made a firmanent, and put a pond of water above the firmanent. How large that pond in heaven was, is not stated. But the rest was on earth. And on the third day He spoke and the waters of the earth were gathered into seas, and the dry land appeared; then again He said the word and grass and herbs sprung up yielding seed, and trees bearing fruit. Then on the fourth day He spoke the word and the sun, moon and stars, were made to light the earth. On the fifth day He spoke, and little and great fish were made in the sea and birds to fly in the air; and on the sixth day He said the word and the earth brought forth little creeping things and cattle and the beasts, and last of all made man and woman.

These are the legendary inspirations of the bible writers, or they are not inspirations at all, but simply the fictions of sensational writers long after the time when it is said they were written. But as they have been taken for the inspirations of the God of the Jews and christians for thousands of years, it is right to consider them as His inspired statements. We have seen this God differs from the natural God in taking rest; now we will consider His statements regarding the power he manifests in other special works.

The first thing this God did was to make the earth, and the next was to make light without the sun. The first thing the God of nature did, according to reasoning science, was to make the sun. This was the work of the first day, or period of these Gods. It shows they were at very different kinds of work. Here is a great difference in the first occupations of these Gods, and shows they were very different kinds of Gods. Since modern science has demonstrated that the work could not have been done in six days of our earth's time of twenty four hours each, the Jews and christians have changed or shown a wish to change the bible record from days to periods, we will call them periods although it is plainly stated it was the morning and evening each day, which distinctly carries the idea of a twenty-four hours earth day to all common sense people; and besides, the bible God had nothing but earth time to measure by. But nature's God had not an earth to measure the time by, and therefore it was naturally a long period of time that was needed to grow the sun. The earth was made or created by a word, the sun grew by a law. These are the different kinds of work of these Gods, and the different plans for doing it. Nature's God commenced the second period by making one planet or star in the solar system; how many stars were made outside of our solar system is not attempted to be stated. But Neptune was prepared and rolled into the heavenly space. On the second day, or period the bible story makes it appear their God was making a firmament that would hold water, and put as large an amount of the water in it as would make a Noah's flood. In the work of this second period all will see the work of these Gods was more unlike than it was in the first period; and it shows more distinctly that the God of nature is an entirely different person or principle from the God of revelation.

In the third period nature's God sent off another planet or star to mark the beginning of the period. It had been a long time in preparing or growing this planet called Uranus or Herschell; there may have been grown many suns of other systems or stars in the heavens, but we have no means at present to determine that matter. But the third day or period of the work of the bible God was of a very different kind. The waters of the earth were gathered into seas, and the dry land appeared, and grass and trees bearing seed and fruit appeared. Here we again see the great difference in the work of the God of nature and the one of words, or revelations. The one made a single star and satelites added to our solar system, and the other was ordering the waters to run together into the seas, and ordering the grass and trees to appear and bear seed and fruit.

Will any one pretend that these very different kinds of work were done by the same God in this time? Nature's God had not made the earth. The revelator's God had made it and covered it with grass and trees. They are two Gods, and very different in all their ways and works. In the fourth period another planet and its satelites appeared; it had grown until it was ripe; and took its place in its orbit. Its advent marked the beginning of this period. This star is called Saturn. It was the greatest work done in our solar system in that period by the God of nature.

In this day or period of the word God's work, he made the sun, moon and stars to light the earth. The natural God had grown the sun and many stars long before this, and had not made the earth or moon. Here the contrast between the natural God and the revelator's God is marked and distinct; one of them must be a fiction of the human brain, and that one must be the one who made the book that declared him a jealous God. The natural God who is governed by the laws of nature is too great, powerful and noble to ever make such a low, threatening statement.

The all powerful law of nature makes no threatening explanations, or excuses; does not deal in words, but in works. The fifth period in the natural order of events was commenced by Jupiter's rolling into its orbit. In this period this planet or star with its satelites were the only great productions well known to mankind that were added to our solar system. There is not in the bible revelations any period that agrees with the fifth period in any respect; the wordy God was engaged on his earth making fish and birds, and this was a long time before, by the law of nature the earth was made. The sixth period under natural law was commenced by rolling the asteroides into their orbits; there is more than one hundred and forty of them; that is, little stars. This was the great work done by nature's law God in our solar system in that period. The sixth day or period of the revelator's God was so different, they have no connection with each other. He said the word, and forthwith the earth produced little creeping things, cattle and beasts and finally a man and a woman.

These last two days or periods of the word God's commands are put here simply to show that there is no connection at all between these two Gods making the heavens and the earth. The God of words has finished his work in this time, and man is upon the earth surrounded with earthly troubles and comforts. But the natural God has not finished the growing of the stars of heaven, nor has he commenced the making of the earth, or it may be growing in the sun's substance but has not rolled into its orbit, and will not until after another period has passed. And these remarks are put in here so as to have bible days or periods put in with the period in nature to show the contrast and great difference in the periods of time; but the bible days will be referred to as we come to them in the periods of time that nature points out as the actual time when they had grown into existence, or really did exist.

The seventh period in nature was ushered in by the rolling of Mars into its orbit with its satelites. This was the only great distinguishing work of this period in our solar system. This was done when the Jew and christian God was resting.

The eighth period of time was ushered in by the earth's rolling into its orbit, accompanied by the moon, its satelite. But according to the word God's declarations, the earth was spoken into existence the first day or period, and the moon on the fourth. But reasoning from nature's inspirations and works, we see they both appeared and were ushered into existence in the eighth period; the difference is great and explicit.

The ninth period was ushered in by Venus and her satelites rolling into their orbits. This was the great work of the natural God in this period in our solar system; and the God of words does not mention or seem to know anything about it.

The tenth period was ushered into existence or marked by the planet Mercury and its satelites rolling into their orbits. This was the great work of the natural god in this period in our solar system. Here are ten immensely long periods of time that belong to the modern inspirational portion of astronomy. These are the reasonable deductions from the facts which astronomy gives to the people. They show that the ancient inspirations were no better than fictions, whether they were inspired by god or man. And when they are read and inculcated as truth to the people, they do them great injury; but when read as fiction they are as useful as other novels of the same character, and will be as useful as Robinson Crusoe and the Arabian Nights Entertainment.

Now we will leave inspirational Astronomy and turn our attention to the inspirational modern geology. It must be remembered that all the inspirations are what are made in the minds of geologists by the facts they have gathered, or they are the reasonable deductions from these facts. This is the way the modern inspirations are got up; all must finally be corrected by what is known, or from the reasonable deductions from what is known.

The eleventh period in the natural order of law and the first under the science of geology. The white hot molten lava period. This day or period is not noticed by the God of words in his holy book. It seems he had a hell to burn the spirits of the wicked people in; but the exact period when he made it is not stated. The probability is that he made it when he was angry with the wicked; in fact so mad that he did not note the time. But however that may be, the first period of the earth under the natural law was a term so heated that it consumed everything that was not needed in the productions of the earth. It would have burnt up the God of words if he had been composed of any substance; he was thinner than ether; he was a vacuum which nature despises; and in fact did not exist in this period nor for many periods after this. Not until man was made and had made words for centuries; then the word was God. The twelfth period or second geological period was the time the granite rocks were formed. The God of words did not notice this period. Here is the difference between the God of nature and the god of words, showing they are two distinct powers. The thirteenth period, or the third geological period, or the dawning life period of earth. This period is peculiarly the natural law period; no intimation of a dawning life period is hinted at by the god of words. He did not need such a period; he had only to say the word, and out come the vegetable or animal perfect in all its parts, as we now see full grown animals; the present animals were not the result of previous vegetable and animal growth as is shown to be the fact under the natural law of progression, by the law god. The fourth period in geology, and the fourteenth period of time, gives us the primary fossiliferous rock period. These rocks give to the common observer the plain sight of the impressions of the vegetable and animal life of that time, and some petrifications. Here again the word god has not noticed this beginning of life on earth, that was large enough to arrest the attention of the casual observer. If there is any reference at all to this period in the bible, it is on the third day or period, when it is said vegetable and animal life appeared and each produced their kind. But this period ended, and another set of animal and vegetable life came upon the earth, as appears by the rock impressions that appear in the fifth geological age, and the fifteenth period of time. When the rocks show new formations of vegetable and animal life. The word-god did not make any statement that applies to this time, any more than to the fourteenth period of time. For the vegetable and animal formations of this age mostly disappeared in the next or the sixth geological period, or the sixteenth period of time. In this time the great animals, the product of the fifteenth period, mostly perished, and a better order of animals and vegetables appeared; those more in accordance with the productions of the present time. This age produced fish, more like those the God of words ordered to exist on the fifth day than any other time, unless it is the next period of time. That is the seventh geological period, and the seventeenth period of time.

The quarternary fossiliferous period. It is in this period that the most finished, well formed animals appear, and the best vegetables; and with these animals and plants, man and woman appeared. The earth and air had become sufficiently pure and advanced to have man appear as naturally as the little ill shaped ones and the large sluggish ones appeared in their day; all were better now, and what is better than all of the rest, was that man was made with the foundation powers of a mind that would grow until all these better conditions would be understood and noted, as the scientists of this time are noting them, to enable persons to live better lives than was ever possible before.

But the great point for every one to observe is, that the cause of christian hatred to scientists is made plain in the very beginning, by the difference in the character of the gods they worshiped, and in the different ways they adopted to do their work; nature's god works by law. The Jewish and christian's god works by the word of command. Such is the difference between these gods that the worshipers can never harmonize with each other; nature's god made the sun first. The wordy god spoke the earth into existence first; and there is no unison in their work afterwards. Nature's god made a child-man first, and he grew to be a beast of a man. It is considered that the man that nature made first was the poorest kind of a specimen of a man that ever existed. The wordy god made a full grown man first, and the best man that ever was made was this man, for he pronounced him good; and afterwards he said all were evil, not one good person upon earth.

From all the circumstances, it is futile to attempt to have both these gods become the gods of those who worship the natural god and despise the word god, and his worshipers. And those who worship the word god hate the natural god, and torture those that worship him if they can; because that is the only power in their possession that will overcome the worshipers of nature's god. This is proved by the actions of christians for the last fifteen hundred years.

In giving the seven geological periods of the earth, I have followed rather the demands of the christians to make divisions correspond with the seven days of the bible; then they would turn them into periods, and so make an agreement. But they had killed and abused astronomers so they had not conceded anything to christianity; and the historian of this period can make as true a statement regarding the astronomical periods of time as he thinks most reasonable. If we take the inspirations that are given in Psychometric geology, we shall find that it is much more reasonable to make eleven periods than it is seven. Each of these periods are marked by distinction and formations, so that each naturally stands by itself.

Before any of these periods that are marked for the geologists to examine, was the molten lava period. After this comes the geologist's Granite period. In the third volume of Wm. Denton's Soul of Things, page 96, is a synopsis of the ages in which appear special animal formation. People wishing psychometric geological information, I would refer to his works.

In conclusion of the book of inspirations, I would say that it is a sixth sense, equal in value to any, if not to all the five senses. But when people declare that they have an infallible inspiration from their god, they make the most wicked assumption that man can utter. They at once build up a church that becomes the lazy man's Sunday workshop; the ignorant man's knowledge; the brutal holy man's justification for every crime; and the pious man's orders to uphold every falsehood that he thinks will glorify his god. It establishes an inhuman religion, that has always been a curse to the world. People who wish to establish a humane religion, will use this sixth sense as they do the other five; to get information that will be a blessing to mankind and a joy to all people.

BOOK SECOND.

THE RELIGIOUS TEACHINGS OF THE MATERIAL SCIENCES.

CHAPTER VIII.

ASTRONOMY AND THE RELIGION IT TEACHES.

Astronomy the science of the skies. People were punished with death for looking at the stars and making public the result of their observations. The religious people who did it, did not worship the true God. They made a bottomless hell, that Astronomy proved could not exist. The Mohamedans knew more of astronomy than the Jews or Christians. The natural God or the word God must perish. A converted man hates with holy hatred the natural God. If the Babylonians understood astronomy, the Jews did not. If the Greeks and Romans understood it, the Christians did not. The Jews and Christians teach the same doctrines that they did when they burnt an astronomer for telling the truth. If truth like astronomy was made sacred, they would kill people for denying it. Christianity depends on the war power for its support. Jews and Christians have committed more blasphemy against astronomical truth than heretics ever did against their religion. It is time for all to know that worldly truth is God's truth. Let us have a humane religion. Astronomy shows the order of the Heavens. All the sciences have their special laws to manifest.

ASTRONOMY is the science of the skies; its foundation is laid in the transparent ether. The earth, sun, moon, and the millions of stars lay in apparent stillness and quiet; it seems to the casual looker-on, that in some places they are jumbled together, regardless of order or system; and in other places the stars that are alone, shine in their lonely glory like a brilliant on the forehead of beauty. Who would ever conceive of the idea that it could become a heinous religious crime, so great that a person would be punished by torture and death, if they looked at the brilliant show of the heavens, and calculated the distance of the earth from the sun, moon and stars, and proclaimed that there was constant motion of all these brilliants of heaven; and all was harmony, and there was no jumble about it, and never one of them fell to the earth; but all had their orbits and special duties, and the channels that they must travel in to do their duties. And the most curious part of the whole matter that occurred to the observer, was that there was nothing but this ether to be seen to prevent them from going in any direction; but it seemed they loved to go in their places and would not turn and go in any other path.

But persons did suffer the death penalty from christians and other religious people for studying the heavens and proclaiming the truth and beauty of their order and harmony. From this the question naturally arises, why did christians and other religious people do such monstrous wicked deeds? and the answer is distinctly understood. It is because their god was the enemy of the god that made the earth and all the heavenly hosts of sun, moon and stars. These were made by the law god, but the christian religionists worshipped the god of words. If these gods were one or are one that made the stars and the bible, why was this enmity got up? Why were the star-gazers murdered by the bible believers? And why now are they slandered by the bible believers, when the astronomers declare they do not believe the stars and the bible were made by the same god? or were dictated or inspired by the same god? The differences are too great, and the distinctions too manifest.

The heavens declare the glory of one god; it is the god of nature; it is the god of the natural man. The god that made man. The bible declares the glory of another god who declares the natural man is at enmity with him. And if he does not have a change of heart and believe this word of god to be the truth, he is damned. The man must have a new heart to be on friendly terms with this god, and then he becomes an enemy of the natural god and the natural man, and commences his depredations upon his property, his rights, and his liberty, and his life. Right here begins the conflict which can never end until one of these gods perishes from the minds of the people.

Now which in the nature of things must perish? The one who says the stars were made to give the inhabitants of the earth light by night, and swears by himself because he can not swear by any greater, or the god that made the stars and never swore a word nor even thought of swearing, but has left his works to speak for themselves, and the natural man especially the Astronomers, to tell what they think the stars were put in the heavens for. And their conclusions are that they are worlds like our earth or the suns of systems of worlds like our sun, and that the light and beauty of the star spangled heavens at night is only an incident that the people of the earth may admire, but was of the least possible importance and use of the stars. Astronomers do not find stars laying around loose in the heavens ready to fall to the earth, and the sun has other and much larger worlds to give its light and heat to; so that not more than one hundreth part of its light was made for this world. There is such a vast difference between the heavens that the god of the bible made and the heavens that the god of nature made, that we look up to, that the followers of these different creators have been constant enemies, and at open war with each other in words and swords for centuries.

It is said an undevout Astronomer is mad; must he be thought mad because he would not worship a god who had no conception of what the heavens were made for, nor of the plan that was adopted in making them, nor of the movements of the earth, and the heavenly bodies? and is not the christian much more undevout who kills an Astronomer? The earth was not the first world that was made by the law of nature. This natural god made the sun first in our solar system, but it is by no means certain that this was the first sun that was made. But the greatest source of the enmity of christian priests to the Astronomers was that they proved that the earth was a globe that rolled over every day, and to go down was to go towards the center of the earth; and there was no place for their bottomless hell; this proved that the word of their god as written by their inspired saints was a lie made out of the malevolence and ignorant superstition of the writers.

But this falsehood invented by the barbarous natures under the guise of the pretense that their god had given them a new and loving heart, the priests used to frighten all the people they could to join them in threats more barbarous than natural hearts could possibly invent. The ignorant savage natives can torture and murder people, and glory in doing it. But to invent a loving god to make a bottomless burning torturing pit to put the spirits of people in, to continue in its torments to all eternity or everlastingly; can only be invented by educated savage natures, with changed hearts that love god with all their might, mind and strength, as the christian priests did who ordered Astronomers tortured and murdered. They loved god so much that they had nothing but hate for an independent thinking man; and with this hate and their education the priests invented the everlasting tortures that ignorant savages could not think of.

And now when the priests know that there is no flat earth that serves as a cap for their hell of fire and brimstone for tormenting the spirits of wicked men, they proclaim the bible teaches such horrible doctrines as their god's truth; and hold on to the creeds that certify to it; and induce their converts to sign them, when they say they are converted and their god has given them a new heart. Then they hate with holy hatred nature's god and the natural enlightened and truth loving portion of mankind, especially the astronomers who have proved the falsehood of their holy bible in every material respect regarding the heavens and earth.

One of the worst phases of the christian and Jewish believers, in their scriptures, is that they continue the superstitions of the writers who were ignorant of astronomy; and when a comet appears, they are easily excited to the belief that the appearance presages war, pestilence or famine, or great disasters to the human race. And when an eclipse of the sun occurs, that their God is angry with them and stops the sun from shining upon them in His anger. And when little meteors are darting about in the atmosphere and falling to the earth, it presages the day of judgment, the destruction of the earth; the destruction of all unbelievers who would not come into the folds of the churches; in them were the only places of safety. There is no more record that the Jews and christians ever taught people the truth regarding these phenomena; than there is of other superstitious and barbarous people!

The Mohammedans were far ahead regarding astronomical knowledge, of either of these people, at the most enlightened period of the Moslem rule. If the Babylonians understood astronomy when the Jews were captives there, none of it crept into the Jewish biblical record. If the Greeks and Romans understood it, neither the Jewish or christian biblical writers noted it, so as to stop the superstitions that naturally attach to ignorance. So they have fastened the worst phases of superstitious delusions that existed when the biblical texts were written; and ever since they have tried by deception and murder to keep people as ignorant and superstitious about the uses and movements of the heavenly bodies as they possibly could. And as people got knowledge and would not worship and bow to the commands of their god, the priests were constantly harping upon the sins of the people, because they looked upon the heavens as astronomers do, and worship the god of astronomy and reject the gods of the Jews and christians and pronounce them frauds.

One of the most singular phases of the Jewish and christian religion is, that nearly four hundred years ago they burnt an astronomer for telling astronomical truths; and yet in this enlightened age, when they know he did tell the truth, and they tortured and killed him for it, yet they teach as truth the lies that made them murder him. And the same kind of lies made the Mohammedans and Jews murder astronomers centuries before that time, when the dark age of those religious people was inaugurated in Spain and throughout the Mohammedan dominions. Not only astronomers, but all learned scientists that proclaimed the truths of their knowledge to the world, were proclaimed dangerous people, and their utterances were suppressed with a strong hand. This is the result of the dogmatism of the religious people, that makes a despotism in the interest of falsehood, and causes the religious to murder the most truthful and intelligent people in their midst.

Supposing the Christians, Jews and Mohammedans had been sufficiently enlightened to take the knowledge of Copernicus as God's truth, that to believe is salvation and not believe is damnation to their souls. We should at once have been in the same kind of trouble to-day and for a hundred years past. In his time it was supposed the sun could not be more than five millions of miles from the earth. Then some years after it was thought to be thirteen millions of miles, at least. This change in the estimated distance could not have been proclaimed under a despotic religion that had proclaimed five millions the sacred number, until they had killed Tycho Brahe and Kepler for disturbing their sacred number, that one of God's greatest prophets had proclaimed. Then suppose after they had got thirteen millions as the sacred number of miles of the sun from the earth, and then comes along Cassini an age or two after and proclaims that the sun is at least eighty-five millions of miles from the earth; now the blood of Cassini must be poured out for telling this nearer approach to truth, and then his number becomes sacred; and then comes another estimate a hundred years later, that the sun is ninety-five millions of miles from the earth. Then since that time this great number is found too large, and the true estimate is nearer ninety-one millions of miles.

In these estimates we have the changes, in the calculations of men as they obtained more knowledge; and if these estimates had been sanctified and become holy as the Jewish and Christian records have been, and proclaimed by a dogmatic priesthood, the same kind of tortures would have taken place as there has under the older sacred records. And the priests know just as well that these old records are false as they do that the estimates of Copernicus of the distance of the sun from the earth are false; yet they proclaim them true, and are ready to denounce people and say all manner of evil of them who pronounce the Mosaic record as false.

By doing this, the priests are sanctioning the murders that have taken place because of the despotism of the religious people, who thought it necessary to declare the falsehoods truth, and to kill those they could not make agree with them, when they had power, and say all manner of evil of them when they could not kill them. Now the question is, are not these priests who proclaim the same doctrines with the same God and Christ and the same prophets, with their followers, guilty of approving of the murders of their predecessors? are they not assuming the bloody garments of the murderers of the martyrs to science and truth? Their predecessors had no mercy in their religion, and it took all, out of their hearts and minds and put in a murderer's line of practice; and when they could not murder any more they took to the line of defamation and vituperation of the character of their truthful opponents.

When the Pagan, Jewish and Christian priests do these things, as they are doing them to-day, does not all the blood of the martyrs rest on them and besmear their garments? Just think how the churches have gained the power to exist to-day; it is because they have slain the devoted truthful persons of the past ages. If the people of this country will make it just as much blasphemy to speak against the truths of science as it is now to speak against characters of the adopted gods and Christ, christianity would not last longer in Christian countries than the Christian can maintain it by the clash of arms. For it would soon be known that the priests were thirsting for the pap of government as their predecessors had for their blood in past times. For christianity got possession of government control by the war power, and must lose it when they can not have special privileges and the war power to enforce them.

It is generally known at this time that the amount of truth contained in any of the old religions is not enough to enable them to stand by the power of truth. Let the priests be subject to blasphemous libel when they speak against modern scientific truths as they did against the truths of astronomy when that was a new science in Christendom, and it would put a new phase on the pompous priests, if they were subject to fine and imprisonment when they denounced the truth as devilish.

Blasphemy is more of a Jewish and Christian fault against truth than ever a heretic committed against the gods that Jews and Christians have set up for people to worship. And if such laws were enacted it would put the ignorant, fanciful religious notions of the ancients on a par with the well proved truths of science. But instead of giving truth an equal chance against ancient superstitions, the laws give the priests that retail the superstitions that they know are false, the entire power over science. It is no legal fault for them to denounce well proved truths as devilish, dangerous falsehoods, and to say all manner of evil of the persons who promulgate these truths. It is time to make the priests know that worldly truth is as much to be respected as their religious assertions, or those of any of their gods' most precious words. It is time to protect every truth as God's truth, and to put down every lie as the devil's lie, and to call all persons who insist upon teaching falsehood as truth, the devil's imps.

The truth of any statement shall be determined by scientific tests upon scientific principles, under all the lights that free speech and free press can give. Then comes up the question, what shall be the punishment of these lying imps when convicted of promulgating their falsehoods? The humane answer is the true one. Their punishment shall be just as light as it can be, and be sufficient to cause them to reform, and stop them from retailing their falsehoods. It may be that instruction would be all that the person needed. Community might require fine and imprisonment of the person to protect their lives and property. And by these mild means see if we can not teach Christians and other religionists a lesson of humanity that they have never shown toward their opponents, especially astronomers, when few in number and struggling with all their power to find out the truth of their science, and make a scientific religion that shall be as true as man can make it, and as humane and just as it is true; and their God shall be the astronomer's God, that made the heavens and earth of the spirit and matter in space.

CHAPTER IX.

THE RELIGIOUS TEACHINGS OF THE SCIENCE OF GEOLOGY.

The rocky crust of the earth is the book of nature. The first leaf or cover was the granite rock. Then comes the secondary rocks with the impressions on them of crude animals and vegetables. First, the lava period. Second, fundamental rock period. Third, dawning life period. Fourth, Primary Fosiliferous period. And so on until man appears. Geologists have been at work on these rocks for about 200 years. They were not killed by christians very much, as Protestants were allowed free speech. The rocks give the basis of a true history of the earth. The new heart is an enemy of the natural God. This includes all religions that worship a God who saves people because they offer or believe in sacrificial offerings. Geology gives the best illustrations of the laws of order and progression.

THE science of geology has its basis in the rocky crust of the earth. It illustrates the plan adopted by nature's law abiding God, in making the layers of rocks and its soil that now composes the surface of the earth, and its underlying strata. These layers are the earthly leaves of the book of nature's God. The hand of man had nothing to do with making the leaves, or putting the figurative writing on them, and the natural man said nature's law did it or nature's God by nature's law; and these natural people began to look at the figures and impressions on the leaves of this rocky book, and to turn them over, until finally they concluded that they had looked the book over and understood its teachings, and modestly declared their opinions of what the writtings on the rocks declared in regard to the age of the world, that it had existed millions of years, and in fact that it had existed millions of years before the first leaf in the book was made; and fully realized the saying as true; that the mills of the gods grind slow, but they grind exceeding fine, when applied to the rock book of the earth.

The first leaf of this book that was laid down according to their ideas was changed from an impalpable powder to a granulated rock; or from a liquid lava to such a rock. First it was put down fine grained lava rock; then it laid so long as to become the coarse grained rock now called the granite rock. This was the first leaf in God's earthly book, or it may be better to term it the lower cover of the book that was put there to protect the book from being injured by the ever moving molten lava, as the whole mass of the earth had been before this rock was formed. But now after this first rock was formed, commenced the second, with marks of animal and vegetable productions upon it. Here was a leaf, and it may be a number of leaves that contain a number of the forms of different kinds of animals; but all of the simplest and most coarse and ugly looking kind; just such as we should expect would be made out of such bad materials as the law of order and construction had to use in making these vegetable animals. It was the dawning life rock making period, where there was impressed the first appearance of life on earth; and after all, this dawning life rock is considered more like the primary fundamental granite than like the primary fosiliferous rock which follows it, or lays above it.

These periods run into each other. First we have the molten lava period, when the whole face of the earth is covered with waves of lava at an incandescent heat, and all rolling in waves like the oceans of water at the present time; nothing like vegetable or animal life could exist at this time. Then second commenced the fundamental rock making period. But the lava did not harden alike all over the face of the earth; in some places it was boiling lava, in others it was lava rock or hardened lava, while in others it was granitificating; and some of it had become granite rock.

Then commenced the third or dawning life rock making period, where the granite rock was cool enough to permit it. From this it may be that the last part of the first period and the first part of the dawning life period existed at the same time. The rocks of this period bear the first impressions of animal and vegetable life on earth. Then commenced the fourth or primary fossiliferous rock period, as shown by the petrefactions and impressions found on the rocks of that age. And yet the lava is boiling up in some places, and the rock is being granitificated in others, and the dawning life rock is being formed; and still this is the real beginning of the vegetable and animal life, of sufficient size to make an impression on the rocks that a casual observer would notice.

In this period the molusks and fish appear, and the coal tree forests appear, and the immense coal fields are laid down. The period can as well be divided into three periods, as that is the age when molusks first appear, and when fish first appear, and when the coal forests appear. After these ages comes the fifth or the second fossiliferous period, when the rocks show new formations, and the old are not found among them to any great extent. Fishes become abundant in this period. Reptiles appear and become abundant, and of monstrous size in this time, and had a curious resemblance to birds, and birds had reptilian affinities. The mammals appear the first part of this age. They are small and mostly marsupial. Then comes the sixth or tertiary fossiliferous period. In this the most of the monstrous formations of animal life became extinct, and many of the animals of a kind now on earth appear for the first time, and trees and other vegetation which was found before this time became extinct in this period, and new kinds of vegetation appear for the first time on earth. And monkeys and fossilized man appear in the last of this period.

Seventh, The quartenary fossiliferous period, with the later times, too recent for fossils, when monkeys and man abound in great numbers upon the earth. And other animals for the use of man, and vegetables, bearing fruits and grains, that sustain man, as he could not have been sustained before this time. If we could get a complete skeleton of a fossilized man of the sixth or tertiary fossilized period, we should be very likely to have one as near the present species of mankind as the fossilized horse of that period is to the present races of horses.

Geologists have been at work on these rocks to discover their language and meaning for about two hundred years. Their works had not become of sufficient importance before the death penalty in Christian lands, for searching for natural truth, had become mostly inoperative; therefore but few if any of the geologists were murdered by the Christians because they delved into the rocky coverings of the earth, to find the natural God's truth about them, and to learn the order of their creation. But all was done that the civilization of the times would permit by the way of persecutions and prosecutions to prevent the geologists from searching into these rocks to discover the religious teachings which they inculcate. Can any one imagine a more innocent or just undertaking? because if there is God's truth displayed anywhere on earth it is in the rocks. They give us the best specimens of all the past ages of the world, when dug from their native place in mountain or valley; where man could not have altered their figures or impressions, they unmistakably give to the intelligent mind the truth of the world's history. And what is that history? It is that law and order were the gods that ruled. No special providence or wordy god is found; no special catastrophe god is printed there, but growth and decay are marked on all the rocky leaves of the earth; and a progressive development is noticed to be very distinct in each period, from the first to the last. Here is shown to be a natural religion that agrees with the natural man and a natural God; and there is no change of heart necessary for a person to obtain before they can believe and be saved; and there is no persecution of the geologists except from the priests, who have changed hearts and belong to some Christian or other dogmatic religion.

We find the same kind of religionists opposing the facts of geology as we did that opposed the facts of astronomy.

Just as soon as a person has such a changed heart from nature to grace, so that he religiously believes that God made the heavens and earth in six days, and there was a morning and evening to each day, and that on the seventh He rested, such persons are ready to persecute the geologist who proves that there were millions of such days on earth, before man was created, and millions since; and in not one in all that time has the natural God rested or needed rest, as appears from the improvements in the natural earthly forms of animals and vegetables of the present day compared with the past. And the only persons who would question the purity of the motives of the geologists in investigating the rocks of the earth and persecute them, are those whose hearts have been changed from nature to grace, and who have adopted a word God instead of a natural god.

The same kind of persons who killed Astronomers and would kill geologists, if they were sufficiently numerous and strong to do it to-day. They are the enemies of natural truth, justice and humanity: and their history shows them to be the most heartless and bloodthirsty of any that ever inhabited the earth. This includes all the sacrificial religious people, whether they make sacrificial offerings, or adopt the principal that they are saved by sacrificial offerings.

The special laws that geology is best calculated to illustrate, are the laws of order and progression. Here we have order for millions of years, that is marked by successive steps of the progress of the condition of the world to produce better vegetable and animal life, until man appears; and then for thousands of years since man could live on the earth to the present time, until man shines forth with all the intelligence that clear, precise, practical thinking gives to the most intelligent people of the age. Many geological facts and theories have been given when treating of the time that the earth has existed.

CHAPTER X.

THE RELIGION THAT THE SCIENCE OF CHEMISTRY TEACHES.

It agrees with Astronomy and geology. These sciences teach the same kind of religions. We are not to throw these sciences aside when we take up the mental spiritual sciences. We should follow the true prophet. If religion does not teach the sciences, it does not teach systematised truth. Chemistry considers the movements of the ultimate invisible atoms of matter; matter has intelligence. It is as difficult for spirit and matter to make a God as it is for them to design all things. Spirit and matter have had an eternal existence. Chemistry does not show an accident or miracle. All is under law and order. Atom joins atom to make a chemical composition. Chemical proof has been mostly gathered in this century. It is not found in holy books. Crystalization the work of the laws of nature. The different kinds of crystals show the different substances of which they are composed. The fundamental forms of crystals. The idea is that they have a polarity. It may be a crystal begins with cells like animals. People not to be condemned for not believeing it. The four elements of the ancients. The twenty-nine elements known in the last century. The ether above our atmosphere 58 degrees below zero. The sun's rays do not heat it. No heat in the sun's rays. Heat expands articles, but does not increase their weight. Heat travels with the veloscity of light. Heat is a spirit of matter. Light is a spirit of matter. The rainbow. The dark surfaces absorb the heat of the sun more than white surfaces. Mercury is whiter than Neptune. Twenty billions of miles makes a sun appear like a little star. It is strictly under law. Light travels about 186,000 miles a second. Light the most important power in the universe. Electricity is one of the spirits of matter, like mind. Spirit cannot exist without matter, and matter cannot move without spirit. But law governs. B. Franklin discovered Lightning and electricity were the same powers. It travels about as fast as light. In this subtle power we find law is God. The religion that places a God above law, was made by persons ignorant of the facts. Attraction and gravitation. The earth attracts all things towards its center. Who would think that people that pretend to be the best in the world would be the only ones to murder the persons who searched into chemical truths? Professor Hare at Albany. The chemist first to suffer, and may be the last martyrs.

We have seen that the religion taught by astronomy and geology was one founded on law and order in nature. Now let us look at chemistry Man can not regulate the movements of the sun and planets; they are too large for him to handle; so of the rocks. Man has not interfered in the making of the rocks as they are laid down in nature; these works are too large for him. Here are other works that are too small. The handling of the atoms of matter. Man cannot interfere in the great and small deeds, so nature shows her works uninfluenced by man. The chemical works of nature show that all atoms of matter find their places exactly, and the different kinds of matter unite in the same proportion every time to make the same kind of compound chemical substance. In all these sciences, man stands by and looks on and sees what nature does, and the way it does it so far as man can comprehend the works of nature. The lessons learned by these scientists are not to be forgotten and thrown away when we take up the mental and spiritual sciences. Where man becomes the principal agent and often proclaims himself a God or some kind of supreme being; or the right hand assistant of such a being. When we bring these persons down to the making and moving of worlds, and handling the little atoms of matter of which great worlds are made, they are exposed, and show their powers are nothing to compare with the tasks that are required of them. We ask them to so change the movements of this world and the sun and moon so that eclipses will not occur as the astronomer has prophesied, yet they will occur in the regular order of the movements of these bodies; and if he does change them or they are changed according to his plan, then we shall say the Astronomer is a false prophet, and he the true one; and greater than the God of the Astronomer who prophesies falsely at least. But if the Astronomer is right, every time, and the mental spiritual prophet is wrong, then the astronomer is the true prophet and the god of the mental prophet, without pretending to be his god. It is about time for peopl to begin to follow the prophets that are true, and prove by their prophecies that turn out true constantly, to be the true prophets; and prophets who make an occasional hit, but are often false, to be put among deceviers.

It has been said that religion does not teach the sciences. This is equivalent to saying it does not teach systematized truth, which has been the fact about all religions until the scientific religion began to be taught. And the scientists did not think they were teaching religion until the religionists began to persecute and murder them for presuming to question the statements in the bible and other religious text books, or rather because the systematized truths of the sciences proved the falsehood and inconsistency of biblical statements. And chemistry seemed to be as far removed from religious teaching as any science could be. Yet the lynx-eyed christian religionist saw in it the truths that would be joined with other scientific truths, and finally overthrow their unsystematized and disjointed religious statements and sentiments, that their priests are ever proclaiming but never putting into form so that they can be practically and and usefully adopted in the ordinary affairs of a good life.

The Christians and the other religionists of the great religions of the world, have been engaged in a most dastardly, cruel and murderous war against the acquisition and systematizing of knowledge, for the last six hundred years, not to go back of Roger Bacon, whom they imprisoned for years because of his chemical discoveries. Chemistry takes into consideration the movements of the ultimate invisible atoms of matter, and the power that moves them, and finds there is an intelligent principle attached to every particle of matter which directs it where to go and where to stay, and when to move and when to be stationary. It finds every particle of matter has the wisdom of a God, and they do not find that a few particles of this matter combined with spirit is made into a God. They find a designing law, but not a designing personal God of that law. They find that a certain kind of combination of matter and spirit makes a mental brain power, that is superior to any power on earth except the power that makes the brain; and that power they find in every atom of matter under the direction and order of the animal's and man's personal life-giving powers and laws.

It is as difficult to understand how this matter and spirit can combine together to make a God to design all things, as it is to understand how matter and spirit can make the design and execute it, without making a God first to establish the plan, the design and the execution. It is easier for an intelligent person to think that matter and spirit made a personal God, than it is for them to think a personal God made spirit and matter. It would seem that spirit and matter, law and order, have had an eternal existence, and force and motion are brought into existence when required by law and order to make a beginning for any purpose. And if a personal God was ever made, he is subject to law and order so far as by chemistry people have been able to discover, and so far as scientists have yet been able to learn in any of the departments of knowledge. There is one point especially to be noted in chemistry; there are no accidents or special providences or special catastrophies or destructions in chemical combinations. However confused things may appear to the uninformed, all is directed by law and order. Water is always composed of one part hydrogen and eight parts oxygen, no matter how many other substances are mixed with it, however roily it may be; pure water is always made of the same kind of atoms combined in the same proportions. So all matter when combining chemically, always does so in certain fixed proportions which must be determined by experiments; there is no other way by which chemists can know. They must find out by an analysis; that is by, decomposing, or separating the various kinds of atoms from each other, and so determine what quantity of each was contained in the article analyzed, or by synthesis they must take the elements of the substance and put them together and make the article, and thus determine its composition.

In this way chemists have separated oxygen and hydrogen in water, and determined the quantity of each, and then they have combined oxygen and hydrogen together and made water; and by these two processes they have demonstrated the composition of water, beyond a doubt. The theory is that atom joins atom and makes the chemical composition, or one, two, three, four or five. Atoms of one simple substance join with one atom or more of another simple substance and make different kinds of compositions. But there has been no discovery yet that a half atom of one kind unites with a whole atom of any other kind to make a chemical compound. That whole atoms unite with whole atoms, is the theory.

It is better to refer persons to chemical works for further information on this subject than to give it here. But it should be remarked that this proof has been given principally in this century; there was none for religious people to make their observations upon before; they would look in vain in their holy book for this information; their God had not given it to them, but had given them such instruction that for centuries they had persecuted the persons who were trying to find out nature's God by searching into the works of nature, as the chemists have done.

The poets had said long before this that order was heaven's first law, and rebuked the christians sharply for not permitting people to find out all they could about it, and prove that it was earth's first law also, if they could. Now this has been done, and the chemist has established the God of law over all things on the earth, and have relegated the God of words and commands to a place of very little consequence only as an instrument to deceive and degrade mankind. He is the God of man's ignorant imaginations, and only used by the learned to degrade mankind; or he is the God of the superstitious, who are fearful that he will bring untold misery and condign punishment upon all who do not worship him by words, forms and ceremonies; and the rule of this God is the rule of the malignant, superstitious or ignorant, all over this world; and the bible that does not rebuke such worshipers and uphold the God of nature as he is demonstrated to exist by the modern chemist in this world, is not a fit bible for the people of this age, when the material and spiritual sciences have given them so much knowledge.

The crystalization of the various substances of the earth are the most beautiful and orderly works of the laws of nature that has come under the observation of chemists in this world. Each substance assumes its peculiar form. Common salt always crystalizes in cubes, alum in octohedrons. Salt Peter in six sided prisms; and Epsom salts in four sided prisms; and other substances take on their peculiar forms. This is so certain that chemists often tell the composition of a crystal by its shape. All crystals are laid in scales or lamina so that they have a beautiful cleavage that jewelers take advantage of in shaping their brilliants for settings in their various works of art. And the chemist takes advantage of it to determine the primary and secondary formations. There are said to be six primary or fundamental forms of crystals. There are a great many secondary forms, all of them are modifications of the six primary forms.

The cause of this variety in the forms of crystals is one of the most interesting studies of the chemist. The general opinion is that the atoms of the crystals have a polarity, or are under the influence of the electrical or magnetic forces, and are obliged to form under the direction of this power into the various shapes in which they are found in nature, and in the arts, when the laws of nature are allowed to have the entire control, when crystals are being formed. Yet back of the primal forms before mentioned, all crystals seem to be in a circular or egg shape form; then after the peculiar life giving magnetic forces begin their work. This life gives the especial kind of form which its composition demands. It may be that there is a cell to the crystal the same as there is to vegetable and animal life, and the power of the life in that cell determines the kind or shape of the crystal to be formed, the same as the life power in the vegetable or animal cell determines the kind of vegetable or animal that must be formed.

This is a very plausable theory, and if adopted in the religion of science after many experiments and observations, it will not oblige every person to believe it or be damned. Our religion will not permit of such profane denunciations, because our God does not use such language, and profanity will soon cease to exist in a community where the scientific religion has a dominent power over all the individuals. We do not condemn people for their belief any more than we condemn the boy who breaks a valuable jewel to find how it is made; but we try to impress upon his mind that such works are not well calculated to make the discoveries he is in search of, and are too expensive to be practised until he acquires more knowledge or less valuable crystals.

The boy is said to be the father of the man; and we should instruct him how to acquire all knowledge with the least possible destruction of valuable articles. We should condemn all wrong acts. But every avenue to knowledge should be opened to him or to the girl of like enquiring mind, that can be legitimately done, and where there are wrong laws in society that condemn persons for trying to get knowledge, they should be repealed or made null and void.

FIRE—CALORIC OR HEAT.

The ancients regarded earth, air, fire and water, as the only elementary substances of the world; and it may be truthfully said that their knowledge of fire was as accurate as any kind of information they had upon any subject. Their knowledge was wholly sensual, and the little reason they obtained, from injuring or burning themselves. And this only enabled them to think it best to keep out of the fire and away from other hurts, but did not enable them to go back of appearances to the facts, as is the habit of scientists in this age. In this way the modern chemists have not proved fire to be matter, but only the action of matter. It was for a long time thought by chemists to be an imponderable substance. But to-day it is thought to be the motion of matter only. But scientists never put people to torture or death because they do not believe it, matter or not matter. In the beginning of this century there were but twenty-nine simple substances known to the chemist. Now we have sixty-two or more.

The discovery of thirty-three new simple substances in this century does not shock the scientific world. Any little change in the religious world frets the priesthood, and it is time we had a religion that would not be shocked at the discovery of God's truth in any department of knowledge. The ether or atmosphere above the earth's atmosphere is said to be fifty-eight degrees below zero, Fahrenheit's thermometer. The sun's rays comes millions upon millions of miles through this ether and the outer portion of our atmosphere, and does not heat it perceptibly, but when it gets to a certain density of the atmosphere it begins to heat it; and when these rays fall plum unobstructed upon the earth they create great heat on the level of the ocean. Yet, strange to say, there is no heat in these rays, as is proved by the experiments of trying to burn white paper in the focus of the light of a convex lens, where black paper would be ignited almost instantly, while a coal of fire would burn the white as quickly as it would the black paper. It is curious to note that heat expands many articles, such as iron and other metals, and yet does not perceptibly increase their weight. Now the question is, what is it that expands these articles?

Heat is not a substance, and can nothing expand something? The wave that causes heat is something; can that enter the iron and weigh nothing? When it is in the ether of space it seems to have the velocity of light, and when expanding substances it goes slower than a snail on a rail. Here we have a law that rules, and if any god attempts to rule it he may burn his fingers or freeze them, according to the effect of the law which he attempts to overrule; for the law is commander here as well as elsewhere. Heat or caloric is not matter, but one of the spirits of matter, that is potent in all the life-giving energies of the earth.

LIGHT.

The present opinion is that light is nothing but the motion of matter. It is that physical agent of moving matter which, acting upon matter, produces the sensation of light. It is curious to note that light which is nothing can use matter so effectively as to produce heat, electricity and vegetable and animal life, and make great chemical changes among the atoms of the earth, and yet there is no heat or electrical power in it when it strikes upon a perfectly white surface. And there is another circumstance of striking interest; that is that light can be divided into all the colors of the rainbow, and besides all these colors it has heat and electrical and chemical powers inside or outside of the seven colors of the rainbow or prison light; and yet the atmosphere is proved to be perfectly white, and it never could be heated by the sun's rays if it were not for the particles of matter in it; and so when clouds intervene between these rays from the sun to the earth with sufficient density, you see the lightning flash and hear the thunder's roar.

But when the vapor of water is mixed in small quantities with the pure air, all is so transparent that very little light, heat and electricity is absorbed or lost from the rays of the sun light; so little that the vapor of the atmosphere when far enough above the earth freezes and turns into ice or snow, and remains perpetually on the highest mountains. Nothwithstanding there is little light and heat that is rubbed off, there is some; and this little will require that each planet must be colored according to its distance from the sun. Mercury, the nearest to the sun must be the whitest, and Neptune the farthest off, must be the darkest, to keep the one from a very uncomfortable heat and the other from being to cold for animal life. Our globe is clothed in a dark green vegetation, and the earth is covered in the hottest, most desolate sections, with the whitest colored sand.

The great expanse of water in the equatoral region also tends to make that region habitable as well as the high mountains. The equatorial regions of Mercury and Venus will be found to be cooled in a similar manner, only whiter or more mountaneous and more water. While Mars and all the outer planets will have less of these heat resisting and disipating elements in their equatorial regions. From all these considerations it becomes a very nice and important question to find out how much light, heat electricity and chemical power is lost in the sun's light in a million miles, or how much from planet to planet, that are several millions of miles apart. We see that twenty billions of miles distance makes a great sun appear like a small star. This shows what an immense distance is required for the light of suns to pass, before their light becomes imperceptable to the naked eye, and shows that the comparatively short distance from our sun to Neptune a little short of three thousand million miles the sun will be quite large, and if it has a very dark surface for its rays to strike upon, that it would be capable of producing great heat on that planet. This shows the peculiar structure of the atmospheres and ethers that the light passes through, that does not absorb it, rub it off or disorganize it; so but that it retains all the elements it started with, with a little diminution of power, until finally, after traversing immense distances, like billions on billions of miles, it becomes star like in its light and power. Here we see some of the most intricate and wonderful works of the God of nature, the law God.

Will any one pretend that there is any power of heaven or earth given among men to change such laws in any degree, any more than a tree does when it shades its roots, or a mountain when it shades a valley. Here is prepared a light to pass through the transparent ether, loaded down with heat, electricity, magnetism, chemical power, and the life-giving power of all that has life on earth. Who will say to the law-God, take off some of these burdens of light; take from it the chemical power of decomposition and recomposition, or any other of its powers; will he do it? Is there any such change to be made in answer to prayers and supplications, in the world's true history? No such transaction has ever happened. Light is not matter, but one of the spirits of matter.

It is very difficult to understand how nothing can push something aside and create a wave; we can see how something dropped into water that makes a wave that may extend thousands of miles; and it is possible to see how a breath from man can make a wave that will bear all the inflections of his voice for a distance of many rods in the air. But it is possible to start a substance to make a wave from the sun. The substance of the sun begins a wave of light, and after that it is nothing only a wave; the substance is left in the sun, as the pebble that is dropped in the water remains there while the wave it created goes to the end of the ocean. So the substance that made the light wave remains in the sun, while the wave of light goes millions of miles in the ether at the rate of about 186,000 miles per second.

Light starts from a luminous body and passes through ether and other transparent substances until it strikes some opaque body and is absorbed or continues on its journey until it is lost in the eternity of space. In all its creation and moves it is under the laws that compel it to go where the law directs. It is created by force and propelled by law. Law created the force and took charge of the motion. And it must be considered that every wave of light had its special work to do and did it; and not a particle of the immense light of the sun is lost. There are planets and satelites and other opaque bodies to absorb all that is not needed to keep the ether free and ready to do its duty. Light seems to be the most important power in the universe; it is constantly at work, and the commander of almost all work that is done in nature, while it is itself under the laws of nature. It would seem that an intensely illuminated body contains all the substances and forces in nature, all life and all forms of life; all motion and all forms of motion; and if it has not all these powers when it strikes an opaque body, it seems to have the power to produce in the opaque body these lives and motion. This applies especially to the light of the sun striking on the earth. A wave of light contains electricity, heat, sound, and chemical action, or it finds them immediately on striking the earth or a cloud of the earth, or its atmosphere; whatever has power to refract the light like air and water, no doubt causes it to assume the other wave powers or carry them with it to be ready to do the work assigned to it and them by law.

Now if man is made by the chemical action of light, heat, electricity and the most if not all the sixty-four elements of matter, and besides these he has a special life principle which makes him grow to be a man distinguishable from other animals, and all species of animals have their peculiar life principle that give them their peculiar powers and avocations in life, as well as their size, form, color and strength, and gives them instinctive knowledge of the food they want to sustain life. Where did they get this power and knowledge? Every particle of matter and spirit of which they are made, is governed by law.

The combination of the forces that made them was governed by law, and all the matter had knowledge, or the law made it appear that it had. Then where can we go in nature to find any power that governs law? God is governed by law or law is God, whether we go to matter, organized matter, or to the spirit of matter, of which light, heat, and electricity are the most potent known to man, we find the same testimony; and if a person wishes to prove that there is a power above and commanding law, they must go outside of chemistry for their proof. So we need not go beyond the spirit and matter that composed the intelligence that animals and man have, to find where they get their mental powers or intelligence.

ELECTRICITY.

Electricity is one of the three imponderable substances or motions of matter that seems to hold the same relation to matter that mind has to the brain; they give it life and intelligence or the instinct to obey its commands. They are the spirit of matter and the God of nature, so far as the scientists have yet discovered. They can not do anything without matter, and matter can not move without this spirit, or if we take them separately without these three spirits heat, (or caloric) light and electricity. They exist in all space wherever matter exists, so far as known, and make life in matter that is called lifeless, and cause it to have the same intelligence, when the conditions are favorable, as matter manifests in the vegetable and animal creations.

It may be discovered that light and heat are only certain actions of electricity, but according to present knowledge they are three distinct motions of matter, and for the religion they inculcate they may be so considered; they are a true God that science has discovered that is composed of nothing, and can do nothing only in connection with matter; and yet it has great power to manifest in connection with it. But here comes in another power that makes these manifestations come to time and obey law; and that is the law of nature that has control of all things in the heavens and earth.

Dr. Benjamin Franklin, with his kite and string, discovered that the lightning of the thunder clouds was of the same kind of electricity that was produced by the electrical machines, that followed the same law and was governed or conducted by the same means. Some experiments seem to prove distinctly that there is but one kind of electricity; others seem to make this a little uncertain; they seem to indicate there may be a positive—that is, distinct from negative electricity. When persons try the magnetic forces that keep the needle pointing north and south, they find there is a magnetic or electrical current flowing round the needle that holds it in its place; it flows on at the north end and off at the south end. This indicates that there is but one kind of electricity, and the positive and negative powers are made by one line of movement of one electricity. But magnetism by magnetic batteries have different powers, according to the size of the plates; one size will create great heat, another has great decomposing powers—that is, to decompose water and separate it into its original elements, hydrogen and oxygen.

The velocity that electricity travels seems about the same as light by the magnetic telegraph wire. Experiments seem to determine that it travels about 100,000 miles per second; but in either it seems to keep up with light. Here again in this subtle power we find law is god, and we can not go back of it; and the religion that places a god over law was made by persons entirely ignorant of scientific truths, obtained by the same means that other knowledge is; that is, by experimental observations. Electricity and magnetism are not matter, but the spirit of matter that pervades all matter, and with the aid of the other spirits of matter cause all the movements in the heavens and earth.

ATTRACTION OF GRAVITATION.

The earth attracts all bodies within its attractive power towards its center. All things on the face of the earth are held there by this power, and all things that are above the earth are attracted or pulled towards it by this gravitation power; and when anything is thrown up from the earth it goes against this power. This is as near the breaking of a law of nature as man or God has ever been able to do. And this is as near a miracle as any religious person can point to. That is, by the force of one law to overcome another. Persons can walk on the water if they have either spiritual power to buoy them up, or a material power, and they can walk on the air in the same way; they must have some power to hold them up, that is equal to their gavitation that pulls them down.

A spirit cannot live and be at home in the ether above our atmosphere, unless it is lighter than the ether. They would feel uncomfortable in a situation where the elements around them were lighter than they are, just the same as a good swimmer feels in water, not afraid, yet not at home as he does on his own terafirma. All miracles, whether made by beasts, man or God, have just as much foundation as these have and no more; and theology has its foundation in miracles of that character; the whole range of spirit powers to overcome the laws of nature is not yet fully understood, but it is well known that they can take persons through burning flames, and allow them to rub burning embers of fire on their hands and faces, and remain unscorched, unburnt; but how often it can be done is not established; but that such things can be done is well attested in the annals of modern spiritualism, and by the records of ancient religions. If spirits prevent the chemical combinations according to nature's law, this does not break the law at all; it is only suspended in that transaction by spirit power; but the law continues in force just the same.

Who would think that there could be a class of religious people who pretended they had a changed and a better heart than common people, would be the people, and the only people who imprison, torture and murder the chemists because they looked into the secrets of nature, where the god of nature resides. Yet there is the history to prove it was so; and now these very religious people who have a god of grace instead of one of nature, oppose the investigation of the doings of the law of the god of nature. Just consider the conduct of the religious scientists towards Professor Hare, the most eminent scientific chemist of his time in this country. See one of them jump up in their convention in Albany, N. Y., in 1856, and move that he be allowed a half hour to speak in a lunatic asylum instead of being allowed in that convention. Then hear Professor Agasiz say that was an insult to such an eminent scientist, and then move that he be heard then and there. Then to see another member get up and second the motion; but as that was not a religious body, that they adjourn for the half hour to hear him, and this was done. Was the spiritualism of which he talked any more religion than chemistry? Not a bit. Chemistry shows us nature's god's little works in this world. Spiritualism shows the works of spirits. If God's works are more important than spirit works, then chemistry is more of a religion that spiritualism, ancient or modern. But they wanted to insult Professor Hare, and the christian portion would have instituted an inquisition on him if the popular feeling of the people of the country would have permitted it, just as they did on chemistry a few centuries ago.

The fact is, the sciences have taken from the ancient religionists all their pretended religious truth except what is attached to spiritualism; and what they have of that is proved to be false by modern spiritualism, and if that is to prevail, then they will not have a spiritual or worldly truth to hang their salvation and damnation services upon, and people will not love their God nor fear their devil, nor listen to their harangues on their plan of salvation. But this consummation will not be reached until after a very severe and bloody fight. Not a science has been taken from the religion of superstition and placed to the credit of the religion of science until the harmless, the pious, the loving christians have been beat in bloody battle. Therefore these pretended peaceful gentlemen will not allow their last and strongest hold on the public to be captured until after one of the most terrible slaughters the world has ever seen. This can truly be seen as coming by the hatred they manifested to Professor Hare, and now manifest to living scientists in other countries, and as chemists were the first to feel their inhumanity, they may be the last to suffer martyrdom from their hands.

CHAPTER XI.

THE RELIGION TAUGHT BY THE SCIENCE OF BOTANY.

There are two kinds of Botany, fossilized and present growing vegetation. The law of progress is plainly shown by the fossilized plants. The law of like producing like is shown by every kind producing its kind. When forests and useful plants are destroyed, if we would have useful plants again we must sow the seed or wait for nature to produce the plants and trees by slow growth. Under the laws of production the God of words is a failure. Plants and trees have their particular distinguishing characteristics. Did a God of law or words do that? Botany trains the mind of the student the best of any study. Potatoes and other plants. Miracle God is an uncertain God. Spirits are the best advisers. The first plants seen by a psychometrist. The coal period. The law of progress and order shown to exist. More to be said when speaking of animals.

WE have two kinds of Botany, that relating to plants that are fossilized and plants now growing on the earth. The fossilized plants show the regular progress in the growth of plants, from the most crude and unpromising for the use of man, until trees for fruit and building purposes, and for fire, and schrubs for the berries and other uses of man are the natural product of the times and the soil. Here again we have the regular order of growth and progress, showing that the God of law prevails, and not the God of words. But man is ruthlessly destroying our pine forests regardless of the wants of the time; and unless this is checked, the time will come when the noble pine forests will cease to exist in the lands where man can find them; and the most useful natural grasses for the uses of man in the Rocky mountain section of this continent are being ruthlessly destroyed by herdsmen with their great bands, as they call them, of sheep and cattle. How are these to be replaced, by the God of words or the God of law? Which shall we teach the people to regard in their religious worship in repairing these wrongs?

When we look at the grasses and trees, we find every grass has its peculiar habits, and looks, and all kinds are easily distinguished by their particular shape and color; and every species of trees has its distinguishing form and color of bark and leaves, and the wood has its special hardness or soft texture, and its peculiar color and odor; some of it is light, some heavy, some of it is very elastic; some very brittle; some trees have limbs that spread to a great distance when left natural, others grow tall and the limbs grow up close by the side of the body of the tree. Were all these different kinds of vegetation the result of accident or miracles, or of a God who governed by miracle, or one that could change the law by which they were formed? Just think of the thousands upon thousands of the different species of grasses, trees, and shrubs, each kind having a family resemblance, and yet all different so they are easily distinguished by the botanist. Can there be any doubt that this was done by an all commanding law?

Let any one attempt to describe the stems leaves and flowers of plants, and they will soon find the great necessity of accurate terms; for these plants are so nearly alike that if the description is not exact, it will describe some other plant.

Much is said of the value of mathematics to train the mind to accurate thinking; and there is no doubt of its great value in that line in reaching conclusions; but it does not give persons words for accurate descriptions. The study of the ancient languages, especially Greek, and Latin, are of great advantage in giving persons the true definitions of words, so they can give flowery descriptions, which are of great value in giving persons the use of language which has a general acuracy, but lacks that specific descriptive accuracy which is often necessary in science. The study and practice of law, gives persons great accuracy in describing legal points. But they must learn to change the meaning of sentences so as to be ready to take any side of a question.

Of this kind of language the priests have the greatest range; their plan is to make up a beautifully bombastic sermon with nothing of real meaning in it, except their dogmas; and the real idea with them is to keep them as much out of sight as possible; this is their game; persons who wish to follow such a course, may do well to study mathematics, Greek, and Latin, and law, and they may be benefitted in their deceptive mannerism of speech. But if they want to get at the subject to make them accurate and true in speech, there is not any study or science that will train the mind to so accurate a description of any and every subject as botany. When a person takes a plant and begins a description, they at once feel the necessity of accuracy in their observation of the distinctive peculiarities of the plant, and the necessity of using the exact words that will express their meaning to a nicety; and if they fail in giving the right words in the description, they soon find they have described another plant; and unless the description is altered and amended, it is useless jumble, but when the plant is accurately described, any person who will take the trouble to take the plant and compare it with the description, they will find them to agree; and if they have another kind of plant, they will find there minute but plain differences between that and the description. Who made these thousands upon thousands of similar and disimilar plants, trees, shrubs, mosses, leaves, flowers, fragrance, and different shades of colors?

Was it not the God of law, the God that is ruled by law? Did a miracle God ever do this, and can he continue to make each of these vegetables produce their kind and no other? It is impossible for the well trained mind to conclude that the author of all this variety and unison could be produced in any other way but by a fixed and immutable law. Just look at the sensitive plant; how it shrinks away from the touch of man or beast.

The potato bears its fruit for the use of man at the root. The tomato has its fruit on its stalk above the ground. The cabbage has its fruit above the ground. The turnip in the ground. The bark and buds of the cinnamon tree are used by man for their pleasant flavor and fragrance, and the fruit of cloves for the same purposes; and other spices are the fruit of the spice trees. The rose is raised for the beauty and fragrance of its flowers, and the raspberry for its excellent fruit. How is it that every seed produces its kind of plant or shrub, and that we can calculate upon the kind of fruit or flowers it will produce? Is it by a miracle or by a law?

If man bases his farming calculations upon miracles and sows cockle, expecting to raise wheat, his mistake would be no greater than it is if he bases his religion on a god of miracles and expects to have his salvation made sure under any rule or law of life. The miracle that his god will make next is as uncertain and unreliable as the shifting scenes of a kaleidoscope. Good works may save them to-day, but they may not be of any value the next day. The principles upon which salvation is based may have changed, and this is exactly the condition in which we find christians; the hope one day is sure and certain, next day they are despondent and very uncertain about their salvation; and then comes seasons of the greatest despair; prayers and hopes fail them, and so they live lives of great exaltation and great depression. They have no certain law of salvation that they can depend upon.

How is it with the farmer? He depends upon the law that every seed will produce its kind; no mistake in that. The astronomer prophesies by a law, and is never deceived unless he is wrong in his figures. He has a certain law of motion to guide him. And now the time has come to have a religion that gives the law of salvation just as certain; and the scientific religion does that. The law of nature presents the way, and the spirits are the best of advisers to keep you well posted regarding the best kind of living and works. But do not take them as infallible; the best of them are our best friends, and it is good to hold sweet counsel with them as friends frequently. Can any one imagine a more delusive, deceiving system of religion to be given to mankind than the one that teaches that there is a god that can control the laws of the universe, and the natural and spiritual laws that control mankind, and does control and change them to make a miracle? If he could do this on a little scale to man, he could do it to all vegetables, and there would be no reliable standard for any persons to be guided by to determine what would be the right plan to adopt for the morrow.

We have seen that all the present vegetation of the world is produced, grown, fashioned, made and finished under special specific laws. And now let us see how it is regarding psychometric observations as to their first appearance on the earth, and their subsequent changes in growth and peculiarities. In giving these notes I am guided by the "Soul of Things," by William Denton, the same as noted on the earliest animal life of earth, vol. 3d. The first vegetation observed is sea weed. It is red and short, about half as long as his little finger. This is near the sea shore. Then in some places he sees rich soil and a kind of plant in it that has little branches like fine needles. It is about an inch high. This is all the vegetation that I have noted in the book in the Laurentian and Cambrian ages.

Now we come forward in time to the Silurian age. Here what is first observed as part vegetable, and part animal, is a lily-like growth that is seen in bunches growing like a lot of lilies from a stem; they were at the bottom of the ocean; they were crenoids. He sees many of them washed ashore dry and dead, some sticking to rocks out of water, but dead. He sees floating on the water what look like plants growing, spread out like Irish moss; next he sees vegetation like very fine blades of grass; again he sees other vegetation a little like mullen, but no stalks; the leaves spread on the ground; on looking closely they seem cut up like fern; next, in speaking of the trilobites' eggs, he remarks that they are attached to weeds, and each other. Then he sees some fine Iceland moss sea weed, but no large ones.

This completes about all the vegetable life that I find in this volume, in this Silurian period. The next period above the last described is the Devonian period, denominated also the age of fishes. I do not find any special description of the plants of this period; the psychometer saw trees, but gives no particular description of them. So we pass over this period and begin on the next above it, that is, the carboniferous or coal bearing period, or the age of plants. In this age coal trees seemed to grow very fast and were very soft and sappy, so that it appeared they could not stand, only they grew so thickly together at the top that they held each other from falling. They grew to great size and height. They were where the water was two or three feet deep, and the young trees just coming out of the water looked like cabbages. It seems a curious law of nature to turn these trees into hard coal that is so useful to mankind in the modern ages. A man is said to have turned water into wine many centuries ago, but here nature turned the water, sap, and wood into coal, which is of vastly more use to mankind than water turned to wine. Some of the leaves appeared ten feet long or more. There were a great variety of trees. There was a large tree, hollow like a reed, and are growing where the water is six feet deep, yet there is no water in their hollow trunks, or their hollow roots that go into the ground. There are many flowers, but not a great variety, I should think, in this coal age. There were great numbers of large fungi, or large mushrooms in common language; some of these were so large they could hold a number of persons in their cup if they were strong enough to bear them.

From this period the earth became productive of a greater variety of vegetable life, but the coal period seems to have the greatest amount that was turned to coal. It seemed to be a kind of wood that would not burn or rot, but would turn to coal, that is one of the greatest blessings of this age to mankind. From this time vegetation began to assume its present form more and more, as time passed, until the vegetables were prepared for the advent of man on earth. Here any one can see the same law of progress is made manifest by psychometry as by geology; all the sciences agree that the law rules ungoverned by any power.

When any one looks at the animal kingdom they find the same law rules. There is no commotion or perturbation in all the vegetable and animal creation, more than there is in the starry heavens, that is not designed by law for some purpose which would be accomplished by this to us extraordinary movement. I have followed the vegetable growth from the little needle like appearances, from age to age, as put down by geologists generally, and by psychometrists, until I come to the plant age and coal period. The observations of the psychometers from this time forward do not seem sufficiently marked in vegetable growth to show the distinct ages that have passed. But for these the reader is referred to the chapter on Zo-ology. From these psychometric observations, as well as from geologists, it appears that the greatest vegetable growth was attained long before the greatest animal growth; and the greatest animal growth long before the present species of man appeared on earth, and the present kind of wholesome fruits and vegetables upon which we exist and the animals feed upon, that are killed by man to be used as food to nourish his body and enable him to accomplish the great work which his great mind and refined spirit was designed to accomplish in this world, and all coming worlds.

CHAPTER XII.

ZO-OLOGY.

THE RELIGIOUS TEACHINGS OF THE SCIENCE OF THE ORIGIN AND GROWTH OF ANIMALS.

Progressive improvement of animal life. Man can destroy the useful animals, or make them more useful. Fossilized and living animals. What is it that gives the leopard his spots, and other animals their peculiar stripes and colors and powers? A law god or word god? William Denton's "Soul of Things." Some of the first forms of animal life. Animal life in various periods and ages until man appears. People have got out of savage and barbarous life, except in religion. The law god rules.

HERE we have the same order and progress that we have in the other sciences; the meanest animals were first made, and there has been continual progress until the present time; and man can not change the progressive improvement, but he can kill off the present species of the most useful animals, as he has killed off the best grasses in large tracts of country by over-feeding, and an inferior grass that cattle and sheep can not thrive on is now growing. And the most useful seals and sea lions can be destroyed by man, and an inferior race will be substituted by nature to fill their places; that is, inferior for the uses of mankind. And if man chooses to fill the rivers and lakes and oceans with useful fish and animals, he can do so by the law of nature, which is now being enforced in many countries. The race of men who are the ruthless destroyers of the best and most important animals for the uses of men are disappearing under the direction of scientific persons, and by the support of governments of those who are propagating the most useful of animal life.

In animal life, as in the vegetable, we have two kinds of subjects to consider. The fossilized remains of animals, and the living species. It is one of the most interesting studies in nature to trace the growth of animal life by their fossils in the rocks, and above them in the alluvial soil. We begin with the smallest and most ill-shaped kind of animal life, and as one kind dies off, another and better succeeds them, until we come to the living species of the present time, and man heads the list; and there is an improvement now going on in all animal life. This progress is noticed in my remarks on geology. And there, as here, any one can see that the animal was under the control of the law of progress. Slowly by millions upon millions of years this law has controlled the animal growth. No miraculous god's work in all this time. Improvement upon improvement has taken place, and the law is doing its work now continually, and will be until the earth has arrived at its maturity, and finally passes on to its decaying period. Then there is every evidence that its decay and that of the animals on it will be under that law, and no god of miracles can prevent it.

What is it that gives the leopard his spots, the tiger his stripes, the lion his mane, the rhinoceros his central horn on his head, the elephant his trunk, the camel-leopard his high fore-shoulders and long neck? Who made the bird of Paradise with its beautiful plumage? Who made the peacock with its rainbow colors? The eagle with its strong pinions and mighty tallons? The innocent dove for him to feed on? The drumming partridge, the talking parrot? Then why are reptiles continually reptiles of the same order and species? Why do the various species of molusks, snails, clams and oysters, continue to produce the same orders and species? Is it a god of miracles that does these things in this regular order of having every sort, kind and species of animal life produce its exact kind or species, and no other kind? Or is it the law that is god in this matter, and directs every movement of their production? So far as man is concerned, so far as his powers of mind and spirit have yet discovered, there is no other ruler—no power to alter or amend this law, and all the gods that people make to perform any part of this work is one purely imaginary.

There is not the least scientific proof that such exists, only in the guesses of people whose minds are reaching for a cause back of the law. They reason because man adopts a law, for the guide of people in society, that there must be a God to make the animals of the world, in the order we find them. Inference is a good thing, but persons carry it too far; as they can other matters, when it becomes so weak that it is ridiculous. There is no more use for a personal God, that is less than all matter, and all spirit, and all natural and spiritual law, than there is for people to have a balloon to keep them always high and spiritual.

When we take a psychometric examination of the growth of animals, as given by William Denton in his Soul of Things, vol. third, we find that the beginning of animal life, was very small; specimens that patted the earth. They were from one to two inches long; next we come to little shell fish or other animals of the shell kind. The longest seen are about one quarter of an inch broad, and a little longer. Next is two worm like animals; one with rings around it, as though it was articulated, the other with bushy ends. These were some of the first formations of animal life discovered, and said to be in the Laurentian and Cambrian age, which is first above the granite rocks and minerals. Here we see how small the animals are, but there were undoubtedly millions of smaller ones existing before this time. These ages are called the age of the Radiates. Now we step forward in time to what is called the age of mollusks, to the beginning or lower part of the Silurian rocky formation. The first animal the psychometer observes is a little ant-like insect crawling in the dirt. Next he mentions the little animals that slap the earth with their tails before mentioned; thousands of these were seen. He next sees an animal crawling like a clam, but is without a shell. Then we come to the Trenton lime-stone, in the Silurian period. Life at the bottom of the ocean. Here the the first of animal life observed is a fish about two feet long. Next is described an animal, part lizard, and part fish. There is seen a dead custacean or fish. It is about three feet long. Then he sees smaller water bugs. He sees one of these bugs sucked into a crenoid, a kind of lilly-shaped vegetable animal that lives on the animal life, and fish live on the crenoids. It should be observed here that it is the age of mollusks, of geologists, and a long time before the age of fishes, as they appear in the rocks that geologists have found. There is a probability that their frames were cartilage, and have not been preserved. Many other animals presented themselves in this age, but none of them seem to belong to the bony kind.

Next we come to the trilobites of the Silurian age, in the time of the formation of the Trenton limestone. The first of animal life that attracts the attention of the psychometrist are what he calls, short-tailed trilobites; they were about two inches long. Then he obsevrves the long-tailed trilobites; these were about three inches long. Then again appeared the kind of fish about two feet long previously mentioned. These fish seem very soft bodied and slow in their movements. Then he sees a crustacean crab that is four or five inches long; next he sees a crustacean about half an inch long, which may be a crystidean. Geologists do not find the crab until we come to the permean age which may be considered millions of ages after the Silurian period of the Hudson rock age, where these animals are supposed to be seen.

Next we come to the Devonian period, or the age of fishes. The first observation of the psychometer was that she saw a large fish ten or twelve feet long, with a peculiar shape, largest at the head and tapering almost to a point at the tail. Next she sees a nautalus or sailing fish. I have been unable to find many observations in Denton's "Soul of Things" that I can put to this age; but the above is gathered from first volume, page forty and after, and shows that a finer quality of fish structure existed than in the ages before. And now we come forward in time to the Carboniferous period, or the age of plants; and we turn to Denton's third volume, where we find the general statement made that the animal life of this period as known to geologists, consists exclusively of radiates, moluks, a few articulates, fishes and amphibians. And the sensitive first observes there is very little of animal life. Then he sees some animal that looks like young crocodiles; the feet are webbed, and the animals are about two feet long. They seem to live on vegetables. Then he discovered they lived on bugs and animals, and when he saw them biting out pieces of the trees, it was to make a place for their house and nest.

After this he sees grubs, water bugs, moths, lizards, land snails, a peculiar kind of crab, and a snake five or six feet long. He also sees beetles, wasps and bees that live on the sweet sap of the trees. From the above statements it will be seen that the psychometrist saw much of animal life that the geologists have not yet discovered in the coal age. From this time we will pass on to the age of reptiles, next above the coal age, called the secondary period. The particular part of the country psychometrically examined was the Connecticut valley. The first observations of the sensitive is that he is in a very filthy place. Mud and water stirred by animals, birds, reptiles and fish. Then

he sees great tracks of birds; then birds twelve feet
high. Bird reptiles and kangaroo reptiles. Ptero-
dactyls, with wings like bats, were seen flying about.
They were of great size. He sees one whose body is
seven feet long. Then a very long reptile with horns
all over its body. Then he sees a humped-back reptile, very large, and thirty feet long. Then a swan-
necked reptile that partook of the character of reptile,
bird and fish. Then he saw a frog as large as a cow.
Then there is the penguin reptile, and beetles, and
butterflies, and walking fish. Then he sees a mam-
mal about the size of a rat. He thinks there are just
as curious animals away from the water as near it,
and sees an animal about the size of a cat; but he says
most of these animals are deficient in color. This is
better than some that have zig-zag brown marks, and
the rest dirty white. The last we will mention are the
bird reptiles that have four feet instead of wings. Then
some curious reptiles, with small bodies, about seven
feet long, and enormous heads. Then a large snake
about fifteen feet long and about six inches through.
This account will give the reader some idea of the animals of the reptile age; and now we will take up the
age of mammals, or the tertiary period.

When animals arrived at their greatest bulk, such as
the mastodon and Zeuloden or carniverous whale, that
seem to have more bulk and power in the water than
the mastodon did on land. Apparently these animals
existed with the greatest strength, the first part of this
period, and were killed off by the glacial period. The
psychometer saw many animals killled by the falling
hail stones, and does not think any animal could live
which was exposed to the storms and weather of this
time, and place. There were before this time many of
the same kind of animals that existed after that icy
time had passed; and mankind were apparently among
them. But I think, notwithstanding they belonged to
the same class and order, they were a different species,
the same as the elephants and whales of the present

time are different from the carniverous crocodile whale and mastodons previous to the cold glacial time. If a Zoologist should say these ancient monsters did not belong to the same order at all; then we will say this cold period killed off one order and the warm term since that time has introduced another class of monsters less bulky and more refined, and adapted to the ages that have followed, a purer atmosphere and sweeter and more nourishing food.

If we are to rely on the description of the man (Indian) which the sensitive saw previous to the glacial period, as appears on page 142 third vol. of the Soul of Things, then men existed so far advanced as to be in the stone age. They had lived through the wooden age; could make holes through stones so as to hang them around their necks. He had a wooden spear with a stone at the end, and he could throw it with great accuracy. There was the same gradual improvement in the animal formation after the cold icy period, as there had been before; and finally the earth was prepared for the advent of the present species of mankind; and the age of man, or the quarternary period, was introduced. And man has acquired a wonderful degree of intelligence out side of their superstitious religions. In their religions they are still in their infantile prattles, and their youthful vagaries and malignity, untutored by correct thinking; and barbarous to prevent free thought. And like the savages and barbarians that were the ancestors of our special species; three or four thousand years ago, and like the savages and barbarians of other species like the Indian and Negro, the Australian, the Hottentot, and Mongol Races.

While the religious mind is on this plane, they will be kept in mental bondage, and favor barbarous practices upon unbelievers. By the pompous forms and ceremonies of their priests, and by their solemn voice in prayers, suplications and exhortations, and their grand and solemn music; and the announcement of the great and sublime goodness of their God to those who worship Him; and then their declaration of their own pureness of heart, and their show of tinsel in their great churches—just the pageantry to captivate the youthful and barbarous mind.

Now the question is to be settled whether there are enough minds among the people to establish a religion of science that will save people spiritually, as fairly as the sciences have established the principles that will save the body from unnecessary pain and premature death, if lived up to faithfully, or that will do as much to make the spirit happy here and hereafter as it has to make bodily happiness for persons on earth. These religious ceremonies and practices got up by christians and others are about as useful in saving souls as the beatings of tom toms by savages are in keeping off witches; and every well informed, unprejudiced person knows this to be true. But the governments and priests have been united so long to enforce these ceremonies and practices upon the people, that they have become natural, and it is very difficult to break away from them. By psychometrical observations it is seen we come to the same conclusions that we do by the ordinary common sense or scientific observations; that there is a law of progress and order that rules all things, and so far as man has discovered, these laws are their own designers; and when we go back of them we find matter and spirit through all space under these laws; and if they made the design from the beginning, they gave up the execution of that design to the higher power, the law.

The past progress of animal life from the least to the greatest, and from the greatest to the best in present life, fully sustains these views, and proves conclusively that there is no god of miracles or catastrophies in existence with any power to alter, change or influence these laws only so far as these laws give him the power, the same as they give power to man to act with all the power of his being, bounded by the restraints of natural law. Can there be anything more convincing that the law god commands, than the fossil remains and imprints of animal life, together with the animals at present existing on earth? And the gradual improvement of animals since we have a history of them? A person can not look at the animal progress by the light of the science of paleontology; that is, the fossil remains, and by the light of the history of animals, since we have had a history of them, without coming to the conclusion that the god of law and order prevails from beginning to end in all past time, and now has entire control, and animals and man and all spiritual beings are subject to this law god.

In conclusion of the book on the material sciences, we would say only a few of them are mentioned; but where can a person look and not find the handy work of the law god of nature? Every science is made in accord with this law, and all are made because the natural laws are found to be commanding, and the sciences could not be established if the laws were not always acting in the same way; and as they are, every truth in the sciences becomes the law god's sacred truth. And if any are to be fined and imprisoned for blasphemy against the holy ghost, the persons who speak against the proved truths of the sciences should be fined and imprisoned for blaspheming the holy truths of science; for the law god's scientific truths are the most sacred and holy things that have ever been given to man; and the legislatures of every state in this Union and the Congress of the United States should be petitioned to have all the laws repealed that punished people for speaking contemptuously of the Jewish and christians' God, Christ, or Holy Ghost, or enact laws to punish persons for speaking contemptuously of the sacred and holy truths of the sciences and of the law god of the sciences. Give the scientists an even chance and as fair play as the priests have, and it will be proved that the scientists worship the god of truth, justice and humanity, whether the priests do or not.

BOOK THIRD.

THE RELIGIOUS TEACHINGS OF THE MENTAL AND SPIRITUAL SCIENCES.

CHAPTER XIII.

THE SCIENCE OF REASON, MATHEMATICS AND PHRENOLOGY.

Reason a science. It shows the difference between beasts and man. Religious people denounce it. Reason is as near a science as common salt is to a salt. It is time to have a reasonable religion. The ignorant will err. Christians condemned the reasoner to eternal punishment. The Science of Mathematics. If persons will lie with figures, they will much more with Theology. Theological falsehoods paid for. It is more important that priests present a proof balance sheet than for cashiers. Criminals make innocent Mathematics lie. But priests make innocent theology a more dangerous liar. The law of spirits is the God of spirits. Two and two do not make four a necessity by the word-God religion. Phrenology gives the basis of the science of the mind. The brain has special organs for special parts of the mind. The size of the brain indicates the power of the mind. The size of the organs of the brain indicates the special power and faculties of the mind. The front brain gives the intellectual faculties. All back of the front organs belong to the unreasoning part of the brain. Knowledge will give the greatest happiness.

THE science of reason consists of the laws of mind, that confine it to certain modes of thought and facts, by which other sciences are established. Reason is not generally considered a science; but as it is the mental power by which all other sciences are made, it certainly should be mentioned among the sciencs as one of them. It consists of memory, knowledge, intuition, impression, and the power to receive revelations, and of combining facts, and making conclusions, so as to arrive at truth. It enables persons to learn causes from effects, and to establish effects from causes. It is the great distinguishing difference between beast and man. It is the faculty of mind that enables persons to tell coming events by calculating the movements of the earth and of heavenly bodies; and also the power of men and beasts to accomplish certain kinds of work, and invent machinery to do the work better and easier for man and beasts, than can be done without the use of reason. In short it shows the difference between civilized man and savages.

The reasonable man is a civilian, the unreasonable one a savage; and the religion that puts reason up as a guide for the people, is a humane, civilizing religion; and the religious people that denounce it as dangerous, are a barbarous people, and are trying to put man on a level with the prowling beasts that live on the flesh of their victims. And if reason is not a science, it comes as near it as common salt does of being a salt, when in a dry state. Scientifically speaking, a salt is made by uniting an acid and an alkali. But dry salt is made of clorine and sodium, so its component parts are neither acids or alkalies, but simple substances. But when you have a solution of common salt and water, the oxigen of the water unites with the clorine and soda, and you have the muriate of soda, which is a salt composed of muriatic acid and soda. So with science; when you have hard, dry, good sound reason, it may be a science; but when it is wet and sloppy and slipshod, it may not be a science, or even scientific in any sense. That is, such kinds of reason as christians use to show how dangerous reason is.

To be reasonable or to be guided by reasonable principles at all times, is a great art, and requires a person to be very steady in their principles, and wise in their thoughts. It is said in the religious faith founded by the word-god, that the principles of salvation are put down so plain that a person though a fool need not err therein. And yet the persons who profess this faith, have committed more errors than any other class of persons of the same standing in society, and education, and mental powers that have ever appeared in the world. And it is time to have a reasonable religion that will teach people that they must have knowledge and wisdom to live correct lives; and it is the duty of every person to acquire an education; and all should be united to see that they have a fair chance to get a reasonable education, and have a religion which proclaims that a foolish ignoramus can err, and will err in precepts and practice, until he gets knowledge.

The religion that professes to be so plain that a fool can understand it, is the one that has deceived the wisest and best of men, and continues to lead them astray, and will continue to bewilder and betray as long as it exists; for it is the religion that proclaims the great mystery of godliness, and has denounced and decided reason as an element of religion, and pronounced it so dangerous as to be the cause of the eternal punishment of persons guided by it.

The abominations which resulted from this rejection of reason for sacred revelation are too great to name, and stamp the plan as one that was conceived by malice or the unholy ambition of priests, and resulted in hellish tortures that can not be justified by any humane principles or people. Reason is the chief corner stone of true religion, and the building without this stone in its true place is a hideous object to behold, and unsafe to the occupants, and the religion a wicked fraud and a diabolical institution. Persons may be reasonable and not logical, and they may be logical and not reasonable. Reason is a mild, steadfast, moderate, firm, even, temperate enunciation of truth and justice, or what the person deems truth and justice. It is tolerant, and is the mental foundation of the sciences.

That is, back of reason are the facts of the sciences, and the truth and justice of them. The religion of science must be the religion of reason, while the religion of belief and faith must be the religion of feeling, sentiment and passion.

This makes the two religions as distinct as possible, and they never can be joined as one. It is curious to note the advantages that Jewish and christian gods promise shall take place if the people will come and reason with him. Isaiah 1:18, "Come now, let us reason together, saith the Lord; though your sins be as scarlet, they shall be as white as snow; though they be red like crimson they shall be as wool." That was just the god that David wanted to make his gory record as white as snow, and his adultery and murders have all the virtues of innocence; and the character of Solomon requires such a god to be tolerated by decent people. And it is just this class that need such a god to turn their vices into virtues, and their crimes into justice; but reason has no such power.

The science of mathematics or numbers is a purely mental science, so calculated that it proves its truth, so that it is called the exact science; it is a law unto itself. It needs but one witness, and that is in a just summary way to get a balance; the sums must agree; no other witness is required or permitted to settle the question whether the true sum is stated in the conclusion or not. It is said figures will not lie; but it is proved that men will lie mathematically as well as theologically, and make results that are a lie, while they declare them true as gospel, and they appear true; but cashiers and financiers have made lying figures that have deceived many people, especially in these latter days. This is very singular, when the statement is made that figures will not lie. This statement is only true when the figures and sums are truly stated, and there is no necessity of a forced balance, as the saying is, in accounts.

Here is a science that can not lie, if every sum is

truly noted and every numeral in its true place; but it is made to lie most egregiously when not submitted to the proof that all things are truly stated. Mathematical statements, when not subjected to proof, may be as false as the theological that are not subjected to the closest scrutiny. And if the great and good men in reputation will lie mathematically, where it can be easily proved on them, how much more will they lie theologically, where it is the most difficult to prove them liars. The lies of the priests are not regarded of much consequence; it is only when they are guilty of the most atrocious tortures and murders of the innocent, that people begin to sense the enormity of their acts.

Then they begin to look back to see how the priests became villians and monsters in crime, and discover it commenced in the falsehood which they proclaimed as truth; and the only plan left for them to sustain their false Theology was to silence the people that questioned it by every crime known to mankind. But gradually and steadily the protestors gained power, until they were allowed to live. Then the enormity of the crime of accepting unproved theological statements as religious truths, and calling upon all people to believe them or be tortured here and be punished eternally hereafter, became fully known to all intelligent people. But they had infected the minds of many people so much that they still continue to utter these dogmas, when they know they are false; and the people who hear them know it, yet they continue to support the preacher that utters them, because there is beauty in these forms and ceremonies, and harmony in their music. Bankers may make innocent and true figures show a lie; Statesmen may swindle the people by falsehood; Thieves may break the safest safe and steal; but all these crimes put together, and add all the others in the criminal calendar, and they are insignificant compared with the falshoods of the priests in corrupting the people and making them diabolical in their acts.

From all these considerations, how much more important it is that the priests of any religion shall present a balance sheet that will show proof that any statement that they make is true; than it is for a cashier or accountant to show such a balance sheet. It is time that religious people were called upon for such proof; they say their God is truth. But the disasters that follow the practice of the word-god's precepts, are greater than ever followed any people who were led by the most deceiving financial accountant that ever was trusted, by a nation or people. The accountant has to deal with mathematics that cannot lie or deceive, unless there is a knave, fool or mistaken person having the handling of the items. It is pure unadulterated truth, proved to a dot by truthful competent persons. The question is, is god like mathematics perfectly true and entirely innocent in every way, and in all things, but more helpless than an infant in the hands of rogues and criminals? This one thing is certain, that mathematics represent a law-god; if any one intends to be mathematically true, they must be true to the law of numbers. There is no miracle to help them out if they vary from the law. There is no special providence to intervene that will make right wrong, or wrong right.

The fixed facts have the entire control of this science. Sophistry may bewilder an accountant, and pilfering may prevent a just balance; but the facts govern, and the competent mathematician will not be bewildered, and will show the exact amount of the stealings. This exact mental science comes in squarely and fully to prove that the law rules; that the law of nature is the god of nature; that the law of mind is the god of mind, and sanctions the principle that the law of spirit is the god of spirit. It would be one of the mysteries of godliness to make what is just and true mathematically, unjust and untruth theologically;

but the fact is, there is no such mystery by the law god of nature and spirit; but such kind of mysteries must always exist where the word god is proclaimed, because he is an enemy to the law god, and his proselytes are always fighting the true god; and some of the persons who have been deluded by the word god theology will even deny that two and two make four. Their god can change it; and there is no doubt but that he can, as well as he can any other fact or law of nature. It is no greater miracle than they claim in other matters.

Phrenology gives the basic principles upon which the science of the mind is established; it shows that mind is made up of a great number of different elements, like memory, comparison, causality, calculation, destruction, and firmness, and many other mental faculties. These facts make it apparent that certain fibres of the brain make their special faculties of the mind. The general principles are that the size of the brain, other things being equal, shows the power of the mind, and the size and length of the fibres of special portions of the brain determine the powers of the mind that these portions of the brain represent. There are malformations of the brain, as there are of other portions of the human body. Large brains indicate great mental power as surely as large bodies in man indicate great physical power. It is often found that small men have much greater strength and endurance than large ones; but when a hundred large persons taken as you come to them in communities, and compare them with a hundred small persons taken in the same way, it will be found the large have very much more strength than the small ones; and so it will be found in brains; large brains as a rule have more power and endurance in accomplishing mental work than small ones; and the largest organs in a head have the most power. The general principles of phrenological teachings are that the front part of the head gives to the mind of the individual his intellectual faculties, such as judgment, reason, memory, discretion; it is the planning, the discovering of the ways and means to do things, that other parts of the brain and other parts of the body instinctively give notice that they want done, or what this intellectual part desires to do. A good front brain gives good and correct judgments in the line of business, that its powers are calculated to judge well of; and when the frontal brain power is sufficient to keep the sensational brain and body under its control, the person will be a self controled individual, and his acts will have the sanction of his mind. But when the frontal brain is not sufficiently developed and powerful to command the instincts, passions, and appetites that the other parts of the brain and body demand, then the person is governed by his feelings, appetites and impressions, that do not have the sanction of his judgment, and causes the person to be vacilating.

At the base of the brain on the sides of the head are the organs that call for food and drink, and the organs of destructiveness and combativeness. When these organs are large and caution is small, which lies above them, they tend to make the possessors bold, reckless and unscrupulous about the way they get their living; and when caution is large, they are sly, careful and tricky in their way of supplying their needs, unless the intellectual and moral powers are so large as to have a commanding influence over these selfish organs. The back of the head at the base of the brain is amativeness, and above it love of children and the love of home. When these organs are large, they tend to make people licentious, and have too great a desire to have children as pets, and gives them a senseless attachment for home. When the organs of the top of the head are large and have commanding power over the mind and other organs, it makes people stubborn and mulish. If the organ of benevolence is large, it makes people too free in giving property to support unworthy objects and persons. How can these large portions of the brain be commanded? There is only the front brain to do it; that is, the intellectual portion. The intellect must be educated; people must have knowledge of themselves and their surroundings, and learn to use it wisely, or they will be more or less beastly in their habits; and the mental powers have a great work to do when the animal organs are large, and small work when these organs are small, in so far as these organs are concerned. But the calls of nature are imperious. Cold and heat, hunger and thirst, make people exert themselves as animals do with but little reason, or as man should by correct reasoning faculties. The instincts given by veneration and hope make people fanatical in religion, and absurd in their expectations; and the organ of acquisitiveness makes them thieves, unless they are governed by reason. The child takes all that he can find that he wants, and has no compunctions of conscience or any knowledge that it is wrong, until educated; and men without a correctly educated conscience or a just knowledge of what is right and wrong, are like children, and must be educated as children are to know good from evil; and any religion that has a damnatory and false creed or bible that they refuse to correct and make true according to the proved facts of the age, tend to keep the people in their childhood condition. There is not any well established religion in the world, and never has been, according to history, that made an intellectual education their greatest and safest and most certain way of salvation. But the scientific religionist turns to phrenology and asks, what are your demands of people who wish to establish the true religion? The answer comes, people who have veneration commanding them will worship anything, and people who have it small, and it has little influence, will not worship anything worthy or unworthy. Then if you wish to establish the true worship with the true religion, you must educate people not to be governed by their feelings, sentiments, impulses or passions, when they differ from the intellectual judgment of what is right and just, as established by reason, founded upon experience. But to make the worship consistent, humane and reasonable, the front brain intellectual organs must take control. So of moral principles; they can not be established by the organs of conscience or the feelings of what is pure and virtuous. The many bundles of brain in the sides, back and top of the head are too conflicting in the feelings they produce in the mind to make them a safe guide for people; and all these feelings must be brought to the intelligence located in the front part of the head to be considered and reasoned upon to gain a just judgment. The conclusion of the whole matter is, that the science of phrenology falls into line with other sciences, and proclaims that the law god has made mind to be subject to law, the same as matter is; and if the people will acquire knowledge, they can learn to make the most of this life, and get the greatest amount of happiness that is vouchsafed to mankind on earth.

CHAPTER XIV.

THE RELIGIOUS TEACHINGS OF THE SCIENCE OF MAGNETISM PSYCHOLOGY, PSYCHOMETRY OR MESMERISM.

The subtle invisible power which persons or animals have over each other. All animals and man have this power. It is the vital life power. All have the same kind of love and hatred. Earth and Rock have the same Psychological power, and this is called Psychometry. It makes matter have a mind, and connects mind with matter. All space and the stars have this power to some extent. It is a subject of great magnitude and power. The life of all the living and of worlds. Priests of Christ do not deserve the name unless they can heal the sick as He did. The law that governs the psychological and magnetical worlds are the nearest to God, of anything known to man. The dirt of the earth gives facts, not reasons. Its memory is better than man's. Man and animals can pervert truth. Study nature by Psychometry rather than ancient bibles. God of law will not reason with men until men obey the law; perhaps not then.

THE science of psychology treats of the magnetic powers of persons and animals over other persons and animals, or of the subtle influence of one person over another without physical contact or fear to make them obey his will, or it causes some to be influenced by others by their mere presence, when there is no wish or will to influence them. It is called evil eye, witchcraft, or the works of the devil or god, by the ignorant and superstitious. It is an influence that has been felt and known to exist for a long time, for centuries; but it was left to the intelligence created by the scientific era to explain it, so that its origin and powers are somewhat understood; so much so that it is ranked among the sciences. When Mesmer called the attention of the learned world to this subject, it received his name, and was called mesmerism. Then it was called animal magnetism, because it resembles the magnetic power that holds the magnetic needle to point north and south, or nearly so. It is a quiet force, imperceptible to the senses of ordinary persons. It surrounds the world, and mankind and animals have it; some more than others, so that they can overpower the weaker by their magnetic influence. Yet this vital or animal magnetism is somewhat different from the worldly or chemical magnetism. It is animalized or humanized so as to be better adapted to cure diseases of the body or mind of the afflicted persons. This may result from its being mixed with the vitality of mankind. This vitalized magnetism in one person can take entire control of another by the will power through the connecting threads of magnetic influence that hold us to the world and bind us to each other. This is the power that is used to make all animals and all mankind, and make all men related; that is, brothers. They are made of the same kind of matter, the same kind of spirit, and this magnetism is used to bind them together so they all have the same kind of love and sympathy, and the same kind of hatred and revengeful feelings, so they require the same kind of laws of society and government. All have the same kind of appreciation of what is right and just and true. But they do not have these feelings in an equal degree, and there is great difference of opinion of what is right in special cases. But all are so near alike that when expressing their feelings and opinions, they understand where they agree and where they differ.

But the most convincing proof of this universal element of the union of the people as a brotherhood, and of all these people with all the earth and its productions is, that a small piece of the earth, or rock, or of animal matter will so psychologize some sensitive persons as to enable them to read its history, and much of the history of its surroundings; this phase is called psychometry. This power is a greater God

than any that the ancient religionists ever dreamed of;
it is a power that fills space and unites the heavens and
earth and the people of the earth with the spirits of
heaven; it makes matter have a mind, and causes
mind to unite with matter; in other words, it converts
mind into matter, and matter into mind. The works
of psychologists have been spoken of extensively
when treating on psychometrical geology. There is
something wonderful to contemplate about this psychological psychometrical magnetic power. First we
discover there is this power in some persons by which
they influence or command others, give them new life
or energy, and cure or relieve their diseases. Then
we find persons that can be psychologized by a piece
of metal or coin. Then that bones, rocks, and earth
will do the same thing; and these things give their history to the psychologized person; this is psychometry;
and when we look into the universe of space, and to
the stars, we find they have an influence over people of
the same character. Astrology is as old as witchcraft
and evil eye. It belongs to that class of phenomina that
the ignorant seem to get by intuition, and to the class
of persons that are despised by material philosophers
and scientists, because the forces are intangible to the
materialist's mind; and are placed among the religious
notions that are without foundation in fact, and are
established by ignorance and continued by priest craft,
ignorance and superstition.

But the spiritual scientists discover that this influence of the stars has a sure fact basis in this psycho
logical magnetic power that fills all space, and gives to
the sun, moon and stars certain powers over the earth
and its surroundings, and its animal and vegetable
productions. The sun and moon have a palpable and
acknowledged power that materialists see and feel; but
besides these, there is a subtle magnetic power that
comes from all heavenly bodies, especially the planets,
and affects every individual. The whole subject of
the magnetic influences upon mind and body is one of

great magnitude, great power, and of the greatest magnetic, electrical and spiritual importance for mankind to know, to enable them to live lives consistent with their destiny. Is there a power that shapes our ends, rough hew them as we will, that we can know and practice so as to make the best of life? Can we find out our destiny by any means in the power of mankind? This is the great question to be settled by scientific experiments and observations. We find this magnetic power existing in all nature and spirit, and is either the power that makes the law or the law itself that accomplishes all things, in the scientific phrase, or in religion, it is God or the hand of God. It is the spirit of all matter and the life of all the living. And when persons get into the inner circle of the law by which men are ruled by this psychological power, the best way for them to act under its influence can be determined. The priesthood makes itself feared by its prophetic denunciations among the ignorant, of the pains and disasters that will be inflicted upon them in this world, and the world to come, if they do not follow them. But as people become informed, they prophesy only of the tortures of hell to unbelievers, and the joys of heaven to believers; and when the people become informed that there is no hell, then the priests give up all such denunciations, and give their time to persuasion to make people believe they will have more joy to believe in the Savior than in any other way. But all the time the priests mix in some prophesy of coming events in time or eternity. But these prophets had and have only the opinions of other prophets to guide them.

But the astrologer like the astronomer is governed by the law of magnetic and electric motion to determine the truths of his prophecies; and when they determine as correctly how people must move by the power of this law, as the astronomer does how planets must move by their law, they can prophecy as truly what will happen in each day of a person's life as they can in astronomy where a planet will be in its orbit because we find each governed by law, not by word or accident. And when the psychometer traces the magnetic influences of moon or planets on individuals, their power may be sufficient to trace their influence on each individual, and in that way get a better view or realization or influence of all the heavenly bodies or a person's life than has yet been found possible. If a piece of rock can psychologze persons, it becomes a question how much a distant planet can influence them.

The ancient religionists made gods of those persons who raised the apparently dead, and the moderns who adopt the ancient superstitions continue to call them gods. But many persons are raised from the apparent dead who have no person near them, nothing to cause them to live but the shining stars, sun and moon above them, while they are surrounded by air, earth, water and the habiliments of the grave, it may be. When such things occur, does it not prove that each of these elements or bodies are gods, as truly as man proves he is a God by doing the same thing? They all have the psychologyzing power in a greater or less degree. The sun and moon have vastly more vitalizing power than man has; and if Gods are made out of the power of raising the apparent dead, it is much more sensible to worship the sun than any man. When a person fails to get the magnetic powers of life to maintain bodily action, they appear lifeless and dead; then when a wave of magnetic life-giving power reaches them, they revive and live, no matter where that power comes from, whether from man, earth, air, water, or the heavenly bodies, or all of them combined together. As persons study more and more into the occult sciences of the ancients, they find how simple, ignorant and superstitious were the persons who made their religious sentiments and established their worship, and how silly or wicked those persons appear in modern times who proclaim these doctrines.

Priests proclaim that the mantle of Christ has fallen upon them when they can not even ease the pains of the sick or do any deeds to prove that they have any faith in the Christ that cured the sick, and even as they say raised the dead; such priestly shams should be abated by all persons except those who believe that words are Gods and worldly works are devils. Most of the man-gods have had great magnetic powers over large masses of people. Magnetism is the great unseen secret power which is used by wicked persons to make slaves of the people; and the great magnetizers will always be leading people in any community; yet among the intelligent they cannot make many persons blindly obey them unless they have great worldly power, such as commanders of armies or the rulers of nations, or great wealth. But it should be remembered that the law that commands the scychological powers of heaven and earth are nearer to the god powers than any other principle and powers known to man. This law seems to govern all persons and bodies in the celestial or terrestial worlds.

We have but just commenced to learn the great scope and importance of psychometry. It shows that the dust of the earth has memory and the five senses of hearing, seeing, feeling, tasting, and smelling, and that its memory is much better than that of any person, for it seems to tell the particulars of events that occurred millions on millions of years ago. How many more faculties it has that man has not discovered in his mental composition, it is not known, and can not be known to man until he learns to use other faculties that lay dormant in his mental and physical being. But there is one faculty not discovered in the dirt of the earth, man possesses; that is the faculty of reason. Man and beasts possess reason to a greater or less extent; but the dirt of the earth has not yet given us notice that it is in possession of that faculty. Yet what is the probability regarding its possession of this faculty? Most assuredly that it has it; in a much greater degree than man; some may say that spirit alone possesses reason; that it belongs especially to the life principle of man and beast, and that it is in the spirit of the air; but not in the solid materials of the earth. The solid earth and the moving air, are composed of the same materials in different kinds and degrees of combination; and every faculty that is in one is possessed of the other. All is filled to a greater or less degree with the spirit of truth; man and animals have the power to pervert this truth, and make truth appear like falsehood and falsehood appear like truth. This is shown by the cunning of the fox and the maneuvering of the successful warrior, and by the double dealings of the politician, and more than either of these by the pretentions of priests; all of this class of people hate the psychometrists who go to the ground, to the heavens; and to their writings, and even their clothing, which tells them the truth regarding their characters and their designs, and the infamous acts they intend to commit if they can get the power.

It is this knowledge which the earth gives that makes the sacrificial priesthood hate the natural law, the natural god and the natural man. He is an enemy of natural truth, as well as spiritual, and when we can once get the religious to turn their attention from the ancient bibles that ignorant people wrote, to the earth, the rocks and the sun, and other heavenly bodies, and talk with them through psychometry or psychology, they will soon learn how deceived the ancient religious writers were, and how silly it is to take their wild statements, when the earth can give, and will give, the true ones, if truly consulted; and when people have these facts they can reason together and conclude what is best to be done to be saved from trouble in this world, and in the spirit world, where all spirits will go. All the religious facts are about us, and at present mankind must reason among themselves from these facts, as there is not a god that has come to man to reason with him, that is well known. And if a god should come to reason with man, he must reduce his reason to the capacity of man's reason, or they would not be understood by man. And it is not at all probable that the law god will ever reason with man until mankind come to their senses enough to submit to the laws of nature as their god, and man and his spirit shall reason together to learn all that man can know on earth. Then we may expect the natural law god will give a reason for every law and every act under the law, and peace will reign on earth among men.

•

CHAPTER XV.

THE RELIGIOUS TEACHINGS OF THE SCIENCE OF SPIRITUALISM AS PROVED THROUGH MEDIUMS IN THEIR VARIED MANIFESTATIONS.

The basis of this was discovered by children. It spread from them to all people who were hungering for this knowledge. They were anxious to learn about heaven and hell. Spirits have no knowledge of a word-God, nor a God on His throne. Word-Gods have no power only what man gives them. The spiritualists must claim the right to make these observations and experiments. The Jewish laws were only calculated for a barbarous people. The fresh Mohammedian inspirations were better than the old christian ones, so are the fresh protestant inspirations. The right of private judgment better than any ancient religions. Where is the inventor who depends on a word-God to make his invention work? Who will say a little piece of spirit and matter is greater than the whole? Such persons will make Gods of wood, or stone. Priests prove your bible true. Spiritualists sought information. Prof. Hare. History of christianity and spiritualism. Christians never believed in spirit communications, but murdered mediums as witches and wizards. Christ could not be above the barbarisms of His age but a little. People will not submit to so many falsehoods in this age. Different kinds of spirit manifestations. People were deceived by ancient myths that the word of God was all truth, also that of Angels. People must use their own judgment. If priests can not prove there is a hell and a little heaven, there is none. Slate writing. Incontrovertable facts. German scientists. Wm. Slade. Mrs. Fletcher. Salem witches. Readers of Moses and lovers of his law live in his age. Photograph manifestations. They raised persons and floated in the air. Home. The Davenport Brothers. Fire tests. Hell has no terrors for spirits. Materalizing spirits. Brooks and Wallace. Clairvoyance. Clairaudient. J. V. Mansfield. Flower mediums. Solid bodies pass through each other. Articles appear and disappear. Epes Sargent.

Every age should make its own bible. Spiritual religion is very different from the christian. Mormon religion. The growth of spiritualism. Try the christian and spiritual questions. What kind of governments do they call for?

MODERN spiritualism is a science that was discovered by children; girls in their girlish play at Hydesville, Arcadia Township, Wayne County, New York, March 31st, 1848, at night, by Margaretta and Catharine Fox, the first 14 and the last 12 years old. They observed that when they rapped a certain number of times, the same number of raps were heard from an unknown power. They told their mother, and she asked questions, and learned that the power that made the answering raps to the raps of the girls, were the spirits of persons who had departed from their earthly bodies; or in other words, were the spirits of people whom the priests and people generally pronounced dead. Then she inquired about her own family, and got correct answers. The neighbors were called in, and they got correct answers, and the news spread that the spirits of the dead communicated with the living by means of these Fox children, and thousands of people rushed to their house to get information from spirits about their spirit friends that had left their earthly bodies, and learn from them their condition and the condition of spirits generally in the spirit land. The people showed that they were absolutely starving for this spiritual food.

All the ancient spirit manifestations and communications paled into nothingness by the side of this new revelation, and the Fox family soon removed to the city of Rochester, N. Y., to be in a better condition and situation to meet the great public demand for information from their friends in spirit life, and compare it with their earthly knowledge. So the investigation went on in the modern and intelligent form; took the dress of modern thought. Superstition and previous opinions were laid under the explanations of the spirits, to be altered as information dictated. The people wanted to know all about God and heaven and hell, and they soon learned that the ancient description of hell was a falsehood, and their description of heaven was far from true, and gave the people no correct idea of the spirit's condition in the spirit land, and no true idea of the best way to live on earth that would give them the greatest happiness when they went to the spirit's home. And it soon appeared that the God of the ancients was not greater than the spirit friends of those who came to consult with these mediums.

The whole matter of spirit manifestations and communications were subjected to the proof of their truth and usefulness by the common sense people that characterizes this age, and gives it its progressive reputation in arts and sciences, inventions and discoveries, greater than was ever known before, and more useful to mankind generally; and especially beneficial to the great working middle class of the people, who are the principal inventors and discoverers of the most important principles and implements of the age. These common sense people, educated principally in the common schools of the day, demand spiritual truth as much as they do material; and in all cases they call for proof on the common sense plane that this age is noted for.

No superstitious belief or opinion is allowed to stand for truth that is not proved to be truly based in the nature of things, spiritual or material. Under this inquisitive search for spiritual truth, modern spiritualism has grown to be a power in this land and throughout the world, among intelligent people. The shafts of ridicule from the learned, and warnings to beware of it as a devil, from superstitious religionists, have had no other influence than to make investigators more careful in their investigations and observations; and great and wonderful have been their discoveries. They commenced with a belief more or less established in their minds that a personal God ruled the heavens and earth by his words; but soon they found that the spirits did not have any knowledge of such a God. If he existed, he was as far from their knowledge as he was from the knowledge of the people of earth. They got the information that the God that ruled in heaven and on earth was the god of law, and so far as they knew, God was law, and law was God. There was no personal God that was sitting on a throne in heaven in their sight, and there were no visible thrones on his right hand or left for Christ and his twelve apostles.

All these descriptions that the ancients had put in their religious books were without the shadow of foundation in the heavens, so far as their observations were extended. They said instead of a despot on his throne with his assistants, judging the spirits of the people of earth who had left their earthly bodies, and sending some into heaven to be blessed and happy on the right hand of God, and sending others into hell to be cursed and tortured on the left hand of God, they were their own judges, and went to their own place by their own judgment. They lived under the rule of republicanism instead of despotism, and heaven was a great republic instead of being a kingdom. And Christ was a spirit like other spirits, judging himself and not others; and he and his apostles and disciples were so quiet and distant or reserved, that many christians who wished to find them were unable to see them or make their acquaintance in any way. And these christians were so disappointed at not finding God on his throne, surrounded by a brilliant staff of assistants, angels and little gods, that they were dumb with astonishment, and so disconsolate that they did not know what to do with themselves for a long time, because they could not worship before the throne of their god of words, and fall down at the feet of Jesus and proclaim his greatness and goodness, and their right to exaltation, because they had praised him so much in their earthly life.

By such communications the minds of the common people were so changed in regard to the character of

God, heaven and hell, that they do not hear with pleasure the doctrines of the wrath of God, the tortures of hell, 'or the despotisms of heaven, that formerly were so charming to those who thought themselves the elected of God to be assigned by Him to eternal joys in His presence. They have learned from modern spiritualism that real goodness, not praises of God and Christ and belief in any bible, is the road to the highest heaven and the purest happiness. And the threats of a bible-swearing-wordy-god are of no avail in heaven or hell, and no influence in making the people happy or miserable in spirit life; and the only influence on earthly people, if they believe in such a bible as the word of an all powerful God, is, that it makes them proud, haughty and happy if they think such a god is on their side, and very miserable, desponding and insane, it may be, if they think this god is not their friend.

This has been the effect of all the religions upon people that have through the superstitions adopted a god of words. All ancient religions have had one kind of god, the god of words. And spiritualism is based on another set of observations, that establishes another kind of god, the god of law. The law is supreme, so far as observations have yet determined this matter; and talking gods have never been heard by scientists, unless they were little gods that had no power over the laws of nature and spirit, and were entirely dependent on these laws for existence and the little power they have. Here is the ground of the conflict between the christians and spiritualists; and there is no chance for a peaceful settlement of their differences by reason.

The modern careful observations of the characters of these gods, shows that the christian's god is only the spirit of fallible man, and has no power over the laws of nature or over mankind, only what man and the governments of mankind give him. But the god of law asks no favors of man or his governments. His laws man can not break, alter or amend. People must obey the laws of this god that give health and happiness, or they can not have the joy that this obedience gives, and they must suffer by disease and be miserable just in proportion to their disregard of the health and happiness giving laws. Now for ages the christians have passed laws that forbid man to investigate into these laws of nature, and obey those that give him the most comfort; and they still insist on making such laws, regardless of the god of law and his laws. The spiritualists and their spirit friends have a different god and a different heaven, and a different spirit home from the christians; so different that there can be no reconciliation between them.

The spiritualists must have the right to make their experiments to determine what the laws of health are, so they can live in accordance with them. And they must have the right to make their experiments and observations to determine what are the best social and moral laws, to enable them to live most in harmony with the laws or nature's god, and have the greatest peace and justice among themselves. And the christians with their god of words insist that they know it all now; notwithstanding the diseases, troubles and afflictions that distress mankind at this time. Their god tells them all about it; they must pray to him and have holy days and sabbath days, and keep them in such a way as to reconcile god to his people; and adding fast days in the spring and thanksgiving days in the fall; then we must believe he is the great ruler that he professes to be in the heavens and earth, and we shall have health and happiness, and blessings beyond the present comprehension of mankind.

But the difficulty is in believing in such testimony, when it is well known that Jews, Pagans and Christians have tried it, by nations, societies and individuals, and their failure to reap the promised advantages and rewards show that their god is not reliable. For those nations that come the nearest to fulfilling the commands fared the worst, and finally the Jewish nation was destroyed, and their people were sent among all nations; and when the christians attempted to put these wordy god's laws into force in the Roman Empire, the people became base, ignorant slaves of the hardy north men, who were not tied down by the commands and words of the Jewish and Christian Gods. These northern men had their own superstitions and their own inspirations to guide them; and when any people are guided by their own inspirations, obtained at the time they are used, they are stronger than any ancient or foreign inspirations can make them, because these inspirations are fitted to the times and people that get them.

The inspirations of Moses and the prophets of his time built up a great and glorious nation, according to their history. But any one who looks carefully into their history sees that it was not fitted for them at a subsequent age, when they had become more nationalized and civilized. They obeyed old and cruel laws and prophecies that were well calculated to subdue and subject a barbarous people to rules and laws, but were wholly out of place when the people were brought into a semi-civilized state, as the Jews were under the judges and kings. The laws and prophets that were good for them, and brought them safely out of Egypt and into the promised land, were old, worn out and barbarous, and caused them to be conquered by the Babylonians, and held in captivity for seventy years. These prophets say that it was because they did not obey the laws of Moses and his God. If this is true, then there is no hope that any people will ever succeed in obeying these laws, because they are entirely out of place to any other people, and to the Jews also only for a few hundred years. I never read of a people that tried harder than they did to obey these laws, and repented more sincerely when they failed, or when their prophets told them they failed to keep the commands of the God that brought them out of Egypt.

And many times they were accused of doing evil, when people who receive the best of modern principles say they did not do evil, but good.

When people obey an unjust law, they do evil; and many of the laws of the Jews were and are unjust. Were cruel, and only useful to make savage natures obey law, and are an absolute curse to more enlightened people, and will make them become savage in their acts, and destroy the nations that enforce them, as they did the Jewish and Roman nations, or make them slaves, as the same kind of cruel laws have the Chinese. These remarks apply especially to old laws and old inspirations that the people have observed the wrongs they have done for a long time, and the outrages of the priests and rulers who enforce them.

The fresh inspirations of Mohammed were of great value to the Arab people of the time. Low and false as they were, they made them a better people than the christians of the dark ages, who obeyed their old inspirations and laws; and they established better governments and institutions of learning. But when these inspirations became old, and the priests added superstitions and horrid cruelties upon the people for not obeying the mandates of their rulers and priests for ages, they began to decline, and finally are in their dark ages, while the Protestants are in their enlightened ages, because for three hundred years and more they have been guided by their new and fresh inspirations, and have made changes in the laws to meet the growing intelligence and humanity of the people.

While the Roman Catholics are guided by their priests and the old Jewish and christian inspirations, and uphold their most cruel and false laws and prophecies, and are using all their ingenuity and power to bring upon Protestant countries the dark ages again, when the priests and rulers can indulge in every kind of disgraceful acts and crimes that they did in the dark ages which they made in the Roman Empire, and after it was destroyed. Their only hope of continuance in any power on earth is to enforce the laws and inspirations of the Jews that destroyed them as a nation, and of the christians that made them the ignorant tools of the priests, or the slaves of the Mohammedans.

When the Protestants demanded the right of private judgment, they demanded that the new inspirations of the people should be heard. This sentiment took root among the Mohammedans and christians more than six hundred years ago, but was wholly rejected by the Mohammedans long before it was fully accepted by the protestant reformers more than three hundred years ago, as before stated; now mark the contrast between the Mohommedan and christian nations and the protestant nations that are falsely called christians and call themselves so. For although they hold to the Jewish and christian text books, they were guided by the inspirations of the ages since they proclaimed the right of private judgment; the old inspirations were proclaimed by a paid priesthood, and supported by the governments in a greater or less degree; but notwithstanding this, the new inspirations had a commanding influence; the people believed in the knowledge which the new inspirations gave them, and in the god they proclaimed; so chemistry was first established as a science, then astronomy, and mineralogy. Geology, Paleantology, and Botany, Zoology, Ornithology, Entomology, Agriculture, Phonography, Photography, Telegraphy, Phrenology, and Psychology, and many other sciences not mentioned in the previous pages, and last of all, the sciences that people have become sufficiently civilized to permit the experiments and observations to be made to establish as a science, spiritualism; and every one of these sciences and all others that have been established are based upon the principles of a god of an unchangeable law, of a law of an unchangeable god. The god of word's commands and threats are not found among the inspirations that make a science.

The scientist bases all his calculations upon an unchangeable law, and this law is god so far as he knows, and apparently so far as he can know. Then again the inventor bases his power to make his inventions work for the benefit of the people upon an unchangeable law, that no god or man can change; all his inspirations point to this law as all powerful. And all the inspirations, thoughts, and ideas of this age point to an unchangeable law as the ruler of the heavens and earth, and of spirit and matter on the earth, and of the spirits of the spirit land in space around the earth and to all known distances in space. And in all the world and heavens where man and his spirit are known to exist, not a miracle can be done that man or his spirit can not do. Every material and spiritual science proves this in these modern times.

Just compare the whole array of the sciences, and of scientific knowledge, and of inventions and improvements to benefit mankind spiritually and physically; see the benefits that knowledge has conferred upon mankind to keep them healthy and allow them to live comfortable lives. And compare these people and the cheerful enjoyments they have, with the poverty, disease and wretchedness that people have who live under the laws and inspirations of the ancients who believed in a god of commands and words, and the cruel laws that people inflicted on themselves because they had faith in such inspired words, as the words of a god, compare the power of the people and nations on earth who allow the right of private judgment to be practiced with those that do not. And you see where this right is; they are the most powerful nations and the most wonderful people that was ever on earth, and the others are common place and ignorant, and under the control greatly of these free people and nations.

Where will you go to find an inventor who depends on a god of words to make his invention work to benefit mankind? Where will you go to find a scientist that relies on a god of words to make his prophecies come true in his astronomical or his chemical calculations? none can be found; they rely upon the unchangeable laws of nature's god to fulfill their prophetic calculations. But says the believer in the god of words, who made these laws? There must be an intelligent maker of all these laws that makes the beautiful crystals of the earth and the sparkling stars of the heavens. Why, its the same power that made spirit, matter, force, and motion.

We find matter so intelligent that it will form the crystals of different kinds of matter in different forms, and the same kinds of matter in the same form. Who lived before spirit to teach it? Who lived before matter to teach it? Who will say a little piece of spirit, and a little piece of matter separated itself from the great mass of spirit and matter and made a god of itself and learned the rest of spirit and matter, to obey the laws of nature, and then went on making the laws of nature to suit himself and had power to change them as often as he pleased.

Will any one suppose that a little part of spirit and matter has ever had more power and more knowledge than the whole? If any one thinks so then they can form a little god made out of these little pieces and worship him as a personal god that has power to regulate all things according to his feelings and desires. But the scientist has not found such a god; and the spirits have not found such a god. And the conclusion is that such a one does not exist. Only to work under the control of the law that pervades the entire universe of matter and spirit, because we find spirit knows enough to do its work under law without help, and matter knows enough to do its work under law without help, and law knows enough to control all their movements in exact time and with the exact force required to have all movements orderly, without help. If any one says that spirit or matter does not know enough to do its work, then the law takes charge of it and directs it; or forces it to do its duty. The scientist finds the intelligence in spirit and matter, but has not been able to discover yet how it came there, whether by their own intuition or by the force of the intelligence the law gives to them or either one of them.

The law with its intelligence, power, and controling force that obliges motion to obey its orderly movements of spirit and matter, seems to have been in existence eternally; and if it is the educator of spirit and matter, it has had an eternity in the past to educate them; and time was never started in the midst of eternity untll the spirit and matter required to be used to measure time with, was educated to be completely submissive to the order of time, and to the laws of progression. But persons who think a little spirit is better than all spirit, and a little matter is better than all matter, and a little law of nature is better than all the laws of nature, and will make a more powerful omnicient and omnipresent god, will make a man-god or a ghost-god, or a bull-god, or a wooden-god, or stone-god and proclaim them the gods of the heavens and earth, and all powerful to judge and reward and punish mankind for their good and deeds, or beliefs. Such persons will lay great stress on the importance of believing in a little personal god as changeable as themselves, while they pretend and declare that he never changes.

Spiritualism teaches people that they need not fear an angry god, or a malicious devil, for neither of them exist only in the imaginations of ignorant or malicious people. But whether god made all things, or all things made god, or little parts of them made god, one thing is certain, all the modern sciences proclaim law as the ruler; and spiritualism as the last science that has been established, agrees with all the others, and clinches the evidence that law rules supreme so far as known. And the god of words is so different from the god of law that there never can be an agreement between the worshipers.

The god of words rules by laws that he can alter, and make miracles and cause catastrophes that cannot occur by the unchangeable laws of the god of law. This makes the god that the scientists worship so very different from the gods of all the ancient religions, that one or the other must be thrown out of the public councils. In Protestant countries each has maintained a precarious existence for centuries. The god of natures laws has been constantly gaining power and influence among the people, and the governments have adopted more and more the laws and institutions that are required by the people who believe in the unchangeable laws of nature, and if people wish to be healthy and happy, they must learn and obey the natural laws that produce such conditions.

The science of spiritualism has given people direct information of spirit power of the spirits of mankind on earth, and the thousands upon thousands of spirit communications and manifestations that show their power and give information of themselves; and descriptions of their spirit homes, and the advice and admonition they give to people regarding their conduct to secure the most happiness on earth, and in their spirit home when they drop the earthly body, is sobering the people down to a calm consideration of what they shall do to be saved, that the threatenings of the bible god and his priests can not change among intelligent people; and when the priests denounce people for inbelief, they quietly ask him if he knows absolutely what punishment his god inflicts on innocent unbelievers, and he reads his bible denunciations and damnations of unbelievers; and then they quietly ask him if he knows his bible is a true record, and his reply is that he believes it, and knows it only through belief to be true; he can not prove it so by direct and unimpeachable testimony of witnesses who were cognisant of the facts and testified to them under oath to tell the truth, whole truth and nothing but the truth, and that the magistrate who administered the oath duly recorded it and signed his name certifying that such was the testimony; no he has not such testimony, so well certified to. Then how near to such certified testimony does your bible come? Why the fragments of the bible were collected together and put in book form and authenicated as true in the fourth century. And what was the character of the priests who put the bible together and testified to its genuine truth; and that it was written by the persons that they pretend it was, who were the companions of Christ and heard these words from him and recorded them? They were all liars, says Mosheim, one of the most learned and most reliable authors in the christian ranks, and is accepted by christians as such. The best of them according to this authority would lie to promote the glory of god in that century, and afterwards for centuries, when the bible was entirely in their hands, and under their control. Now Mr. Priest if this is anything like true of the priests and persons who put the bible together. There is no reason to believe that they hesitated one moment in altering the texts of the writings that came into their hands, and giving the names of Christ's companions to books that they never wrote one word of and would have condemned if they had been consulted about it spiritually at the time the priests put them in the one book. But the lying priests could not hear the small voices of pure angels, and would not have heeded them even if they could have heard their voices; so determined were they to palm lies off on the people as truth. That they did so is abundantly proved by christian and pagan writers, that the christians now have to acknowledge as true, and many passages are now said to be interpolations that were thought and taught to be canonical for centuries.

Under such a state of facts, would it not be best, Mr. Priest, to take up the science of spiritualism and consult the spirits about what is true and false in the Bible and all religious systems? But the Priest may say that he did not know that there was a science of spiritualism, as many of them have said to me. But that does not alter the fact that there is such a science more than it did when they denied that there was a science of Astronomy when they put Bruno to death; or that they did not know that there was a science of Chemistry when they imprisoned Roger Bacon. Their knowledge or ignorance did not alter the facts then, and does not now. Spiritualism is reduced to a science now by a system of co-related facts obtained by tests, experiences, experiments and observations, combined together into a system by reason in such a way that they can not be denied any more than the facts in other sciences.

The only object of the greatest number of spiritualists is to know the truth and abide by it. There is nothing that christian priests hate and fear so much as systematized knowledge, because it tends strongly to stop their ceaseless meaningless diatribes against sin, which they can repeat day after day by a little alteration before the same audiences, because they have no scientific beginning or practical conclusion, and because it tends strongly to stop their preaching continuously of the love and glory of God without telling exactly what his love is, so we can gain it to a certainty, or how we can add to the glory of God or understand and put in practice a plan that will be sure to end in glory to God or man. But they always leave a doubt in the minds of their hearers, so they must come to them again for another sermon on the same subject; and this continues for the lifetime of the preacher and the hearer, and the next preacher and the next generation must preach and hear the same kind of discourses, that are always pretending to inform people what truth, virtue and justice are, but never telling them so that they are understood.

The science of spiritualism will put an end to such endless talk upon spiritual subjects, the same as the material sciences have on those subjects. Spiritualism was given to the world by a child who discovered that the spirits rapped as many times as she snapped her fingers. She told her mother the facts, which she soon verified. There was no theory about it. It was simply a fact and nothing more; the snaps of her fingers were answered by just as many raps. The mother discovered intelligence in this, and here commenced the science of spiritualism. The spiritualists by the advice of spirits formed circles to get spirit manifestations and communications; and no ridicule or threatening could turn them from investigating into the facts of spirit life and manifestations, in all ways that could be thought of. And the most renowned scientists came to their assistance, with all their experience in manipulating experiments, and of observing their progress and noting specifically every movement, so that the spiritual facts might be as accurately known and verified as the facts in the material sciences are. And any one wishing to know how carefully a scientist made his experiments and noted their workings and results in the early stages of the spiritual movement, will find them in Prof. Hare's book on spiritualism. There was not a point neglected to make his experiments reliable in every particular, to establish the facts which such experiments were calculated to determine.

Then if any one wishes to see how contemptible theoretical theological scientists are, let them take up a history of his life after he was convinced by his experiments, observations, and reason, that the spirits of mankind lived, and manifested in various ways to the people of the earth; this fact. They silenced him in their conventions by the most approved gag law conventional rules, and called him an imbecile in the most approved christian slanderous style; but never attempted to show that his experiments were not made with the utmost care, and wholly upon scientific principles; nor did they attempt to duplicate his experiments and show their mistakes; but they took to the most contemptible of modern christian tactics—vilifications and falsehooods, to put him down in the public estimation; although they knew him to be one of the most eminent chemists in America.

The spiritualists who were not eminent for their scientific attainments, took the utmost pains to obtain the facts, and be right; and were determined not to adopt any theory, that would interfere with their free investigation into the spiritual facts; so organizations to do anything more, than to obtain and establish the facts upon which spiritualism was founded, have had but a precarious existence in their ranks. Just compare this little history with the history of christianity in the few years of its formative stages in the life time of its founders. The founder of christianity is represented to be a man about thirty years old, when he commenced his spiritual work, who was possessed of large magnetic powers, and surrounded by many spirits who did many wonderful works by means of his mediumistic powers. But it was not his powers, nor the power of the spirits through him that make his character among christians, but his pretentions, or, the pretentions of his followers, that he was the life and light of the world; that he was the way and savior of mankind. That he was the god of this world, equal with the god of the universe. That he and his father god were one. That he was the word that was god These and many other pretentions were set up by him. or for him by his followers, and upon these pretentions and the theories that arise naturally out of them, churches were formed in a very short time. And the belief in Christ as the savior of the world was promulgated by these churches, and want of belief in these dogmas was declared to be just cause for the eternal punishment of the unbeliever. This made such belief, the greatest virtue in the sight of God, and want of this belief the greatest vice that man can commit.

In this way these church organizations made virtue to consist of a belief, that the natural man considered foolishness; and they made vice to consist of a want of belief, that the natural man pronounced absurd and ridiculous in the extreme. So the common sense of humanity has always been at war with the church sense of christianity; and when the sciences began to be formed, they agreed more with the opinions of the natural man than with the artificial church sentiment. So the common sense of mankind and the learned in the sciences have been opposed to these church ideas. And the christian church men have made war upon the common sense people and the scientists.

The scientists stood their ground and were tortured and murdered by the christians, and many common sense people have done the same, until a civilization has arisen in some parts of the world that shames the christian church members into some sense of human feeling, and forces them to acknowledge that wrong doing is vice, and right doing is virtue, in an individual or nation. This gives the reader the real grounds of the conflict in christendom for all the centuries of its existence since it became a potential power by gaining control of the Roman Empire. The christians never have believed in the spirit manifestations and communications as a source from which we could get true spiritual knowledge, and learn how to live here to have the most happiness in our spirit homes when we go there. They did not consult the spirits to know from them how they live in their spirit homes, but instead were ready to murder those who did, as witches and wizards in this country less than two hundred years ago, and did murder them. They did not want to know what the spirits of heaven said about themselves and their home, and about what was virtue and vice in this world; but they consulted their bible to learn what that said about these matters, and then under its inspirations and the priests who were supposed to know more of the teachings of the book than any others, they went forth with venom in their minds and committed the barbarities which history relates of them.

Then the precise difference between church and bible christianity and spiritualism is that the christians make a Savior and a God out of a medium and assistant Saviors out of his apostles and disciples, and that this Christ will save believers and damn unbelievers, and that God, the universal father of all people, has given them the power to do so in their spirit home. This theory and theology the christians are trying to fasten in the minds of the people so as to crush out all investigations into the facts that will enable them to know the truth of their assumptions and belief. The spiritualists began without any theory or belief in the matter that prevented them from investigating and learning everything that the spirits had to teach, and then comparing it with the christian sense, and common sense and scientific sense; and the final conclusion that has been arrived at after more than thirty years of tests and experiments and observations, and considering and reasoning the communications is, that the spirits agree with the good common sense of the people and the scientists, and disagree with the christian that the natural man is at enmity with God.

They teach us that our natural body is not a cursed body, and our earth was never cursed for man's faults; and heaven's spirit home is a natural home, not under artificial dictational gods or men; and they teach us that the bible account of the lives and employments of the spirits in their summer land is no nearer true than is their description of the making of the heavens and earth; and that the bible makers and church makers departed immediately from spirit manifestations, communications and advice and instruction, to making gods of spirits and infallible prophets of mediums, and formed churches and instructed the members to murder the persons who had familiar spirits, and so cut off all spiritual instruction, while pretending to be guided by the spirit of god or of gods. But the moment people became too humane to allow them to kill those who had familiar spirits, the power of these churches and their priests and bible began to decline, and all the barbarities of the christians have been caused by their theologies, and all the spiritualism that there is in christianity is just enough to prove the divinity of Christ and the Apostles, disciples, and prophets, and confer divine rights on kings and rulers. The Jews carried their theology one step further, and the christians accepted it; that was, that their nation was blessed with the great privilege of being selected by God, as his favorite people, and the entire gist of their spirit communications goes to prove this. Now it must be remembered that the Jews and christians killed the mediums, or those who had familiar spirits, as the only way that it was possible for them to prevent these frauds upon the people from being discovered.

When the child discovered intelligence in the power that made the raps, she had no theory to support, or destroy; she simply told her mother, and investigation proved that they had familiar spirits, and the most intelligent spiritualists soon learned why they had not had them before; and the priests who were in the secret and knew perfectly well that if these communications continued their crimes would be restated and added to them, would be their duplicity in pretending to be guided by the spirit of god and the angels of heaven, and it would be known they were utterly opposed to the true God, and pure angels being known to the people. But this time they had not got the ignorant brutalized Roman people to deal with, nor an ancient ignorant nation of Jews, but an intelligent people who said the mediums should have a fair chance, and have their say the same as the priests' and the trial commenced.

The spiritualists soon found they had the basis for a science which would be established just as other sciences had been by repeated experiments, and observations; and when they had accumulated sufficient knowledge it would be systematized by reason, and take its place among the sciences and become of great value to the scientists by preventing them from being seduced into theological errors by dogmatic priests. There would be the science of spiritualism before them in books with all the most important facts to support it if they desired to have a knowledge of spiritual science in place of theological opinions. The spiritualists have used their facts just as other scientists have used theirs, that is, to prove true what they absolutely did prove. They have not turned them aside to prove what they are not calculated to prove as the christians have.

The spiritual facts do not prove Christ any more the son of God, than they do that other persons are his sons or daughters. A christian spiritualist is like a Mohammedan spiritualist, or an Astrological Astronomer, or an alchymist chemist. The Astrologer seeks a horroscope instead of a telescope, and the alchymist seeks to make gold out of other metals instead of seeking to know the composition of all substances, and the number and uses of all simple substances in their simple capacity, and in their combinations.

The question is: Will spiritualists allow their system of facts to prove anything but what they do prove? Many of them think Christ has a noble character, and they wish to honor him. This can be truly done by calling him a man with the power of a man and a spirit medium with the faults of a medium. His inspiration could only be understood by being in accord with the Jewish information of his time; and he approved of the inspirations of thousands of years before his time, which every humane person of this age considers cruel and wrong. He described heaven as a kingdom, with its ruler on his throne, or his followers did for him, and he is represented as sending the spirits to the right and left in the most despotic manner. He did not vary from the spirit and knowledge of the age one half as much as our mediums have in our age.

They found the people steeped in the belief of an orthodox hell and heaven; and they said such a hell did not exist, and the real heaven was a republic or democracy; and our mediums have quietly continued to say these things by spirit power and directions, and orthodoxy has had to change its front and stop its hellish discourses in a great degree.

There was too much barbarism in Christ's age to allow him to live but a short time even with the slight changes he proposed to their old laws and institutions; and it is very likely if he had proclaimed that his familiar spirits worked through him, instead of saying he and his father, God, were one, and other expressions indicating his own opinion of the great powers God had given him, he would have been crucified just the same, because Jewish priests had no more mercy over persons who had familiar spirits than they had over persons who proposed to change their religious laws and practices, nor any more than christian priests had over witches. The cry was, kill them; crucify them, and pardon robbers and murderers in all countries and times where priests have power to have such awful crimes committed.

The spiritualists of this age are considering the claims of all modern mediums, and when they are Christ's, or that Christ's spirit controls them, they call the people devils, as he did, and it is generally found that the devils are in the mediums, as the people in Christ's day said they were in him; and finally all pretentions of that sort are without any other foundations than that the persons can be taken possession of by spirits, and do many wonderful things, curing diseases and giving tests of great value to mankind; but this only proves they are men or women mediums, not Christs, not saints, not God's agents, in any other sense than that they are the agents of the spirits; of the spirit land, or of the angels of heaven.

It was very easy to deceive the people in Christ's age, and for ages and ages after; and besides it was very easy for the mediums to be deceived themselves; they were in so much danger from the ignorance of the people, and the priests were constantly trying to find them, and hunting them down with all their power, so they had very little time to think and observe the facts, and make just conclusions from them regarding their own powers, and the power and characters of the spirits who could manifest through them. Besides the laws were cruel and blasphemous against them. All these things combined to mislead the mediums and people regarding the persons who did these wonderful deeds. But in this age only the relics of these barbarisms and ignorance exist in the most enlightened portions of the world, and the intelligent will not be deceived by any kind of modern manifestations for any great length of time.

The priests have so long preached and persecuted people to make them believe their ancient records of religious manifestations, that people will not submit to their falsehoods much longer than they will to any such modern frauds and falsehoods; but all the unjust laws and ancient dogmas and fabrications are losing their hold on the minds of the people as fast as they can be supplied with the new truths, and make them practical under the present civilization; and slowly and steadily as other sciences have done their work, spiritualism is doing its legitimate work of putting spiritual truth into the minds of the people. It commenced with the raps, and after that kind of manifestation had been practiced by the spirits for some time, and the religious scandalizers and scientific doubters had got their arguments all fixed, so as to prove to their satisfaction that the spiritualists were wholly wild and mistaken, for the raps were made by fraudulent means, or by an odic force, or by the devil, who was going about the earth deceiving the people.

When all these arguments were made as strong as falsehoods and false logic could make them, lo and behold all at once they were not of the least consequence, for mediums began to write by spirit power; ignorant persons wrote learned essays; children too young to have any education wrote wise, intelligent sentences; and even sentences were written by spirit power without the aid of a medium's hand; pencils were moved by an invisible power, and wrote correct answers to questions. The devil explanation was good yet, and as he was a spirit, it was an acknowledgment of spirit power; but the knee-knocking, toe-cracking explanation would not apply; the odic force and fraudulent plan of mediums would still apply; but when nothing of the kind could be said of the medium, then came unperceived muscular action. Then came impersonation, where the medium would take on the appearance of some person who had gone to the spirit home. Most frequently the death scene.

These actions the priest and their supporters were always ready to lay to the devil, and the material scientists to chicanery, or to an unknown power. Then the mediums began to lay their hands on the sick, and they would recover. Here was an absolute good done that all had to acknowledge. But the christians said it was the devil working to deceive the nations, and the scientists said, it was only an imaginary work; that really no one was cured, but only thought they were for a little time, then the disease would return; but when the doctors had said that a patient must die from the disease, and the mediums laid their hands on them and they became well, it was pronounced the work of a good spirit and was no work of the imagination, but a reality that would be a recommend to doctor, priest, or scientist to imitate, and would give them a great and good name if they would go and do likewise. But instead of this the proud priest walked by on the other side, denouncing the medium as an anti-Christ, and the self conceited scientist went about bewailing the superstition of the spiritualists who approve of the good deeds of the spirits through mediums; and not only that but demonstrate that their good works are done by the magnetic power that they possess the same as successful magnetisers have; but beyond that the spirits can see the wants or needs of sick persons and can apply the remedy best adapted to the patient, whether it is magnetism or some other remedy.

The spirit power to heal the sick, shows itself to be very great through mediums and without them, and comes as near raising the dead as the power of spirit ever had; all that was ever done in ancient times by gods, Christs, or prophets is duplicated in this age by spirits and mediums; and it is curious to note the opposition and enmity of christian priests and their pals to these spiritual healing powers; when we hear them applauding to the sky, Christ and His followers for doing the same kind of curative work, or rather attesting to the truth of the accounts of such medication that is in their bible, as the work of these ancient mediums, but the only real proof that such a class of men ever did such deeds is that the mediums of this day duplicate them. Because it is a historical fact undisputed by any reliable authority that the new testament was got up when christian priests were known as the most consumate liars that ever walked the earth when they could do so to glorify God. After this, and with these healing manifestations, the spirits began to speak through mediums. These speaking mediums attracted a great deal of attention, the christians had taught the people for fifteen centuries that the word of their god and his angels always spoke the truth; and although many of their priests and deacons were liars and scoundrels, it was impressed upon the people generally that the words of Angels must be true, and many among the spiritualists believed them to be true, and they relied implicitly on them for correct council to direct them in the right way, to do and to act. This caused many spiritualists to act foolishly, unwisely, and unjustly; as all other religionists have done, who have relied on God, Christ, or

Angels to direct them; instead of taking these persons in as advisers, and determining all matters by their own judgment and taking all the responsibility on themselves for failures and wrongs, and for success and right doing. It was one of the greatest triumphs of spiritualists that enabled them to break from this old religious wrong that all religions had taught, that people must rely on the judgment of God, Christ, or angels to keep themselves right instead of upon their own judgment.

After twenty or thirty years of experience, spiritualists were convinced that they had as pure and truthful spirits to direct them as ever came to the earth to advise people; and yet the natural god had given them a mind of their own, that they must use or they would suffer for neglecting this important duty. It came to them to take all the counsel they could get from any one else, but then they must consider this as the advice of friends, and use it in making up their judgment, as they would use the advice of other friends. It is found to be one of the most difficult tasks in the world to convince people that they are possessed of a mind that is of more value to them to direct them what they shall do, and what they shall refrain from doing, than all else that they possess. They do not seem to think that words from heavenly sources are to be taken as advisory counsel, the same as words from earthly counsellors. But the inquiry will be made, what should mediums do who give themselves up to spirit control? They must take their chances, whether it turns out good or evil to them. The medium then becomes responsible for the good or evil the spirit does that controls them. Sometimes they are exalted, and do the greatest good that mortal can do. At other times they do as great evil as mortals can do. The theory is that good persons attract good spirits, and evil-disposed persons attract evil spirits; and as such was always the law, all ancient communications must be tested by known truth to find out their real value.

The change that has come over the minds of the people since spiritualism has been before them in this regard is marked. Our first good speakers, like Achsa W. Sprague and Selden J. Finney, would find large numbers of people ready to listen to them in all parts of the country where intelligent people could conveniently get to them. Large halls were filled to listen to their spiritual instruction. But at the present time our best speakers only have good congregations in special localities; the people do not want words and philosophy, however richly ladened with eloquence. But they want tests, facts of spirit presence; and only speakers who can give these tests, are greeted with large audiences generally. This shows how hungry the people were when spiritualism first came among them, for spiritual food; trance-speaking was a god-send. But now they not only want trance-speaking but tests that prove the presence of spirit friends.

The demand of this time is that every speaker and priest must prove their assertions true by satisfactory tests. Wordy proof is no longer received as satisfactory. It is well understood that priest craft with all its diabolical work has been done; because the people took the priests' words for what they asserted as truth; when now it is well known that nine-tenths of what they asserted was false. The intelligent people are objecting to the old priesthood, that was built up in ancient days on the plan that words are gods, or god's truth; because it has so much evil in its works; not only falsehood, but barbarism. And they object entirely to making a new priesthood upon that plan. From this it will be plain to all good speakers, that if they wish to succeed, they must have good test proof that what they assert is true, in the spiritual cause; and the christian priests have to prove the words of their bible, or explain why they cannot do so, to meet objections to the truth of its assertions.

The division in the society to-day is that some people take the words of priests and bible as true, and others demand proof, that statements be proved true, no matter who makes them. That is, if a priest cannot prove there is a hell of fire and brimstone for the wicked to be sent to, to suffer eternally, then there is no such place. If they cannot prove that there is a little new Jerusalem heaven, prepared for the elect good spirits to go to; then there is no such place. The bible and priest's assertions that there are such places is a fraud and deception. And the assertion was made that there were such places by bible makers and priests, to drive people to madness or into the church. The spirits that come back to earth, and tell their experiences through modern mediums, say, they do not find any such heaven or hell; and as these statements are made by thousands upon thousands of the spirits, right from their spirit homes, it must be taken as truth, and the enemies of modern spiritualism have very generally come to the conclusion that this spirit testimony is true, and it modifies the sermons of the most heartless priests so that they denounce eternal vengeance much less vigorously than they ever did before.

The next phase of mediumship was slate writing by spirits, without the use of medium's hand. The medium would hold the slate under a table, or over his head in plain sight with a small piece of pencil on it, and the pencil would write by an unseen power, communications signed by some person that was known to be in the spirit world; often the writing would be like the hand-writing of the persons when they were in their natural body on earth. This phase of mediumship was first made generally public, through Wm. Slade, who has since become famous by the spirits writing on slates under test conditions; that is, persons who wished the tests, brought new slates and had them locked together with a little piece of pencil between them into the presence of the medium, and the pencil was heard to make a noise, as though it was writing; and when the slates were unlocked, writing was found on the sides of the slates, that had been locked inside. The different ways that these manifestations have been tested, to prove that they were done by spirit power, are too numerous to mention here, and the number of mediums that the spirits have power to do these writings through, are many, and there is no other way to account for them, only slight of hand fraud, or the devil's work, or the spirit's writings, who sign their names to the writings.

This phase of spirit manifestation has vexed the scientists and the priests equally, who thought modern spirit manifestations were frauds, because their most critical observers could not detect any; and there was no way to account for them, but as the works of good or evil spirits. The scientists, especially of Germany and generally on the continent in Europe, who have taken interest enough in the manifestations to thoroughly investigate them, are convinced that it is spirits or an unknown intelligent power. This brings the scientists at loggerheads with each other. The scientists that do not know anything about the matter by experiment, are as abusive of those who do, as the priests are of all persons who question the statements of their divine priestly or bible authority. These facts prove that it makes no difference who it is; as a class, when they are governed by belief, or faith, they are ready to persecute and slander those that disagree with them; only those who are guided by experimental knowledge had the true basis of settling questions by reason; they can appeal to proved facts; and all the persons who will either stand by them, or are willing to hold to the decisions which well conducted experiments indicate are true, and reasonable deductions from such truth.

When English jurists class mediums for spirit manifestations with witches, and refuse to admit testimony that goes to show that the mediums are honest, and that the manifestations are of the greatest importance to mankind, because they truly represent what the spiritualism of the world teaches. Spiritualism never taught that Christ was the savior of the world, nor that He was the first that was ever raised into the world of spirits; although spirits have taught these things, the same as man have. But all such ideas are far fetched, and have no real foundation in the general teachings of spirits, and such ideas could never have obtained a general belief among mankind, especially among the well informed, if mediums had been allowed to live and give spirit communications; but Christians and Jews especially, would not permit this, and they were silenced, or killed, under the names of babblers, witches, and wizards.

The English judges, in the case of the trial of Wm Slade, favored these views, but they were brought out more plainly in the case of Mrs. Fletcher. The truth of her spiritual statements was not allowed to be proved, nor the facts that she did give spirit communications, that she had not committed any crime, was well proved, but she was sent to prison for a year, really because she said distinctly, that spirits did manifest through her, and she was ready to prove this was true, by reliable witnesses, but the court would not admit the testimony, the judges preferring to judge her by their belief, than by evidence, and preferring to consider her as deceiving people by her witchery, under an old law than by admitting the facts in testimony in the case.

The same views are taken by many judges and people in this country, and all they want is a public opinion back of them, and they will not stop at imprisonment, but would commence the ancient witch killing; because people who are governed by the ignorant superstitions that made the ancient witch laws for the Jews of Judea, and the christians of the middle ages in Europe, and for the Puritans of New England that caused the cruelties at Salem, Mass.

You hear it constantly repeated that this is the last part of the nineteenth century, but it must be remembered that the persons who read the laws that were made, some where between the fourth and fourteenth centuries before Christ as God's true laws to govern mankind, are living in all the dark ages which have been made by those laws, since they were put in force; and wherever enforced these witch-craft and priest-craft people never have lived, and never will live in but one age, the age of Moses, and Saul the first king of the Jews. If any one claims that they have been amended for the better, let them read the amendment and blot the other out of their readings; if Christ repealed these laws, why have christians murdered the mediums until humane people prevented them from doing it?

The reason is plain, those persons who read the Bible as God's truth are living in the Bible ages, and the after ages that were fashioned by the Bible. They are not living in this age, that is fashioned in its humanitarian principles, by the sciences and knowledge; and will not permit the spirit mediums, who present the simple angelic religion of the spirits, to live and proclaim it, without prosecuting and persecuting them to their utmost of their ability.

The question is; shall the laws and government, religion, ignorance, superstition, judgments, spiritualism and the abominable falsehoods and barbarities of the Jews in the fifth century, before Christ, and the superstitions, ignorance and the religious, spiritual lies, with all the horrible judgments, and tortures of the fifth century after Christ, which were practiced for a thousand years after, by Christians; be the guide of the intelligent people and their judges in the trial of spiritualists in this age? Or shall we be guided by the humanitarian principles, laws, religion, and spiritualism of modern times, is the great question now before the people to be decided.

The next phase of spirit manifestation was the photograph ; that is, a person would set for his photograph and a spirit-picture would be formed by his side, or sometimes the person would be hid by the spirit-picture ; there were a great many of these photographs taken of persons, that had no likeness on earth; that had been in the spirit land for years, and these photos were so good, that their friends often recognized them at once as being the picture of a long lost friend, or relative, it may be Father, Mother, or other near and dear friend, whose features were clearly fixed in their minds. In such cases it would seem to prove the presence of the spirit beyond a doubt.

Frauds may have been committed in some cases, but that there has been many of these spirit photographs there can be no reasonable doubt, because they have been recognized by so many persons who knew the person well, while they were in the body. The most unreasonable critics, who proclaim that all the spirit photos are frauds, are those who pretend to believe all the spiritual stories recorded in their bible where they have no proof of their truth ; but, here where the proof is palpable and positive, they have no faith that spirits ever have done any such thing as making a picture of themselves on the sensitive plate.

A Mr. Wm. H. Mumler first drew attention to this subject, and took many pictures that were prized very highly by the friends of the spirit represented—and when any one questions the truthfulness of these personal statements, and say they believe all the stories in their bible to be true, it is apparent that they have filled themselves so completely that there is no room for another truth; they believe that spirits have manifested, but when it is proved true, that they commuicate, they are as mad as hornets when their nest is disturbed. It is more than they can bear to have their belief destroyed by the knowldge, that it is true. The reason is it destroys the influence of sensational talkers and preachers, and puts sober, earnest, truthful teachers in their places.

The next phase of spirit manifestations, to be considered, is the power of spirits to raise heavy substances and persons, and float them in the air or in water. Many objects have been thus raised and floated in rooms. Among the persons thus raised, D. D. Home is one well known that has been levitated many times and seen floating in a room that was somewhat darkened, but yet there was sufficient light, to enable persons in the circle to see him. The Davenport Brothers caused many articles to float in the air, when giving their public sceances in darkened rooms, the articles being marked with phosphorus, so their movements could be seen. Hundreds of other mediums have caused these kinds of levitations, and they have been witnessed by thousands of people, and there is no more doubt that spirits have this power, and use it to benefit mankind many times when people are not aware of it, than there is that spirits in the body can raise heavy bodies by their hands.

The principles are not as well understood about the way they do it. But that it has been done, not many intelligent people deny; but there are vast numbers who deny that it can be done now. Ancient times were very different from the present, in their estimation; then these things were done as miracles to show the power of God. But they do not believe He does such things now, but modern spiritualists believe spirits have, always had this power and used it by the law of nature and never by miraculous power, unless all the powers of nature are miraculous.

The next kind of spirit manifestation to be noted is the fire test. Mediums have taken up coals of fire when at red heat rubbed their faces and hands on burning coals of fire in a grate without the least injury to them; their hair was not singed, and there was no smell of burning substances about them. The spirit power to prevent fire from burning the medium, for fire tests are well proved. D. D. Home is the most celebrated of these mediums, but many others have shown this exemption from being burned by fire when under spirit influence. This power disposes of the idea that the spirit of man can be tormented by flames of sulpher that our good Catholic and orthodox clergy have threatened the wicked. If they can surround our fleshey bodies with a substance that will resist the flames and prevent them from burning, they can protect their spirit bodies from being tortured by fire much more easily; and all the tortures of hell which they have depicted in their bible, and in their pulpits are proved to be simply falsehoods that the preacher has used to frighten ignorant and command the superstitious to do their bidding. If evil spirits as the orthodox say all spirits are who protect the mediums from the torments of burning by fire, have this power, surely they can protect themselves and make the most delightful heaven out of the most diabolical hell that the most wicked priests ever depicted to a listening people.

The next phase of spirit manifestation that has attracted a great amount of attention is of spirits materializing themselves so as to be seen by the common vision of people and felt as persons are in their natural bodies. Historically this is no new phase of spirit manifestation, but under the modern science this was introduced by Mrs. Andrews of Moravia, New York, and has attracted more attention, than any other phase since the raps were first heard at Hydesville, that called the attention of people to a scientific phase of spiritualism, that finally is to result in establishing a scientific religion that will be in harmony with the material sciences of the day. The English scientists, Crooks and Wallis have tested the truth of this kind of materialization, and come to the conclusion after putting the medium under the most scientific test conditions, that the materializing is real, that the bodies of persons appear and disappear as though made and unmade right before them by unseen forces.

When scientists of their high reputation proclaim the facts that appear before them; where they have the entire control of the conditions to detect fraud; and state these conditions; and mark every phenomenon that is manifested under such conditions, it makes a great impression upon all thoughtful people who will permit themselves to think on the reported manifestations of spirits in modern times; they will go back to the reports of the eminent scientist, Prof. Hare of Philadelphia, and inquire what it means that these eminent men who have examined carefully the modern spirit phenomena and have come to the conclusion that the spirits of persons who have left their earthly bodies do communicate and manifest themselves in various ways to the people who are in their earthly bodies. If these conclusions are not correct, how do these eminent scientists and men happen to declare them facts? Let honest thinkers trace the facts stated by Crooks and find if they can discover a scientific error.

But it seems impossible for persons who are touched with faith in modern christianity to look over fairly and considerately the experiments that prove modern spiritualism to be true. Instead of this it appears that they must fall into the slanderous habits of christians to put down truth and smirch the characters of the purest and most eminent scientists. But they can not do this so much against Crooks and Wallis in this day, as they did against Hare in his time; not only because christianity is losing its grip on the minds of intelligent people, but because spiritualism is received as truth by great numbers of the most intelligent people; and this large class refuse to take christian slanders as good arguments against it.

There have been a great many materializing mediums in this country who have given decided proof of spirit power to do this work. Not only have spirits materialized, but have been able to walk and talk with their earthly friends. There had been many partial materializations, such as hands and faces, before there was a materialization of the whole body and clothing. A great many of these hands were seen generally in a moving, quivering state ; but many more were felt in seances, when they were not seen. The prophecy from all these manifestations is, that in a short time spirits will materialize, and walk and talk with a great many people, and give the counsels of heaven and of angels to all mankind. They give this counsel now through speaking mediums; but when spirit forms appear to the natural eye, and are heard to speak by the natural ear, as they appeared when in their natural body, their counsels will have more influence with people than they do when the words come through other bodies.

But such a civilization can not be made, as long as the religious law exists, that persons who have familiar spirits should not be permitted to live. The sentiment is too barbarous for a really civilized people to entertain for a moment ; and as long as people believe in a bible that contains such sentiments as the word of their god ; spirits can not come and materialize and give us their best heavenly sentiments ; and the persons who have such low, murderous sentiments are not capable of understanding the best of angel wisdom.

The next phase of spirit manifestation to be considered is clairvoyance. When a person attains such clear sight that they can see through opaque substances that the natural eye, in its natural condition, can not penetrate, or have a plain vision of actions and things that are beyond the power of natural sight in distance and situation, this is called clairvoyance. The spiritual phase of this faculty is, that they can see spirits and describe them so accurately that persons who were well acquainted with the persons when living in the body, would recognize them. Then, in addition to seeing them, if they are clairaudient, and can hear the spirit talk, they can give the sentiments and words of the spirit; and these together give persons who are well acquainted with the earth life of the spirit a good chance to test the correctness of the clairvoyant's and clairaudient's vision and hearing; and this has been tested thousands of times, and the greatest number prove that their sight and hearing is correct. But such proof is of very little value to persons who go by faith instead of knowledge. Such persons, after having the most decided tests of this kind given to them, will go away and say they have not seen or heard anything that would convince them that a spirit was present, and was seen and heard, notwithstanding they gave them the information through the medium that was correct, and that none knew but the spirit and himself. Such persons do not determine the truth by the evidence, but by their faith and feelings. The truth or falsehood of the testimony has nothing to do with his conclusions. This is the christian, pagan and Jewish stronghold. As long as they can keep the people in bondage by their belief, they will do it; but whenever a religion, based upon modern spiritualism is established, the people will be obliged to go by truthful evidence.

The next phase of medium manifestation to be considered is that in which the spirit takes control of an arm and hand, and writes messages that the mind of the medium does not notice or know what is written. The most eminent of this class of mediums is J. V. Mansfield. His communications have many phases that are of the most convincing nature. One of these consists in answering letters in Chinese characters, so that a Chinaman could read it. The answer purporting to come from a relative in the spirit land, and was of a character to convince the Chinaman that his relative dictated it, if he did not write it. But much oftener the mind of the medium is attracted to the writings, if it does not know what is written; yet the whole person is more or less psychologized or possessed by the spirit, and the brain, as well as the hand, is doing part of the work. Often in such a state the medium will write back-handed, so that it can be read by a person sitting on the opposite side of the table from the medium, as he writes it, while the person sitting by the side of the medium could not read it until it was turned around.

The next phase of mediumship to be considered is the flower medium ; that is, flowers would be brought into a room where the medium is holding a seance, when the doors were closed, and there was no way for them to get into the room known to the persons who composed the circle. The well-known flower medium, Mrs. Thayer, of Boston, Mass., brought this phase of mediumship into notice. Not only were flowers brought into the room by a process not understood by mortals in their earthly bodies, but doves and other articles were brought there, or were made by the spirit in the room. But the proof is, that they were brought into the room by spirit power, because the flowers and plants would be dewy and fresh, as though recently plucked from the ground, or from the stems of the plants.

This class of manifestations are the most mysterious of anything belonging to the science of spiritualism. How can a good square knot be tied in an endless rope? How can a man's coat be taken off when his hands are tied together? How can a solid ring be put upon a person's arm when the hands are tied together? The material scientists are completely dumbfounded by such spirit doings ; yet they have been done thousands of times under conditions that could be relied upon to test the matter and establish its truth. That is, the principle that one solid substance can be passed through another by one of them being decomposed until the passage is made, and then recomposed as solid as before, or there may be a spiritual process yet unknown to material philosophers, by which one substance is passed through another. It has been the opinion of some philosophers that there is a fourth extension or dimension of space by which these works are done; but such explanations make confusion worse confounded, and are of no value to plain, common sense people, who seek the truth and wish for nothing but plain words to express it.

There is one other phase of this kind of spirit manifestations that should be considered, that is they have been able to make articles disappear and reappear, in such a manner, that the senses of sight and feeling attested to such manifestations as true; and when reason with all its cool calculating and searching powers makes its researches and its reconsiderations, the conclusions are that the articles like tables disappear, and were not to be found, and they reappeared in the room in another place. For a notable instance of such a manifestation, see Eppes Sargeant Scientific Basis of Spiritualism, Pages 81 and 82. From all these considerations it clearly appears that the mysteries of spiritualism are as profound as the mysteries of godliness can be. But all these unaccountable manifestations should not prevent persons from trying to break the veil of mystery and make all things so plain that the human mind can grasp it with ease. But while persons may acknowledge these to be great mysteries, the facts which bring them to the minds of man are no mysteries; the natural faculties of mankind attest to the truthfulness just the same as the growing grass is a fact, but the vitality that makes it grow is no better comprehended than these mysterious disppearances and reappearances.

The mysteries of nature are as great as these or any others, unless we except the mysteries of christians as the greatest when they say prove all things and hold fast that which is good; but when they find a person that adopts that course; they traduce him, and if that will not stop him they murder him if they can. It is very singular that people with such sentiments and such practices can hold the attention of people at all in this enlightened period. This state of religious sentiment must soon cease, when the people see a religion based upon spiritualism, which demands the best of practices, the best of rules, as well as having them for precepts. Spiritualists are making the bible of to-day, according to the highest religious knowledge of to-day, If the most enlightened christians of a hundred years ago, say the Quakers, had made a bible, they would have made it according to the knowledge of a hundred years ago. If the Protestants of three hundred years ago had made their bible, it would have been made according to the knowledge of three hundred years ago; and when the christians of fifteen hundred years ago made their bible; it was made according to the knowledge of fifteen hundred years ago; and according to their ignorance and the falsehood and deceptions of their priests; and when the Jews made their bible two or three thousand years ago, it was made according to the knowledge that religious people had at that time, and the arrogance and brutality of the priests of that time. And as the first bible made in this time has been the foundation for all the bibles and all the brutality in the christian world ever since, because the principles inculcated in it have not been changed by any of these religionists.

A few items have been changed; the christians repealed the law of an eye for an eye and a tooth for a tooth, but kept it in practice. The Protestants proclaimed the law of the right of private judgment, but suppressed it as much as they could. The reason for the continued practice of the old law, was that the spirit of the Moses law was left in the make up of the new. Now spiritualism comes with a new foundation in every important particular; its principles are that laws should be established by the people upon the principles of justice, that are discovered by experience, experiments, and observations in society; the saying is that practice makes perfect.

We reason from what we have learned by practice,

and make the most reasonable laws we can to promote humane institutions in all the departments of government and of religion, where we have not had experience. Where we have had experience and have a true knowledge of what the just humane law should be, it is easy to make it. But this point should be distinctly understood. The laws are to be founded upon justice and humanity. All the experiments are made to find out what is just, and that knowledge gives us the law. True spiritualism will not allow laws to hang upon any other principle. The Mosaic and Christ principles are that they should be founded upon self-love. That is, that on the two commands, you should love God with all your strength and your neighbor as yourself. Upon these commands hang all the law and the prophets. Under the provisions of this constitution the christians and Jews are only bound to make laws that are consistent with the love of self, which they have in them after loving God so much. This little tittle of variable love is the only foundation for humane laws that is left in the christian commands to guide them to make the laws of humanity.

This principle was tried for a thousand years in the Roman empire, and the nations that were formed out of it, after they adopted Christ as their God, and it proved a flat failure; no religion stands more disgraced in the public mind, than that of christianity, and they made laws according to their feelings of loving their neighbors as they did themselves; and if any one can find they had much just love for themselves, or others, it will be news to the rest of the thinking world. They had expended all their love on God, except what they turned into hate of intelligent people who would do their own thinking. These are the radical differences between the ancient religions and the religion that is now being formed by the sciences of which spiritualism is the basis, and like all the other sciences, points to a law-god of an unchangeable purpose.

The Mohammedans have nothing very different in principle from Jews of the David and Solomon type, but they commenced by adopting the arts, sciences, and philosophy of the Greeks and Romans; and prospered as long as they held to them; and they failed just as soon as they left them and went back to their Jewish principles. The Mormans followed the Mohommedans and Jews in their religion, but have adopted woman suffrage in practice which is far in advance of the Jewish or Mohammedan christian practices, and will eventually enable the women to relieve themselves from the bondage that other religionists have fastend upon them. This will occur when there is a disagreement among the heads of the church, or when there is a weak or humane ruler over their church. From this one woman's right principle there is more hope that they will establish a humane religion, upon just principles, than there is from any of the old religions whose members have no more education and intelligence than they have. And already there comes a proposition from the old religionists to abolish this right, and try to overcome Mormonism by classing women with children and fools; all persons who adopt the best principles taught by spirits, will oppose the taking of the franchises away from these women, and will insist that all women shall be endowed with these rights and all others that justly belong to them. Thus spiritualism comes among the people with the best gifts of the angels of heaven, and unites with the wisest men of the earth to carry comfort and justice to the most degraded and down trodden people in society, and is calculated to unite all the knowledge of the world to establish the religion of nature, truth, justice, and mercy with the law-god, as the true god.

The growth of spiritualism, is one of the phenomenal religious events in the history of mankind. The spirit manifestations have great sensational attractions that ordinary people like; not only so, but are very anxious to see, hear, and observe with their natural faculties; these attract the mass of the people for a time, but to hold them, there must be an organizer that will take these interesting phenomena and make use of them in a religious worship adapted to the intelligence of the people. Or the learned must take up the subject and investigate the phenomena and determine their value in practical life. The sensational phase is past, in this country mostly; and now the learned are examining into its truth, and the eminent who have spent much time in investigating into its facts and principles, declare them true to the point, that spirits live, after the death of the body, and communicate with the people on earth who are in their earthly bodies.

This class of spiritualists, keep it alive among the most intelligent people in the country. It is so rooted in facts and experiences, that it is constantly gaining.

> The spirits, ceaseless tread is lighter than noiseless air;
> Their voices softer than finest harp played by zephyrs fair;
> Yet their voices and their tread resound from pole to pole,
> Like music in the spheres are heard by every living soul.

Spiritualism is so strong in truth, and so majestic in the public feeling among the people, so pure in its teachings of justice, and virtue, so undisguised in its principles and so fair in its statements, that it must always command the attention of the high, the low, the learned and unlearned. It joins the sciences and makes a religion. It joins with the humane and makes a just and merciful government. It joins with the moral, to establish the science of morals. It joins with the best socialists to establish a just social science. It asks no privileges, immunities, pay or exemption from taxes by the government, only such as other religions have, and have as much right to promulgate their doctrines among the people. If people are subject to fine and imprisonment for speaking against Christ and the Holy Ghost the same punishment shall meted out to those who speak against the truth, especially spiritual truth.

We say to the christians, come out and expose the body of your religious principles and word-god to the searching investigation that the spiritual doctrines are exposed to; let us have no hiding behind gorgeous tapestry, flowery drapery and flimsy pageantry or college arts and university deceptions and theological frauds and pulpit persuasion and rhodomontade. Bring out your Christ-God and let us see how He differs from our spirit mediums. Bring out your Jewish god and let us see if he differs from our good and bad spirits of this age. Bring out your devil and let us see how he differs from our spirit mediums who have been called evil. Bring fourth your bible and let us compare its communications with spirit communications at present being received, and learn the exact difference, and determine which is most true, most humane, most just, most sensible, and which would be most likely to increase the intelligence and comfort of the people.

Then let us compare the pulpit teachings of the christian priests with the platform teachings of spirit mediums and speakers, and learn which gives the most real instruction to their hearers. Then take up the works of the standard authors of the christians and compare their teachings with those of the spiritualists, and when we have gone through with the comparing of these systems of religious statements, then we will begin to compare them, or the best of our conclusions, with justice, truth and righteousness, in moral, social and religious ethics ; and last and most important, what kind of a government do the religious principles call for? Shall the laws be like those of the kingdom of heaven, or like the republic of heaven? Shall people have equal rights, or the many be subject to the few? These are very important religious questions.

There is no part of the religion of which spiritualism

is the basis, that is so difficult to manage as to prevent the adoption of Saviors, Christs and Gods, like all the old religions. Soon after the spirit rappings became known, there were many Christs, or semi-Christs, that presented themselves for leaders, and small bands of believers followed them. The modern Christs were modeled after the ancient. Those were the saved and righteous who followed after them; and the persons who would not were devils, and damned. Their models were the Jewish prophets, and God and the christians' Christ, and they followed them, to the letter; and when these modern Christs got very wroth, they called those that would not follow them, the children of the devil. See Emma Hardinge, in her history of Modern American Spiritualism, chapter 21.

The greatest number appeared in our conventions; but the great body of spiritualists paid no more attention to them than they did other mediums, because the spirits gave them information that the ancient gods of religionists were abominations and frauds, got up by men to deceive the people; and their modern imitators were no better; and the prophecy is from their present position that the intelligent people of this age will make a common sense religion based upon scientific principles, and they will not accept any other.

Now the question is, what are the teachings of mental and spiritual sciences? A science can not be made without a natural or spiritual law or laws to guide people in making it. Therefore, these sciences must be made by the power of such laws, and the religion which naturally comes from these sciences must be a scientific religion. These sciences agree with the material sciences in being governed by law, and law stands for the true god, until back of the law the god is discovered. And if this god back of these spiritual and natural laws is finally found, the worshippers of the law god will find themselves as near right as it was possible to be, and that they were in harmony with the true god, who made all things, or with the true god that all things had made.

BOOK FOURTH.

THE RELIGIOUS TEACHINGS OF SOME OF THE SCIENCES AND PART SCIENCES.

CHAPTER XVI.

THE RELIGIOUS TEACHINGS OF MUSIC.

The charms of music. Its effect on the Swiss—on the Germans. It is the main support of the Roman Catholic religion. It is the strongest power of religion outside of truth and reason. Puritans rejected instrumental music. When people are very anxious to secure good music they have but little faith in their creeds. It is a science. It is under the law of harmony. See the bell-hangers at work, making a chime of bells. Inspirations not always good in music or religion. Orpheus and Puppets. Blasphemous dogmas upheld by music.

Phonography. A very important science. One alphabet for all languages; one sound for each letter, so all words can be read by all people. Benj. Pitman. Education is in the hands of special providence people, who oppose the adoption of this system.

Photography. This science is governed by law. No miracle or special providence in it. Spirits use a law that is peculiar to themselves.

The echo fastened to be heard at any time. A wonderful discovery that the ancients could not think of.

The science of telegraphing is the art of chaining lightning. It threatens, but is subdued. It is governed by law and controlled by man to do his bidding.

The science of invention. Inventions are made by law. Watts' steam power. Useful inventions that are a great benefit to the poor opposed by word god worshippers.

MUSIC.

IT is not my purpose to give all the scientific phases of harmony and discord in music, nor to dwell upon all the exciting and charming qualities that are so ecstatic to the great majority of the people, and will cause them to do the most heroic and praiseworthy deeds, and also to be deluded by its magic in to doing the most dastardly and wicked acts that curse mankind. When some tunes are played in their hearing, it will make the Swiss soldiers stationed in sunny Italy or la belle France, to sigh for their Alpine homes, and cause them to break from their ranks, and run to get there, regardless of their contracts, their duty and their lives.

When the Germans hear their Rhenish song, they are so excited as to forget their duties when in distant lands, and die of homesickness or flee to their loved valley of the Rhine.

When the Scotch are engaged in battle, and they hear their shrill bagpipe music in their favorite pieces, they rush into the most deadly contests without fear or favor. And among all people, whether savage or civilized, music has a commanding influence to make people do good or evil deeds. When used for religious purposes it has great influence in making people worship where they can hear good music, no matter whether the doctrines taught are true or false; and when people have outgrown one kind of religious worship, and the priests see that their religious doctrines are waning in the public estimation, they turn to music to keep the people in their folds. It is by the charming influence of music principally that the Roman Catholic religion continues to hold its power in the minds of so many people. Its acts and doctrines are repugnant to a great many of their people, and they are only held under its influence by its grand and sublime music.

When it is known that music will excite people to do evil as well as good, any one can understand that its influence, as a religious element, will be used to perpetuate that truth, or dogma, or doctrine, whose members supply the most entertaining music. There is no power outside of reason or truth that is so effectual in drawing a crowd, as music; and if a religious people are determined to teach falsehood, you will see them first at work to supplement devotions and prayers by music. Their solemn devotions are followed by lively music, and their most entertaining speeches by the most solemn dirges, or the most entertaining music for all occasions is selected with care to be appropriate for the time. The sturdy Puritans rejected music as an element to draw people to their meetings. They believed what they professed, and rejected with contempt the introduction of instrumental music in their worship. And when you see a religious people taking the utmost pains to secure the best music, sparing neither money nor influence to obtain it, you may know they have but little faith in their religious professions and creeds.

The scientific religion will put music down as one of the sciences to be learned and practiced as an art; to instruct people in the ways and plan of the law god in regard to the harmonial sounds that can be combined to influence people for good. It is as distinct a science as astronomy, and must be studied with the same care to determine whether it is made by the law of sound or by the special providence of sound; Did the word god make music for a pastime, without regard to law, order or harmony, and change the basic principles of it at every turn when a new class of music was introduced, or a new musical instrument was constructed?

Ask the composer of music how many more sounds he can find in all the world of music than are contained in the octave. Ask him if he is not confined strictly to the law of sound in his compositions. Ask the musical instrument maker if he can find any miracle outside of the law of music to guide him in the construction of his instruments. Ask the most renowned singer, who has spent much time and study in perfecting her voice to obtain all the compass and harmony that she has mastered, whether she has been governed by the laws of sound, and by the laws that govern the voice, or did she rely upon lawless accident or incident to prepare her for success in her charming vocation.

If such laws do not prevail, then there is no science of music, and can not be, and music can not belong to the scientific religion. But every treatise on it makes it a science governed by laws that are in harmony with other sciences. When a person wishes to make a new kind of musical instrument, to give some new and charming intonation, does he ask God to bestow on him a miracle outside of the law of music to enable him to make his musical instrument, or does he study the natural laws that govern sound, and constrct his instrument under principles of the laws that govern the making of the proper intonations? When a person wishes to hang a set of bells for a chime in a church, does he hang them up haphazard and without any regard to size, thickness or shape, and depend upon a special providence god to make the harmonious music which is heard so often to come from these chimes? Most assuredly not. He places each bell in its place, according to its sound; its especial tone; then the hammer that strikes the bell must hit it in the right place, to bring forth the exact tone that is required to make the sound and the harmony that is required. Look upon these bell-hangers and see how carefully they test each bell and each stroke upon it, to bring forth the music required.

When we turn to the classic musician, Opheus, we find it was by his skill that he made inanimate objects dance to his charming music; we find that the heathen gods made music under the knowledge that law governs sound, and the way to get the sound, as it does dancing, and the way to get lifeless objects to dance. The dancing puppet makes great amusement for children, and is made to dance by a law well known to grown up people. The art of adapting words to sounds, and musical sounds to words, ask the composers of songs if they are governed by special providence or by the law of musical harmony in making their charming songs. First they have an inspiration, but whether it will be a flat failure or a triumphant success in harmony and song they can not tell. It is just like the inspirations that the Jews and christians had when they made their bible: they did not know whether it was true or false, and did not attempt to learn by proof, but took it for granted; and that was not the worst of it they made it a dogma and would kill people who did attempt to prove whether it was true or false. But music and song was put before the public and if people were delighted, they manifested that delight, and if not they did not applaud the new song or music. This shows the freedom that is awarded to music and song to catch the popular ear, and dogmatic religionists take advantage of that free expression to introduce this popular music into their meetings and by that means uphold blasphemous dogmas against truth, justice, and virtue, the same as infidels do against the Gods and Saints of the dogmatic religionists. Put religious opinions on the free basis the same as music is, and there will be less blasphema by christian and infidel than exists now; and makes certain kinds of music blasphemous and certain kinds pious, good, and lawful; and the amount of blasphemous music would soon attract the most attention, and the devil, as the Methodist said, would soon have the best music.

PHONOGRAPHY.

This science must turn out to be one of the most useful sciences if it finally fulfills the promises which its advocates claim. This science is calculated to make an alphabet with all the sounds of all the letters that are required in all languages, one alphabet for all people; and while we have a babel of languages, all will be represented by one alphabet and every letter of it will have the same sound by all people of whatever language. From this it will be seen that phonography means that each letter in a word will have the same sound at all times, and in all languages; and shows there need be but one set of letters for all the languages; this will enable the people of all nations to learn the sounds of these letters to read and pronounce the words of all other people correctly; but under the present forms of alphabets people may be able to read the letters of many languages, but as there are different sounds attached to the letters, they can only guess what the pronounciation of a word is, until specially instructed, and hearing the word pronounced.

It is curious to note that all the babel sounds of all the known languages in the world can be signified by about fifty letters so far as yet discovered, that is there are but such a number of sounds to be signified by so many letters in all the variations of all the sounds of the human voice in making all the languages of all the people of the earth. Upon this basis is founded the science of the sounds of the letters of the alphabet, or of phonography, and by this system all words in all languages can be pronounced from the reading, as well as they can from hearing the natives pronounce them. Here is the law of the various sounds of the human voice which the law-god has empowered people to have to express their thoughts; there may be a few more sounds, not yet discovered, that the human voice can be used for in making languages, but there is enough known to determine that the science of phonography is well established, and that the limit of these sounds is nearly reached. Man's mind is found capable of discovering god's will in regard to the number of sounds that man's voice can give, and then to make the sign that shall represent each sound distinctly, and make its shape so distinct, that it will be known as quick as seen; each sound will have its special sign with the peculiar shape, and that shape will always represent its particular sound, so there is no difficulty in pronouncing words as the writer or type setter intended them to be pronounced.

It is impossible for a person to look over the system published by Benn Pitman, and not be impressed with the idea of the system being based upon the law of sound, and all languages are really formed on such a foundation, so the system includes them; and what is more; it is very well proved that a language can not be formed, that the words cannot be represented by characters, that represent certain sounds always, and never put the learner to the task of learning the sounds of the letters in every word. This idea that one letter should have from four to seven sounds could not stand the pressure for one year if the religion of science had the same control over our institutions of learning that the present special providence religious people have over them. In the first place, they are opposed to the common people having an education, and when they have to succumb to the people so far; then they want to make it as difficult to get it as possible, and there they stand to-day against phonography being put in alphabet form and having the common printing done in that alphabet.

PHOTOGRAPHY.

The science of photography is the taking of pictures by light, or the making of shadows enduring, so that they can be seen in the bright sunlight for a long time after the sun or other light has made them. Ask the photographer how he does this, and he will tell you by the power of light on chemical substances. That is by law. There is no other plan to do it. God does not interfere by special providence to produce these pictures, and make them permanent, any more than he does to make the fleeting shadow to follow the substance. The law of shadows is well known; but the law that will make the shadow as permanent to the sight as the substance, is only known to those who make a study of it. This shows, so far as human knowledge can determine at this time, that there is no other way to take pictures by photography, only by strictly following the action of light on substances that will retain the shadow until other chemical substances can be applied to make it permanent. And all improvements are made by studying into laws governing in this matter. The exception may be that when spirits make their photograph, they do it by their own powers that are not known to people in the body. It is a shadow making a permanent shade that we can see; but they must be by law. This is proved by the spirits requiring a special medium to enable them to make the picture.

ECHO.

The cause of an echo is very well understood to be the concussion of a wave of air set in motion by a voice, instrument or explosion against some object that causes it to rebound and come back to the ear less intense; but in other respects but little different from the first sound. This echo has been long known. But the idea that such echo could be laid up and reported in full years after it had been voiced, is of very recent date, but absolutely accomplished by Edison, the great inventor. Now the question is, what rule, or no rule, is followed in laying up an echo? And the answer is that there must be something for the air wave of the voice, sound or noise to float against, that it makes an impression upon; that will retain it so that it can be revoiced or resounded. When placed in the proper instrument or phonograph, and worked for that purpose to do this, there must be complete obedience to the laws of sound, of echo, and of the instruments that will retain the sound and be ready to reproduce it when called upon.

The special providence belief is not consulted in this matter by the scientists; and yet this invention is more wonderful than anything the ancient religionists, Jew or christian, ever thought of that was a fact. They have told many wonderful falsehoods that have caused the ignorant to worship them as gods; but their facts and fancies are childhood's images of mind; surface facts or fancies that bear no more comparison to the profundity of the present thinkers than the cob-house building of children does to the most finished palaces of modern times. And when we think the sensitive psychometrist can hear and see when influenced by the rocks of the earth, we at once can estimate the much greater advantage to be derived from modern thought than from ancient; and if the progress in all these directions is as great in the next century as in the past, the children will know more about religious and worldly truth than the most wise two hundred years ago. Let the people once turn their attention to learning and supporting religious and worldly truth as earnestly as they have religious superstition and worldly bigotry, there will be a new heaven and earth to the people of coming ages, made new by the knowledge of mankind, which is being gained now by worshipping the law god instead of the word god.

TELEGRAPHING.

The science of telegraphing is based upon the principle of chaining chain lightning, and making one of the gods of the ancients a servant of man, and making him carry our messages and do many things that servants are forced to do, regardless of his thunderings and threatenings; and although we may fear his bolts and wish to avoid his burning flashes, as we wish to avoid the threatenings and smashings of other servants; yet we go right on and see to it that it is subdued to do the work assigned to it, the same as other servants; and although we may say his works are devilish at times, and he is devilish willful, still intelligent people say let us command him as we do other servants, and if the devil is in him, and he growls, and threatens, and mutters, and sends his damnations, like the god of the Jews and christians, we know he is weak, because he threatens so much and executes so little.

This christian counterpart of thunder and lightning threatens to send people to hell, when he has no hell to send them to, and threatens to destroy the souls of persons who will not worship him, when he is entirely powerless to do it. As long as he had ignorant Jews and christians to deal with, the threatenings of his priests would frighten them into subjection to their will, as the thunder and lightning did those who worshipped them as God and feared them as they did the devil. But the day is not far distant apparently, when men will command the rain to fall on the parched earth where wanted for human comfort; but whether this is realized or not, sufficient is known to-day to destroy all the religions, made gods and devils, whose priests cursed the people of the earth ever since they were made. It is found these gods are made of the same materials that the christians' god made the world, nothing. Ask any person engaged in telegraphing how improvements are to be made, and they will tell you by the law of nature. They will not study the word of God, but the law of God, to make the instruments that are needed to subdue every element in nature to the use of mankind.

INVENTION.

The science of invention, or of making instruments to be of great benefit to mankind, is of too great importance to be overlooked in the religion of nature, in the material and the spiritual worlds: When a person wishes to arrive at a spiritual truth, they make calculations and inventions to meet all questions, and prevent frauds; and these inventions must be according to the law that governs spirit and matter, and the proof is that material and spiritual movements are governed by the same general system of laws. Inventions are made by complying with the laws of nature, and these useful inventions often lead to the discovery of natural laws that were not before known. Where did Watt look when he discovered the force of steam;

in the bible, or at the steam of a kettle, when it lifted the cover? He looked at the workings of the steam, and the result was he discovered a power that has done more to benefit mankind than all the bibles, with all their religions, that have ever existed in this world. It did not promise to love its neighbor as itself, but it did his hardest and most repulsive work without begging to be excused, or asking extra pay for its noble patriotism. It relieved the poor from some of their most degrading drudgery, without boasting of the great benefit it was conferring on them. The greatest possible; for it took the curse of the Jewish god off of man to a certain extent, and is a prophecy that if people will study the ways of the law god as faithfully as they have the word god, every evil that spirit or man has pronounced on man, that they say he was condemned to suffer, will be proved false; and there is no worship that will please the law god so much as for people to apply all their god-like mental powers to using the laws of nature to do their work instead of forcing the poor people to do it.

The curse that was pronounced on the world was by a people who had such a horror of the drudgery of the world that they never would submit to it only as slaves; and they have never got over the dread, and have never approved of inventions that takes that curse from the poor, by engaging in inventing useful labor-saving implements of agriculture and other productive industries, but rather pronounce the searching out of inventions as a sin against their God. But they were engaged in making images of gold and silver ornamented with precious stones for the poor laborers to worship and to keep them contented with their hard and poverty stricken half starved thankless lives. The Jews and Christians have been in this line of practice ever since they adopted their word-god, Man-God, and Ghost-God, condemning the progress and civlization caused by inventions. I do not include Protestants in this statement, but so far as these are Jews or Christians they oppose this progress, and are trying to curse the people of the world and especially the poor with their horrible doctrines. Such persons are as much worse than the person who seeks to make a perpetual motion, as falsehood is worse than truth, because the perpetual motion worker is obliged to bring his work to the test of mechanical truth and thus end his vagaries in the minds of others, if not in himself. But religionists will not submit their vagaries to a mechanical or reasonable test; but that it is God's truth not to be questioned by man, and thus prevent the truth from being known.

CHAPTER XVII.

THE SCIENCE OF AGRICULTURE.

Agricultural laborers the most oppressed of any in the world. The law-God rules in all the agricultural productions, and farm machinery is made to work by the law of natural forces. The glory of the word God's worshippers, was to have man and maid servants. They know not God's work from the devil's. Seasons and climate must be considered in raising grains, fruits, and vegetables. Stock must be raised from good animals. A nation can not have a worse religion than one that sacrifices the best animals. Protestants are best when they believe least in the sacrificial atonement. Scientific Horticulture is made by obeying the same law-God. Transplanting trees. Small fruits Grapes.

AGRICULTURE, although one of the earliest occupations of mankind, was one of the least understood as a scientific business of any of the useful or indispensable avocations of life, until very recently. The work of farming has been done mostly by slaves or the most ignorant and oppressed of any large numbers of people; this has kept back the necessity for the most intelligent to engage in observing the best modes of causing the best crops to be produced with the least labor. But just as soon as the owners of the soil became the tillers, things began to change; not only were observations made how to get the greatest amount of food from the soil, but also how that could be done with the least labor and the most certainty, and all the skill, and all the experience began to be utilized to produce the greatest and best crops. For many years these enterprises were carried on by private enterprise mostly, but at last governments began to foster such enterprises. Agricultural colleges were established, the soil was analyzed and the elements that were needed to supply the deficiency in the crops were supplied as manure, or to cause the elements to be supplied by the air, water, or sunlight enabling the decomposition, the recomposition that enable the soil to give forth the elements that produce good crops.

To realize this result, the scientific agricuturist makes his experiments and observations to find out the law that governs in the various soils they cultivate and are guided by law in all their movements to get the best crops. They have no confidence in the power of word-gods, or miracle gods, to in any way increase their crops. This shows distinctly where every agriculturist stands, who is guided by the common sense principles of this age, in this matter. When we come to consider the agricultural implements, that have been invented to lessen the labor of farm work; we find that all of them are constructed upon the plan, that there is an unvarying law that has guided the inventor, in the construction of all the useful implements that are used, so the inventor enslaves the law of god to do the work of the agriculturists instead of man as the worshippers of a word-god have done.

The great glory of the worshippers of the miracle-working god was to have great numbers of man servants and maid servants, who were made to be the slaves of their master's appetites and passions; and large landed estates for them to work on to enable them to supply the master's household with every luxury that their whim or caprice could desire, and in this way the masters were rendered weak and sickly by their luxurious indulgences, and the lives of the slaves intolerable by their overwork and unmerciful punishments; and the lives of all were shortened and made miserable, because they would not study and obey the laws of nature's god, and would persist in obeying the man-made gods of words, threats, promises, and the most unmerciful commands that ever emanated from the most heartless and beastly of mankind. As long as people will go after such false gods, they will bring on war, pestilence and famine, with all their misery and wretchedness; and when they turn from them to the god of nature, and begin to use, enslave, as it were, the elements and the laws of nature, then their countenances will begin to beam with pleasure, and the great calamities and hardships that befall persons who worship and pray to the man made gods will be averted, and peace and plenty will be vouchsafed to the people of the world. When people worship the true god, they will receive god-like blessings.

The godfather and the godmother in nature are not stinted in their gifts to those who worship them truly. All the spirits of the air are made lovely, and all the productions of the earth and waters are made to give people health and comfort in their lives on earth; and the stories of the death-dealing influences of goblins and devils will be heard of no more, only in the history of the past, and as existing in the minds of the superstitious, word-worshipping people who did not know any better than to fear God, who was their best friend, just the same as they did the devil, who was their worst enemy, and would not heed their most abject prayers; and in this their god and devil were alike; in fact, when misfortune befel them, they were very uncertain whether God or the devil caused it; and when great good fortune occurred to their enemies, it was always said to be the work of the devil.

But in scientific agriculture the natural law god is the only outside power consulted or thought of to enable persons to obtain the most and best productions of the soil, and the soil, climate and season are taken into account, as well as the kind of seed, to determine what, under the laws of nature's god will yield the most profitable productions for cultivation, or for mankind. Plants, to be profitable, must be adapted to the climate, as well as the soil. We can not raise yams as well in cold climates as we can in a warm one. We can not raise potatoes in a warm climate as well as we can in a cold one. We can not raise the bread fruit in a cold climate as well as we can in a warm one, and apples are raised better in cool climates than in warm ones.

These items are sufficient to impress anyone that the science of agriculture is made by observing the laws of nature; the law god rules here as well as in chemistry. When the farmer wishes to improve his stock of sheep, goats, cattle or horses, they save or get some of the best specimens of stock to raise animals from, and in this way the finest of stock is raised. The law is, that the best animals will raise the best. So here they follow the god of law, and reject the Jewish plan of offering to God the best of their flocks and herds to be burnt offerings or peace offerings, to appease the wrath of their jealous, loving God. A nation can not have a more wicked practice in their religious devotions than to sacrifice the finest animals; the fatlings of their flocks and herds to appease their god's wrath, or get his loving favors, unless it is those that sacrifice their loveliest and brightest children to gain their god's favors, or those that believe that their god demanded the sacrifice of the best formed, and in all respects, the most lovely man that ever existed, as an offering to appease his wrath or gain his favor. The people who worship such a god or gods must, in the nature of things, be the most inhuman of any on earth, just as we see the christians were in the dark ages of christendom, and just as we see the Mohammedans and Mormons are to day.

It must be remembered that Protestants are not christians only in a very limited sense. They worship the God that called for the blood of his beloved son; but they preach and practice to the greatest extent according to the principles of the law god. But if any one looks closely into their wicked, murderous doings, they will see that when they worshipped and practiced most of their bloody diabolical acts, they were most believers in the doctrine that their god demanded the sacrifice of the innocent to prevent his wrath from destroying the guilty, root and branch. Begin with the sixteenth century when this doctrine was believed in the most, and end to-day when it is believed in least, and any one can see that the horrid butcheries were greatest when the people believed most in the bloody atonement, and they are most humane now when they have little or no faith in bloody sacrifices to appease the wrath of God, or gain His love.

Now the Mohammedans, and Mormons are in their dark ages, caused by their taking the greatest amount of their religion from believing in bloody sacrifices as the most acceptable worship to their god. But the humane religion does not allow in any way, that the sacrifices of the best of the flocks and herds, or the best of the babes, or men, is even justifiable in any sense, but is a real crime against God, and man, that must be punished by the law-god of spirit and nature, as a most detestable act, or heinous crime that curses mankind greatly when they destroy the best of their animals, and renders them barbarous, when they thus sacrifice babes, or men, or worship a god that calls for such a sacrifice. Any one who believes the first and best fruits and grains should be given to the Lord as a peace offering to God, lives a religion that is a arce too ridiculous to be practiced by intelligent people. Yet this is a part of the foundation of the worship of the Jews and Pagans; that is, they give to their Lord fruits that he does not want, and will allow to rot rather than to give them to the poor, where they would nourish and make glad the starved beings of earth. That is, this whole subject of sacrificial offerings was got up by the ignorant who feared their God; and has been continued by superstition and wickedness in priestly garb, and the whole religious world has been led to do the greatest wickedness that mankind have been guilty of; and now it is time to have done with it, and establish a natural common sense religion and worship that will bless the people of earth with all the good things this world will produce, that will be the greatest blessing to God and man that we can call down from heaven or raise up from the earth.

If we turn from farming to horticulture or gardening, we find that to be successful in this branch of the science of agriculture, persons must follow the laws of nature, and pay no attention to the word-god's threatenings or promises; one hour's faithful study of the laws that govern the production of plants and flowers will be of more value to the horticulturist than the studying of the word-god's revelations for a life time. The reason is that the life-time is spent in the wrong direction; the word-god says that the laws of production are under his control, when the fact is that He has no power over them, but the laws govern Him and all He attempts to do; and the hours' study of the laws of production of vegetables would be in the right direction, and would put them to thinking in the right way, and will enable them to find what power a god has over these productions to cause them to produce what is wanted; the colors of some flowers may be changed by the application near the roots of the plants of some kinds of coloring matter that the plant will take into its circulation.

When people set out young trees it is said that they are more successful if they plant them as they grew, with the north side to the north; some grounds are best calculated to grow maples, others are better adapted to elm, chestnuts, others to evergreens. A person to become successful in transplanting trees, must become acquainted with laws that govern their growth. When persons wish to raise small fruits like Blackberries, Raspberries, and Strawberries, they must consult the habits of the plants, and the soil that is required, and the climate that is adapted to their growth. Grapes require the sunny sides of the earth's surface where they are protected from the cold winds, to produce their best fruits. It is curious to note the different flavored grapes that are produced in different situations, where the climate is nearly the same. Will any persons say who are engaged in the culture of vines that they depend on a god of miracles or special providences to give them success in their vineyards or in the putting up of grapes and wine to make it best for the market? Will they not say at once, my experience under the laws that govern in these productions is worth more to me than belief in all the word-gods that ever were made.

CHAPTER XVIII.

THE SCIENCE AND THEORY AND PRACTICE OF MEDICINE.

Three schools of medicine since Hippocrates—the experimental, magnetic and intuitional. The learned practitioners despised the unlearned, and try to follow the priests and get to be supreme over the people medically. Diseases are under natural laws; medicines cure by the law of their action. Medical men have done much to rid the people of the idea that they are cured by miracle. But when spiritualism came and cured scientifically, they yet despised them, as they had the priests before. The physician could not find the spirit by dissecting the body. Many quacks have diplomas. Magnetism gives power to the sick to cure disease. The best of the ancient gods and prophets were good spiritual or magnetic healers. The god of battles about the same. Physiology treats of the healthy action of the vital forces. Pathology of diseased action of the body. These movements can not be found out by studying special providences. The nervous system. All the good things are not in one book. Persons must understand healthy action to know diseased action. Organic functional and sympathetic diseases. Polypus. We get pathological information by study, not by special providence instruction. Anthropology. Man the only animal that makes gods and devils. Socrates, Christ, Mohammed, Joe Smith, A. J. Davis, gods that intelligent worship should be selected from among the men that associated with intelligent people, if they must have a man god. J. R. Buchanan. Psychology is best plan to learn the character, except test in practice.

EVER since the old Greek physician Hipocrates, there have been three different and distinct systems of practice of medicine—the experimental or scientific, which in these modern times has become the dominating system; the magnetic, and the intuitional or spiritual systems. The scientific system is divided into Alopathic, Homœopathic, Hydropathic, Eclectic, and other divisions which experience have proved valuable in aleviating and curing the diseases of men and animals. The magnetic system is divided into human and animal magnetism, and the electro-magnetic system, and the different modes of applying these powers. The spiritual system consists principally of two modes of cure, one by means of a medium, and cures patients by means of medicines selected by spirit direction, or by spirit power, as manifested in magnetism by the laying on of the hands of the medium; and the other plan is that the spirit comes to the sick person and relieves or cures them by the direct power of the spirits without the aid of any other medium but the patient.

The wild pretentions and bewildering influence of the magnetic and spiritual medication was in the past so empyrical as to be cast entirely aside in medical science; but as these forces are being better understood, and their medical application to the sick has taken a sensible and curative stand in the medical profession, they are treated with more respect; but when we attempt to go back into the empyricisms of the priests and measure their success with their pretentions, there is such a want of common sense agreement as to make it appear that magnetic and spiritual medication is a wholly bombastic deception and priestly fraud.

When these views became deeply implanted in the medical schools and the minds of the most learned and successful physicians as matter well established, it is no wonder that medical men of the greatest distinction should po-po at the pretentions of those who had become learned in this branch of medical practice in recent times. Then when another view is taken of the subject, it becomes still more reasonable to understand why these practitioners were mostly ostracised by the great body of learned medical practitioners, because they were generally unlearned in the laws that govern diseases; they only knew how to cure in cases where their magnetism was fitted to the patient and the disease. Besides we should not forget that popular medical men began to feel the great dignity it was necessary for them to put on to maintain themselves in society; and they have in some measure followed the priests, and asked to be allowed extraordinary powers over the people such as to oblige them to employ them whenever they call a physician. Then they despise the mere magnetic or spiritual healer as much as they used to priests, who cured the people by the miracle of God's interference, or they set up such pretentions whether they cured the people or not. While educated physicians had learned that diseases were caused by a violation of the laws of health, and then each disease was governed by a law peculiar to that disease, and then they were overcome and cured by the system of the diseased person being strong enough to throw it off and allow the person to live.

Every disease has its law of progress and arrives at its greatest and most dangerous height, and then gradually declines under a law that shows the patient is getting better until the disease leaves the system to recuperate from the waste of disease upon it. That is when the patient lives through the crisis and recovers. The discoveries of the physicians of the laws that govern diseases, removed their theory and practice entirely from the priestly superstitious miraculous cures, and they are natural antagonists and enemies where the parties are low enough to be governed by passion instead of reason, which was often the case in the past centuries. But there was another important discovery made by physicians, that was, that there were many remedies that mitigated or cured persons afflicted with the diseases that human nature is subject to; and all these cures or benefits were done by the law of their action on the system of the person, or on the disease, by the peculiar law of its remedial powers; all benefits arose from a law, and not from a miracle. Then they went on making obssrvations on the peculiar action of the remedies, and by observing their influence, they finally selected a particular set of remedies and applications to cure certain kinds of diseases; and in time a system of practice was established which has obtained control of the public confidence to an extent that never could be done by any miraculous system; because when intelligent people find there is a law for them to observe to retain their health, and when they have violated that, and become diseased, there is a law for them to observe to cure the ailment, and there is no witchery or wizard work in the case, nor special interposition of God. Then they study the health laws, instead of the witchery, miraculous interposition workers to gain their health, and they call upon educated physicians to apply remedies to cure them according to the law system, instead of the miracle idea.

There are no class of persons in the world that have done more to rid the people of the idea that God or the devil, or any angels, or imps of theirs made miraculous cures, or miraculous interpositions of providence in the affairs of men, whether sick or well, more than have physicians in a quiet, unostentious way. Yet it must be acknowledged that they have neglected to study and practice much of the healing art which has been cultivated and practiced by the magnetic healer, and the spiritual medium. This they consider is the same thing that they have fought against in the pretentions of the priests in past ages; and some of them have suffered martyrdom at the hands of these holy murdering priests.

In consequence of these sufferings and the hatred they engendered, the physicians oppose any approach to the priestly medical idea, and as the priests were so badly beaten in the contest that their method of cure was given up by the most intelligent people, and by the priests themselves in a great degree, and finally the gave up the plan of supremacy to the physicians, and only retained enough of the confidence of the sick after the physician had pronounced the case a fatal one, and the patient must die, then the priest was called in, to give the last consolations to the dying, that his office peculiarly fitted him for, or that the education of the dying person required in his last moments of life on earth. Here then was the uniting of these enemies, and their interests became one. Then when the scientific magnetic or spiritualist healers came into existence they were cordially hated by the priests and physicians. By the priest because he interfered with his spiritual teachings and gave the consolations of the angels of heaven, instead of the biblical priestly words. And by the doctors of medicine, because he cured patients just as the old priests had, who had fought them so savagely in times past. They could not see that there was a jewel of priceless value underlying the old diabolical priestly pretentions whom they had just whipped out of their miracle medical notions, and who gave up all pretentions of opposing them in their general practice, although they still performed many miraculous cures according to their ignorant followers' belief.

Now to have this old war over again with these non-professionals of very common place standing in society, was too ridiculous to be thought of. The old physician was impressed with the idea that life was nothing, or at least nothing more than the result of physical organization; they could not find the spirit by dissecting the body, and what they could not find, did not exist, was the wise conclusion of some of the most eminent of the faculty. They did not think that spirit formed the life, that formed the physical body, and that it fled away instantly after it had been interfered with by disease or physical disruption that prevented it from acting to manifest through the body; and as a consequence the anatomist could not find it, and it was too fine for him to see it in the living body, or when it left the body, to go as an organized spirit, to its natural home. But notwithstanding all his natural powers to overcome malignant priests, he found great opposition to overcoming persons who made no pretentions of curing persons by miracle, but did cure by spiritual direction and power, under the laws of spirit control and the knowledge they possess that people in the body have not been able to acquire yet.

Here then is the scientific phase of the spiritual and magnetic practice of medicine that the medical professors have not generally acknowledged, only here and there one that even seems to think that the scientific phase of medical practice can be extended out of the physical remedies into spiritual ones, to the great benefit of the sick in body and mind. There is a good excuse for this opposition among the learned physicians. Many of the spiritual and magnetic healers represent themselves as Christs, and denounce people who will not follow them as the children of the devil, as he did, and put on important airs as ignorant people are apt to; they often proclaim that if people will believe on them they will cure them, but if they believe not they are a faithless set and can not be cured.

These pretenders are like the Christian priests and their Christ; their faith cures them, and want of it prevents their recovery; such foolish and wicked pretenses, whether in priests, magnetisers or spirit mediums, is enough to make any sensible persons reject the entire system of the pretenders, and especially physicians who know that diseases are cured not by faith in any person or any religion or doctor, but by a law of the action of the medicine, whether the curative agent is material, magnetic or spiritual; faith has no more to do with the cure than want of faith; belief than want of belief. But there is one thing to be noted, that often sick people have such a hankering for some particular article of food or medicine or water that they think will cure them, if they obtain their wishes, and it often does them good; but the want of faith does not cure them, it is the obtaining of the articles they want; their minds direct them to the medication and it does the cure ; if a physician or any other person had given the medicine, or made the application without the impression of the patient, it would have done the same cure. Faith does not make people whole in these days, and the people who pretend it does, educated physicians have a right to say are ignorant mountebanks or pretenders.

But notwithstanding all these pretensions and mistakes, there is back of their opinions or belief the fact of great spirit power to cure the diseases that afflict mankind, that must be recognized by all well-informed practicing physicians before they can be said to be truly scientific practitioners; the unseen forces are too great to be overlooked in the healing art; they are closely connected with our very fine active life principle, and have more power to regulate it to a healthy action than any other kind of medication; even the magnetism of a good healing physician is great upon his patients when he prepares the ordinary medicines for them; often the health-giving magnetism of the physician does more to cure the patient than the medicine that he administers.

When this influence is overlooked, the curative qualities of medicines are wrongly estimated, and experiences and experiments are not as valuable as the cures by them apparently indicate; for when the medicines are prepared and given by other hands, there is a failure of the curative effects. This makes a great many experiments necessary to determine the true value of any new remedy, and it requires a person of a very sensitive, sympathetic and correct judgment to become a good scientific practical physician. Merely an education, however critical, can not do it; and these facts should make learned professors less demanding and dogmatical than has frequently been manifested by learned physicians, to have them recognized by law as the only physicians to be employed by the sick; for there are many quacks that have diplomas as well as those that have none; and besides the schools that give the diplomas are often in the hands of professors who reject the magnetic and spiritual forces as entirely worthless in the practice of medicine, when a little examination by a candid man will convince him of their great importance.

In fact, it will be apparent that a scientific system of the practice of medicine can not be established without giving the true value that they have in the diagnosis of diseases, and applying remedies to cure them. In some cases of disease, when the person is taken, the attending physician can be as sure it will terminate fatally as they can when a man's head is taken off by a cannon ball. Then again, there are some cases so slight that the patient will get well whether they have a physician or not. The physician may mitigate the sufferings of a patient in a curable or incurable case; their great work is to break the force of the disease, by a kind of medication that will not injure the physical system or the mind of the patient; the surest way to do this is by the magnetic or spiritual treatment. This practice overcomes the disease by increasing the power of the forces of life to a sufficient degree to enable it to throw off the diseased action and give a healthy action.

There is no other kind of medication that gives this additional power to natural powers in anything like the same degree; electricity, heat, and light may add a little to the natural forces and relieve the patient in that way, but most medication is based upon the idea, that they remove the obstructions to a healthy action of the vital forces; and if they do that successfully the patient recovers by the force of his own vital powers; there are no additional powers given by the medicine; from this any one can see the great importance and usefulness of the magnetic and spiritual treatment. They can see that many times they would save the life of the patient, when without this addition to their vital forces, they would perish. I think all medical men of education will sanction that idea, and they must also agree that any agent that has that power is a very important element in the cure of the diseases that flesh is heir to.

In the short sketch of the principles upon which the practice of medicine is based, it is easy to see how a good magnetic healer could become very eminent, as a miracle worker in curing the sick; then add to that spirit manifestations, and it is no great stretch of the imagination that ignorant people should call him a prophet and a God; and when the priesthood was formed and became interested in his reputation, that intelligent, educated people would proclaim that the testimony of the poor ignorant deluded people testified to the truth regarding the God-like powers of the spiritual magnetic healer. All who will examine into the subject of the foundation of the reputation of the ancient Gods and prophets will see that the greatest and best part of it is, that they were great medicine men; their miraculous cures, and their prophesies about cures that they would make, and the deaths of the sick that they could not cure; or had no chance to try their skill upon. If any person will take away the reputation of any of the Gods, or prophets, what they have gained by their medical practice, there will be little left for them to boast of: they may do many other wonderful things, but unless their reputation stands high as a medicine man, they cannot become to the ignorant masses and their priests a man-god of the first water.

They may be swallowed by a whale and escape death, be cast into the lion's den and come out alive, be cast into a fiery furnace and escape unsinged, or have a poisonous viper fasten on their finger and not suffer from the poison; but unless they can cure the sick their reputation will not be great. There is one exception to this, that is the warrior that can overcome an enemy in battle. There is no god equal to the god of battles, and there is no man so near being a god as the man into whose hands the god of battles gives the victories over enemies; and any god or prophet whose followers are not victorious over opposition from enemies do not amount to much as national gods.

The persons who have come to make peace on earth have not amounted to much as gods or prophets until they or their followers got command of some war-like nation that were victorious over their enemies; you look in vain for a god of justice that did not use brute force to subdue enemies; next to these gods and prophets comes the healing medium, then comes the prophet that makes national prophesy that comes true to the nation either for its success or downfall, so as to bring them prominently before the public. But for ordinary gods and prophets none are equal to the medical ones, to start the name and have a kind of peaceful reputation for doing great wonders that ignorant people think it is impossible for man to do; even the christians' god of words did not get his reputation as a god by his words only, but by his remarkable powers as a healing medium; his ignorant followers thought he raised the dead, so marvelous were his medical powers. But his raising the dead was but a meagre part of his medical work, and people died and were not raised then as they do now, only people live longer now than they did in his time—I mean the average length of life then was not as great as it is now—and this increase of the length of life does not arise from anything he taught, but by the medical profession teaching a better system to preserve the health and lives of the people than he ever taught, or than was ever thought of in his age by either gods or men that has come down to us.

The principles of the science of medicine that at this time prevails and causes the increased length of life of man on earth, is not even hinted at in his history or in the history of the Jewish nation in his age, although a few hints may be found among the Greeks and Romans. From all these circumstances, any one can see how easy it is for the persons in the medical profession to get the name of being great saviors, so great in this day that in many States they are enabled to get laws passed that all persons who have not a license to practice medicine from some medical school or authority, are subject to fine and imprisonment, notwithstanding they were invited by the patient and his friends to try his skill and healing powers upon the sick person. They are trying to get the same over the people, to compel them to employ a diplomated physician, as the priests had in the middle ages over the people, no matter how little practical knowledge they have, or how little their skill in the application of their knowledge to the cure of the sick.

The efforts of the diplomatized physicians to get special privileges granted to them in some States, shows that there is a special corner in every phase of life to shirk the responsibility of contending in open field for the prizes of life. It is well known how doctors of medicine had to suffer before they had a fair field to make their fortunes and fame; and now, when the people want a better system of practice to relieve and cure them of their ills, and think, occasionally, they find a person of great natural skill and adaptation to cure the sick, who is without his diploma, and because he has not he must be fined if he cures the patient. When we see such kind of laws asked for by learned men, it is difficult to see any difference between the ignorant and the learned, in trying to get rights that do not belong to them, and the entire right to do work which they can not do well. It shows that the great effort of most people is to get despotic power, whether they are human or inhuman, and the only way to meet this great demand is for the State to secure the privilege to every child to be educated as well as the capacity will permit, and then say to all, contend valiantly and persistently for the best places by fair means, and the result will be the poor places will not be bad, and the best not so much above them as to exalt a person of ordinary ambition clear above the practical duties of life.

The fact should be inculcated and fully understood, that in peaceful society all the intelligent persons who are at their posts of duty and fulfilling their obligations faithfully and intelligently, and have a special fitness for their work, they should have about the same compensation, and they will be equally honored.

Physiology treats of the healthy action of the vital forces of all animal and vegetable life, and a person who is not educated in the healthy action of the human system is not well prepared to determine the unhealthy action or the pathology of diseases; for the healthy action of the human body is under control of the laws of nature, and any one wishing to understand this science must study these laws and their action on the system; they can not learn what the healthy action is by studying the special providences, or anything like them; and when persons leave the study of these laws and try to come to any correct knowledge of physiology by any other means, they fail because they cannot find the facts by any other plan; when they try to discover by the special providence principles that there is a set of nerves that carry the sense of feeling, pain or pleasure; and another set of nerves that enables persons to make such motions as they wish; and another set of nerves that moves the heart, lungs and digestive organs, that the mind knows nothing of and has no control over; and another set that carry the wish of the mind to the nerves of the muscles and command them to make such motions as it wishes, and see how fast you get along in your discoveries. These discoveries are made by the most careful observations of the physiologist of the laws of feeling and motion, and so carefully have they studied these laws and the facts of the workings of mind and matter, that they have gone into the brain and traced these nerves of feeling and motion to the very point where mind and matter touch each other, so that mind takes the control of matter in the human system. This wonderful combination which enables mankind to make the motions that prove their living existence and power, can not be discovered by the study of the word God's plan; but the farther they go in prayer, supplications and thanks to him the further they are getting from the true knowledge of the wonderful machinery that the god of nature used in making the living, acting human body, with its god-like mind attached so intricately that no amount of study of the word god's revelations would give them the least conception of it. The most that can be gleaned from it is the glittering generality that our bodies are fearfully and wonderfully made; and that is just as useful in a scientific sense as saying that they know nothing about it.

It is just this kind of revelations that the priests have always been trying to palm off on the intelligent people as profound information that they can never study too much. But the practical people of this age demand special information on these general principles, and they will not be put off by the solemn pompous generalities that the worshipers of revelations are bound to force upon them as sufficient for their salvation, and to cure all the ills of the body and mind. These assumptions appear to ridiculous for the thought of intelligent persons, when we compare the revelations of this God with all his priestly followers with the revelations of the physiologists or the simple truthful revelations of man.

This truth is apparent to all intelligent people, that the person who wishes to get a knowledge of physiology, will study the revelations of the modern man, instead of those of an ancient God, and why is this? He knows more about the subject than the God did, and tells it better. Supposing they take up the subjects connected with the brain, the lungs, the heart, and the stomach, and wish information on their various functions, and uses in the human body. The brain is the organ of mind, and thought, and connects persons with the world; it is placed at the top of man, when he stands in an erect position, as man naturally does, and there it is surrounded with the organs of sight, hearing, taste, and smell, and sends its sensitive nerves into all parts of the body, to give it notice of the pleasure or pain that any part of the body may suffer, or enjoy, and all mental observations of movements in the world are made by the brain. The heart has no part or lot in that matter, not even as much as the ganglions of the nerves; these will arrest a feeling, and cause a return movement to remedy a pain caused by some unpleasant position of the body, or one of the limbs; while the brain rests in sleep, or is inactive from some other cause. The revelators of God's words, thought the heart took an active part in mental actions, because it would throb and beat violently when the brain gave it notice of danger or of unexpected success and delight. They also thought that the heart took notice of what was right and wrong, and was a correct judge on these subjects, when it had nothing to do with the conscience that would enable it to decide on such matters.

The feeling of conscience is placed in the ganglionic system of nerves, that are back of the heart and stomach, and give them the feeling of right and wrong, but no judgment to decide what is right or wrong; that is left with the mind; that is supplied by the brain. The ancients supposed the stomach was a kind of a mill that ground up the food for the use of the body, somewhat as they ground it to make it acceptable to the stomach. These crude and false notions pervaded all religious people, when the Jewish and Christian bible was written. They knew nothing of the use of the lungs, only they were the recepticles for the atmospheric air; but they had no idea of the changes it made in the blood when it was inspired or what it contained when they expired it

from the lungs. They knew people must have good
air to live, but they did not know why they must
have it. They did not know that at every expiration
from the lungs, that there was a large quantity of
carbonic acid gas in it that was deadly in its effect on
the human system if breathed in too great a quantity,
or if they did know it, it is not put down in their
bible, and the book is no place to look for the information, and any one who would recommend the bible
or any other book as containing all the information
that is needed in this world, should be looked upon as
a knave, or a fool. One book may contain many useful
things but not all that is needed; if there is any such
book, it is a modern one.

PATHOLOGY.

This science treats of the laws of diseases and the
particular actions or showings which distinguish
one disease from another, or in general terms it treats
of the diseased action of animal life, and may be
considered of vegetable life also. But its great and
special province is to treat of the diseases of mankind. When a person is well informed about what is
the healthy action of the organs of the body, they are
well prepared to detect what is unhealthy. But the
nature of the disease, which the unhealthy action indicates must be obtained by observation and experience
or by an education from persons who have obtained
this knowledge by correct practical work. There
would seem to be an exception where the person has
intuitive knowledge, but it may be put down as a rule
that this intuitive knowledge is spirit knowledge
that is communicated by impression by a spirit, or
by spirit power, and the information is obtained by
the same means that people in this world get it, only
the spirit may have better facilities for obtaining it than
the people in the flesh. But it should be bourn in mind
that some people can reason from effect to cause a
great deal better than others can, and can get more

information in an hour than others can in a week.

The stomach is an organ that requires more attention than any other in the whole body; the great sympathetic nervous system has its centre back of it, and this brings it in immediate sympathy with all the ills of all parts of the body, and all the afflictions of the mind. From this it will be seen, that there are a great many sympathetic diseases, as well as organic diseases; and then there are functional diseases; with all these diseased conditions, it is many times very difficult to learn the true pathological conditions of that organ. Dyspepsia is caused by so many different kinds of afflictions, that it is difficult to determine what is the real cause of it; in many cases it may be irritation, or a slight inflammation, or wholly a sympathetic feeling made by the disease of the liver, or some of the other organs of the abdomen or chest, that cause such feelings of irritation or inflammation. Then it may be a functional derangement, that prevents the secretion of a sufficient amount of good gastric juice, or too much of that fluid. Then again a polypus may be taken for a lizzard or a snake as it swings around on its stem, or pedicle that makes its attachment to the inner surface of the stomach. From all these circumstances, and many more that might be mentioned, it will be seen how many difficulties there are in the way of making a pathological condition of the stomach.

The same may be said of the liver, and spleen, and other organs of the abdominal cavity in a less degree, as they are less besieged by sympathy, and less sensitive; and the same may be said of other organs and parts of the body. But the great idea to be got at, is, how has the information been obtained that has formed the basis of the science of pathology? When any one looks this over carefully, they will find it has been got by study and carefully conducted observations of laws of diseases. There has not been any waiting for special providences to give the information, nor for word-Gods to tell them how it could be obtained but they went on depending on themselves, and the mind the law-God had given them, to get the information regarding his laws, and by observing his laws, they found so many of the secret workings of disease that they discovered the laws that formed the science of pathology, and have not found any other power able to interfere, and change the law, and have disease work to the destruction of life outside of the laws of nature.,

All are well satisfied that the way to get correct knowledge of the pathological condition of a person, is to study his condition according to all that is known on the subject, and proceed to make other discoveries in obedience to laws of nature, and thus get as true a knowledge of the condition of the patient as all this information will permit. And place no more reliance on special providence, and word-Gods, than they would on people who know nothing on the subject; for the law rules, no matter what is said to the contrary, and the science of pathology is one that is established just as other sciences are, by getting all the facts together, and putting them into system and order. This is the law and order plan that distinguishes the sciences that form the religion of science from the religion that makes a theological or guess-God and an unsystematized moral, social, and spiritual religion of creeds, phrases and assertions that are disjointed and may be talked about but give the least possible instruction.

The science of anthropology includes the entire history of mankind in all its varied specialties, from the birth to the death of individuals; and from the beginning of the race to the present age ; and to be continued in coming ages as long as individuals can add new facts to his history. From all that is known on the subject, man is the only animal that makes gods and devils ; other animals are content to take these characters as nature dictates; but man, being himself a kind of second-hand god and devil, has thought it most consistent with his greatness to attempt to make these articles for religious and commercial purposes, and has succeeded to the entire satisfaction of vast numbers of people ; and the best proof that they can bring that they have made the true god, is that they raise to life the apparently dead, and cure the sick. It is the half science, half guess work knowledge, that is the only ground upon which love gods, and hate gods, and word gods, and jealous gods, and devils are made.

So the medical professions stand first in the professional line to prove that the made gods of man's manufacture are the true gods. There are no other professionals that can, by a look or a motion, do so much good to the sick and distressed; and when they are so relieved the ignorant think the person who does it is God, or very near to him, and has his entire confidence. Next to these are the ignorant that can speak words of wisdom or write books, like Socrates, Christ, Mohammed. Joe Smith and A. J. Davis. It should be remarked that when these remarkable persons lived in the most enlightened communities, like the first and last of those mentioned, they were neither pronounced gods or god's prophets. But all the others who were surrounded by the ignorant were at once installed as gods, or his most loved prophets.

Socrates and Davis chose to surround themselves with the most intelligent of their ages, and have little renown as gods, but great renown as wise and grand men. Davis especially, for his wonderful book called the " Divine Revelations," spoken by him before he came to the age of manhood. While the others surrounded themselves by the ignorant and superstitious of their ages to give them a reputation as gods, or very near and dear to the gods ; and now vast numbers of the human race follow them for what their ignorant satelites pronounced them to be.

It is about time that the intelligent people who must have gods made by men should look around them, and see if they can not agree to take one that was made and recommended by the most intelligent people of the age in which the gods were made. For there is not one of those that have been made in any country by any people whose followers have a decent record; not only have all of them gone astray, but most of them have gone astray barbarously, wickedly, inhumanly. We are indebted to Dr. J. R. Buchanan, of New York city, for the introduction and elaboration of this science. His observations of the character of a writer being shown by his handwriting, was one of the first observations that he made that led him into a study. It is one of the tell-tale plans that nature has devised so that persons may know their neighbors or strangers, not by what they say, but by the kind of marks they make when they say it. This psychometry is one of the most beneficent sciences in the hands of intelligent people to enable them to protect themselves from the cheats and frauds of the world. It must be accounted one of the best tests of persons who are suitable to go into large associations; it is next to learning about them by trial and experience.

CHAPTER XIX.

THE SCIENCE OF LAW-MAKING.

Most laws have been made by priests and warriors. Lycurgus. Solon. He abolished debts. He declared the power of the government was in the the people. Athens became noted for the fine arts. Philip of Macedon. Alexander the Great. Rothschilds, Vanderbilts and Jay Gould. Moses and Aaron. Athens. Athica. Mercy to debtors better than giving to beggars. The Greeks show the wisdom of the people to be greater than that of the gods of other nations. Their enlightenment passed to the Romans, and declined under the Cæsars. Christians teach that it is worse to break the Sabbath than to break the bones of a person's body. Man naturally wants to do right. The order from the god of science is to man to make his own laws. Christians warned people not to use their reason on inspirations. The Mohammedan enlightened period. The Mohammedans and Jews did make humane laws for the poor; but you find in England such laws made in the twelfth century. Henry I and Henry II. The great charter John. Bacon and Shakespeare age. Agrarians. The modern Cæsars could not destroy the republics. The Cæsars put working people on the poorest fare possible. The way that imperialists confiscated property. Republicans more lenient; 2,500 years experience. Woman's vote and voice must be heard in the government to make peace. Elections should be annual, and one week set apart spring and fall to discuss the questions and have the elections. All laws are considered more or less religious, and the religious people make war on their opponents.

THE laws that have been proclaimed for the purpose of establishing rules to govern people in nations have been made upon different plans. The most of them have been established by the edicts of priests and warriors, who pretended they were given them by their gods, or their god inspired holy men to proclaim them as the divine laws of their creator, and he would inflict severe chastisements upon those who disobeyed them. This was the way that the Jews and Pagans mostly got their laws until we come to the Greek nations. Man-made laws outside of religious dictation, may be said to begin by the code and constitution of Sparta that Lycurgus prepared for them to be adopted, or this was the first great success in that kind of laws. He is said to have gathered his ideas of what laws ought to be from the laws and practices of other nations, and by his wise laws and regulations laid the foundation of a great nation.

He lived more than eight hundred years before the christian era, and more than two hundred years after him Solon, the great law-giver of Athens, lived, and the Athenians, seeing the good effects of the constitution and laws of Lycurgus to the Spartans, wanted to adopt some of a kind that would unite them; so they could grow in greatness and power, like them, only more important. The wise law-giver, Solon, undertook that task. The first important law that this great wise and most renowned law-giver enacted was to abolish all debts and establish a low rate of interest for subsequent debts, and that debtors should not be sold into slavery, nor be obliged to sell their children. Next he declared the sovereign power resided in the people, when they assembled together for the public business. When the people of Athens had laid this foundation, they began to prosper as no people before that time ever prospered. They soon became the most noted of all the people of the earth in architecture, sculpture, oratory, literature and the arts and sciences. In some of these branches they have not been excelled even to this day.

These democratic laws were continued in force with many changes, for about two hundred and fifty years, when the people were subdued by King Philip, of Macedon, who was soon after murdered, when his son, Alexander the Great, took his place and ended the glory of the Grecian nations. Here we find the result of a wise law-giver to a people who were sufficiently wise to adopt his laws that made no pretense of being the laws of God. They were only the mature results of the wisest and best men of that age, after calculating the effects of all the experiences and trials under all the forms of laws that were then known to the Greeks. In the first place they eradicated all debts and prevented the people from being oppressed and enslaved for debt, and then gave the power into the people's hands to make the laws, and the result was the most learned, intelligent and powerful little nation that ever existed on this earth. It was crushed out of existence by the powers of the most successful warriors of any age of the world. Thus perished the most brilliant example of a government by the people that existed in ancient times.

Could such an example of splendid achievements be founded in wrong, injustice and fraud? Look at the first laws they made abolishing all debts. Can any one suppose the great creditor class were any worse in that day, than they are to-day? were there any worse political rings, whisky rings, Indian rings, mob ring made by masters of helots or slaves, or of the working people, or were the kings and rulers in Attica worse than the kings and rulers of this time? Were the Rothschilds, the Vanderbilts, and the Jay Goulds worse in that time than now? Did they water stock and charge excessive interest worse then than now? In short did the wealthy steal lawfully and unlawfully more at that time, than now? There is no history to prove that they did, yet the rulers were dethroned and the debts cancelled at a single stroke of policy, and the grandest democracy established that is recorded in history.

This legal proceeding was much more important than the proceedings of the Jews who by the direction of their God borrowed every thing they could of the Egyptians and ran away with it by the power and counsel and under the control of Moses and Aaron. But it has never been talked about so much. Yet the nation that freed its debtors was vastly more blessed than the runaway borrowers; as is very well known to every historian. And there are good reasons for this, because mercy to debtors is commended of all good people, while beggars and borrowers are a shiftless set; and have not the stamina to make a great and good nation. Will any one say that the debt of the city of Athens was obtained by any more corrupt means than the debt of the city of New York? And there is nothing to prove that the debt of Attica was made by more corrupt means than the debts of the various nations of the earth. Yet all was repudiated to lay the foundation of the grandest civilization that the people of this world have ever seen; a civilization that sheds glory upon the present people of all nations, where their arts and sciences are allowed to be taught to all the people supplemented by modern sciences, discoveries, and arts. And it warns us to be merciful to poor debtors, and see to it that the laborers are paid living wages for their lowly, dirty, hard work, in the fields and shops of their employers.

There can be no excuse for using our willing working people as badly as we do our criminals, and force them to work as many hours, and some times more. The God of nature finally punishes such overwork, not only on the worker, but also on the people, by sending epidemics that cause great distress and many deaths among all classes of society. If any one should say that these Greeks suffered great trials in bringing about their high state of civilization, that is true, for they were opposed by all the Gods of the Jews, and heathens, and by all the tyrants and many people; but notwithstanding all these troubles, they succeeded, and showed that the wisdom of man was greater than all the Gods and tyrants, and their sycophants that followed them combined together.

From the time of Alexander the Great, until the christian era, the contests were principally between rival military commanders; learning was greatly encouraged, the great enlightenment was inaugurated by the Grecian Republic, and was continued by the nations about the Mediterranean Sea; which were consolidated in the Roman Empire before the last mentioned time. During this time the agrarian laws were enacted to some extent, but were not executed, so as to lessen the burdens of the poor but little; military men kept the control of the nations and the final Roman Empire, and great military chieftains must be tyrants; their orders must be obeyed to the letter; and when they attain civil positions they carry their tyranny with them; this is plainly shown in these ages as well as at the present time in our own country.

Yet while these great generals were contesting for the supremacy, they to a certain extent encouraged learning and the learned; because they knew there was power in knowledge, when in the hands of intelligent soldiers, and their commanders. But as soon as the Cæsars got the entire control of the Roman Empire, learning began to decline; the laws that Solon inaugurated and the Roman agrarians contended for, were completely driven out of the reach of the people, if not out of their minds; and the decline in education was accompanied by a decline of the rights and comforts of the poor working people; one tyrant followed another, until the christians obtained control, when the entire human, and humane laws, were abrogated for the laws of the Gods of the Jews and christians, and the most inhuman laws, that ever disgraced a people were enacted, and there was not a law of the rights, nor the principle of the law granting the just right to the poor honest hard working people adapted by the christians in all of their reign over the Roman Empire, or the christian governments that were formed out of it. Until the people began to get a knowledge of the laws, institutions and learning of the Greek and Roman Republics.

And this education in time caused the wars of the reformation, and finally the wars of the revolutions in christian countries, and human and humane laws were substituted for their God's laws of inhumanity to man. And in this day extremely devout christians consider it a greater crime against their God, to break his holy Sabbath, by having a good frolic, a pleasant hilarious time, than it would be to break every bone in his frolicsome body. The howling about Sabbath breakers indicates how they pray for the thumb screws, and the bastile to make people observe the Sabbath, and keep the other commands of their God.

When men have given laws to people, their plan has been to punish crimes against man, and let God punish those that disobey his laws, or the crimes against him. The plan of every great and good man who proposes the best laws to secure the just rights of all the people in a nation, is to determine to the best of his ability and knowledge, the laws that will best secure these rights to man, and punish those who will not, or do not, obey these laws. He goes to the laws of nature and determines human necessities, and goes to human nature and observes its ignorance, waywardness and tendency to commit crimes and misdemeanors against mankind; and also the strong desire of most of mankind to do right, if they only know how; this makes work for him to teach them what is right; and where the laws are defective to correct them. In this way the man-made laws are vastly better than the laws given by the god of the priests of all, or any religion.

The laws of the god of nature and spirit will see to themselves without the aid of man; in fact, he can neither help nor hinder them from doing their work. The god of nature does not ask to be installed into the work of making the laws of justice to regulate the conduct of one person to another, or to assist man in making laws to regulate his worship to God. But he has endowed man with intellect enough to make all these laws and rules for himself; and if he does not use his intelligence for that purpose, and violates these laws, he can not escape the punishment which should be justly inflicted upon him. The god of nature says, not in words, but in acts, hands off; you mind your own legitimate business and I will attend to mine. If I want a Sabbath day for man to worship, I will order it. If man wants one or two days in seven, let him order them by law. But I never needed a day of rest yet, and never have rested. It was a man-made god that rested, not the true god of nature, of spirit, or of heaven and earth. The order now is and always has been, man make your own laws on humane principles, and you will bring peace on earth that will give glory to God and happiness to man.

We have seen the laws annulled, and the laws of God installed as all powerful and wise; and we have seen the people in darkness, ignorance, denied the use of their reason, and suffering all the penalties of beasts, who can not reason and prepare for the morrow. It should be remembered that the reason of a beast is better than the instincts of man, and also that during all the centuries from the Augustan age, or the era that christians date the beginning of christianity, the people were warned not to use their reason because it was dangerous, nor their inspirations because they were devilish. The people were only allowed the use of their instincts to establish their religion, or make their laws under the christian domination from the fifth to the twelfth centuries, where the priests could prevent it. The last five hundred years was the enlightened period of the Mohammedans. But notwithstanding they adopted a new inspiration and the learning of the Greeks and Romans in their most enlightened periods, they did not adopt their best laws nor institute new ones that are of great value at the present time. The benefits of their inventions of letters and figures are very great in promoting the civilizations of the present time. But we do not find them, or the Jews who joined them, adopting any humane laws, such as are needed at the present period to raise the poor above the abuses of the rich and the powerful.

The first well marked time that such laws as Solon introduced into Attica and Greece was in the twelfth century of the christian era, introduced into England by Henry I., who granted a general charter to the English people, remitted the fines to exchequer, removed many of the feudal burdens, and gave a constitution to London. And in the time of Henry II. the Commons obtained exemption of their property from the debts of their lords. These were faint beginnings or precedents of the obtaining from the great charter, or magna charter from John in the twelfth century. Now the people of England were situated somewhat like those of Greece in the time of Solon. They had about the same rights to make the laws to govern them. And singular as it may seem, the released active minds of the English people produced their Shakespearean and Bacon age in about three hundred years that compares grandly with the age of Plato and Socrates previously noted.

It is seen by this that like causes produce like effects among nations and people. When a reformer wishes to establish the principles of just laws among the people, he will be very fortunate if he judges as well as Solon and his counsellors did in their day, and as the commoners and their advisers did in the time of King John, of England. From the time of the great educational mental period of Greece, or the end of their Republics to the time that Cæsarism was triumphant in Rome, was about three hundred years. And during this time there was a conflict between the common people and their rulers, which finally may be called a war between the Agrarians, and the Cæsars, or democracy, and imperialism. Those who favored the people, who did the work, having a proper amount of the comforts of their labor, were called agrarians and those who oppose this were Cæsarites. When we turn our attention to the history of the various factions that contended for the people, or for imperialism, in the period, we find the general result was that imperialism prevailed over Republicanism. Monopolies were rampant over agrarianism, and the slavery of the working people was fastened upon them, and growing more and more cruel as we approach the time that Julius Cæsar crossed the Rubicon and seized the imperial power. When we compare the struggles of this period, with those that occurred from the days of Shakespeare, to the present time, we find this difference; that in the conflicts of this period, the people have gained power, and their oppressors have lost power. Slavery has been abolished, and the great Cæsar of the last of the eighteenth century, and the beginning of this century, could destroy the French Republic, but it would not stay destroyed; and the smaller Cæsar of England, Wellington, that destroyed the great French one, had to give back to the popular will of England, and to allow a decrease of sovereign power in the rulers of England; and the smallest of all the Cæsars who became the most famous in putting down the slave holder's rebellion, and in freeing their slaves in the United States of America, was elected President of the Republic, and united with the monopolists to increase the power of the oppressors of the people; and the utmost that he and his tools could do, was to bring about a financial crash to make many working people poorer; and many speculators richer; when the people combined and stopped the crushing of the poor, and refused to continue him in power as President, and his most persistent adherents have been pushed to the wall, and their little Cæsar is laid upon the shelf of retirement, and the poor are enjoying the fruits of their labor to a very comfortable extent.

This shows the difference between the people and their wants, and demands of the time of Julius Cæsar and the times of our Cæsar; then the Cæsars could make the laws; now the people that all these Cæsars despise have a great voice in finishing up all laws; when the imperialists get power they confiscate the property and rights of the people who oppose them in the most ruthless manner; and the poor whether they favor imperialism or not, are put to work at the lowest wages, and scantiest fare that will keep them alive. When Rome was under the Cæsars thousands of the poor were given to beasts of prey, or murdered in the Colliseum, and every indignity that it was possible for beastly tastes to invent were visited upon the poor, and masters had the power of life and death over their slaves, and vast numbers of them were murdered. This made thousands of petty tyrants to support the great grand tyrant of the Empire, which was all the world to them at that time.

Now there are many Empires in this world; some of them as large as Rome was in her palmiest days, with no slaves but criminals. And there is only one class of persons now in existence where science prevails to any great extent that is in the position of slaves, and these are married women who are subject to their husbands' whims and wills. And besides this, women of intelligence, and property, have to submit to laws that they have had no voice in making, and that many brutal ignorant men have had a voice in making, that oppress and disgrace women. Then as imperialists and their imps take away the rights and property of the people when they can, when the people get power, what is their duty? Most assuredly they must confiscate the property of the enemies of the Republic the same as the French did in their revolution, and as the Republicans did of the slaves of the slave holders in their rebellion.

The republic of France was maintained by the confiscated property of the King, nobles and church. They had acquired this property by a system of unjust laws and outrages upon the people, and it rightfully belonged to the people; and when they would not allow it to be taxed, and declared war upon the people, then it must be confiscated to the people and become their property to be used for republican purposes. France adopted the Agrarian law and divided the land among the workers, and is the grandest republic on the eastern continent; and if the Cæsarites refuse to sell their land at fair rates, and prevent its being taxed in a peaceful way, and prefer war to the peaceful settlement of the differences between those having republican principles and their opponents, as the nobles and King of France did, and as slave holders in this country did, their property must be confiscated. But republics have been more liberal to their enemies than priests, emperors and kings, and have applied the law of confiscation with a great deal more lenity and justice.

The imperial government of Rome, when under christian rule, adopted the christian principles to take from him that hath little even that which he hath, and give to him that hath much. That is, they made the poor working people beggars or slaves, and gave to the wealthy more than the truly sane persons can desire, or any person can fairly use. It was laws based upon these principles that made the dark ages of christendom; and it was laws based upon exactly opposite principles that made the enlightened periods of Greece and Rome. That is, the reformers from Solon down took from the rich and gave to the poor. And they weakened or destroyed monopolies and slavery, and increased the rights and privileges of the common people. This has been done a great deal better since the christians had to submit to the common and civil laws, as amended by reformers and revolutionists of the last three or four hundred years, and by them they have secured to the present generation the enlightenment they are now enjoying.

When persons look back to the experiences of two thousand years and more, they find then when governments have been formed to take from the rich and powerful and give to the poor and weak, they have made the enlightened periods of the world, the results have been grand and glorious, more so than could be anticipated. It seems that the struggles to obtain liberty give a great start towards civilization, and trains the mind when freedom and justice are attained in a degree to make the persons exert themselves to the greatest degree possible to get the highest possible attainments. This enables all who have any particular faculty or genius in art, science, industry or theory, to strive to be the best and to attain a great degree of perfection. This is shown in a wonderful degree at the conclusion of the Grecian republics after centuries of the struggling masses, in the uses of liberty after it was obtained, or in the keeping and using it altogether. Then it is seen again at the end of the Roman commonwealth in a less degree. There was more wealth and show, but less art and skill in almost every species of knowledge. But when we look over the present civilization, we find it excelling the Grecian as much as our present laws give more freedom, security and wealth to the common working people.

And now comes up the question, how shall this civilization be increased? What laws shall be made? Shall they partake of the principles of Solons or Alexanders of Greece, or of the Agrarians or Cæsarites of Rome? or of the monopolists, or of the anti-monopolists of the present time? or of equal rights, or shall there be class legislation? Shall the most base and ignorant of mankind be allowed to have a voice in the making of the laws, and the most virtuous and intelligent be deprived of this right? The man element in government is the war element. The woman is the peace element in society and government; and if persons think they can make peaceful nations on the earth without giving women a vote and voice in them, they will be as much mistaken as persons well can be.

We have the trials of the Grecians and Romans before us. They stopped short of making the women equal with the men in rights, and they established imperialisms and despotisms at the conclusion of their people's governments. And now there is a large number of persons who wish to end our civilization rather than grant women the same rights that men have. They have adopted a religion that teaches that wives must be subject to their husbands, and women must be subject to men. And the priests who hold these views have great influence at this time, and there is no hope of stopping this class legislation while these priests hold their present power over the minds of the people. And there have not been any principles yet developed on earth that have the power of truth in them to overcome this priesthood and their religion, but the scientific religion that is now growing with the enlightenment of this age. And the humanity of this religion agrees with the humane principles that are naturally in the hearts of the people, and must at no distant time overcome all the fanatical ideas of the priests and persons who believe and worship a man-made god; that is, too helpless to live, in the minds of the people, unless he is supported by the legal enactments of the people.

When people make laws upon scientific principles, all gods will have the same rights under the laws, and neither special gods or people will have special rights and privileges and powers under these laws. The great danger that at present threatens the people of the American and French republics is the making of laws to have biennial elections and biennial sessions of the legislatures of the states. Politicians want it, because when they get office they hold it for some time, and can lay pipes for retaining, by falsehood and bribery, better, because it will pay them more surely than if they only had power one year. They can calculate how to make laws to get their friends in office, or get appropriations for them, and thus work up an influence to enable them to retain the power for evil purposes against the rights of the people. Instead of putting off elections of members of the state legislatures for two years, it would be better to have one week set apart in the spring and one in the fall of each year, to be devoted to the consideration of the laws that people want, and the last day of the week be devoted to voting for the men and measures that are before them.

The first matter that is taken up usually is about taxes, town, county, city, state and national expenses. Some people do not want to pay taxes that exempt church property; they do not wish to support, directly or indirectly, a set of lazy, useless, fat, over-fed priests. Others are in favor of taxing property to support such a class of priests. Some persons want Sabbath laws so strict that a person can not secure his hay or grain on Sunday without being subject to fine and imprisonment. Others want Sunday to be a day of rest to them; and to permit them to choose whether they will secure their grain and do anything else on Sunday that they would be allowed to do on other days, if that will give them most rest, or go fishing, hunting or on a stroll, or go to the theater, or any other amusement that will rest them. And some persons wish people fined and imprisoned for speaking disrespectfully of God, Christ or the Holy Ghost, and call it blasphemy. Others want the persons who speak against truth and justice fined and imprisoned for blasphemy. Some people want chaplains in the army and navy, and in congress and the various state legislatures, to pray that members may act wisely as legislators.

Others object to their expense because when the priests were the legislators of States they passed the most outrageous laws that ever went on to a statute book and if the God they pray to, would not direct them to do justice to the common people, he would not influence legislators who were not priests, a single iota towards justice and truth; and if we must have people to advise our legislators to do justly in making laws, let us have men who worship a God, who has something of a fair character regarding the punishment of his enemies in hell, or on earth, or have persons of common sense, and humane feelings. And if we must have men of peace in our army and navy, let us have men of science who will tell them how to make peace according to the God of law; and if we must have war, how to make it by the laws of science, according to the God of law. Then if we must have chaplains in our penitentiaries, or insane asylums, and poor houses, to be supported by taxes on the people, let us have persons who worship a God of common humanity, and persons who understand human nature enough to know some of the needs of the poor, the criminal, and the insane, and can minister to them words that will do them good; persons who have studied the best modes that have been used to benefit all these classes; do not send priests there who know nothing about humanity but profess to know the God of revelations, from genesis to revelations. But when tested absolutely know nothing of the God of nature.

Some people are opposed to women having the right to vote, because Eve brought sin into the world by taking a bite of the first apple that she picked, and that has made her inferior to man. Others are in favor of giving her that right, becauss she is man's mother, sister, wife or daughter and best friend, and the most virtuous class of people on the earth. This is proved by there being fewer women in prisons for crimes, fewer insane, and begging poor; and this is true notwithstanding man's inhumanity to them, kills thousands of them annually. Some people want God in the Constitution, and are using all their power to have Him installed, in words in that instrument. Others oppose this because his reputation is bad and they assert he never did any thing but mischief in any such law yet? In this way the pros and cons of the laws to be enacted or the persons to be elected would be heard, and if there happened to be any questions before them, that were not connected with religion, the probability is they would be quickly and amicably settled by this week's discussion; but the pious peaceful religious people have always made war, often a relentless war, upon those who oppose them in making laws to guide the people in morals and governments.

CHAPTER XX.

PROPHECY.

Astrology is the only approach to scientific prophecy. Religious prophets have attracted great attention, but have been greatly mistaken; when they prophesied the destruction of the world, they did not mean it, say the priests. The miller prophet of America. Peter the hermit. They could not retain Jerusalem. The Greek oracles were more truthful than the Hebrew prophets. Their best prophecy came from the woman of Endor. Roman prophets. The Jews and Christians could not have a true prophet because he is natural; and they declared war on the natural man and God. Thomas Paine. R. G. Ingersoll. Spirit mediums prophesy by spirit power. The Astral system seems best. Natural prophets are the best, as natural spirit mediums are the best of that class. Systematized knowledge is the only antidote to false religion.

THE only approach to a scientific basis for true prophecy that has come down to this age, unless we put in astronomy, seems to be astrology. The movements of the sun, moon and planets have been carefully observed, and in many instances the forecast of the influence of these upon the occurrences have been as exact upon the failure and success of men as the calculations of astronomers about eclipses and conjunction of the heavenly bodies and the earth. The religious prophets have occupied great attention in the world. The basis of their prophecies have been that, Thus saith the Lord their God. But as it is well proved that their god was a god of words and not of truth, their basis is considered as false as their history of the sun proves them to be regarding the history of the making of the world, the heavens and man. When their Christ, God or prophet prophesied of his coming again on earth and the end of the world, it is done in such a way that his most faithful followers have been constantly deceived for eighteen hundred years about the time he was expected to return, until the christians have given up the idea that they can tell anything about it.

The truthful interpretations of these prophecies is one of the mysteries of godliness, and as great a one as the god of mysteries, or of commands and words have placed before mankind. Some say Christ came upon earth for the second time about the time of the destruction of Jerusalem by the Romans, and from that time to this the christian world has been startled by the cry that Christ was coming, and the end of the world was at hand; flee to Jesus and be saved, or refuse and be damned. The crusades were carried on by the cry, Christ is coming, go to Jerusalem and prepare to meet him. The Miller excitement is one of the greatest in America. But Christ did not come, as it was prophesied he would, and the world rolls on so quietly that the most ignorant religious people do not know that it moves at all; and now under the spirit intelligence these kind of prophets have very little influence, and the preachers and priests back of them are unable to make much of a scare by all their promises and threats.

But there is another interpretation of this prophecy; it is that when they prophesied that the world would be destroyed, they did not mean that the real earth would be destroyed, but only some of the religious and governmental institutions of the world; if this was the real meaning of the prophet, why did he not say so? Or if he meant the end of any kind of a dispensation, why did he say world, or lead the translators of the bible to put the word world in the English translation? When Peter the hermit traveled in the christian countries to excite the people to enlist in the holy war of the crusades, because Christ was coming and christians must prepare for Him at Jerusalem, how did he and the priests, kings, rulers and people understand the bible prophecy? They all had one idea, and that was, that Christ was coming; prepare ye the way of the Lord; or in modern strong phrase, get up and get Jerusalem and the lands that surrounded it; for your prophets prophesied that your Lord would soon be there to meet you; and they went up and took Jerusalem, and their son of God did not meet them to their knowledge, and they could not keep it for the hated Saracen, was upon them, and they left their holy city in the hands of the Momammedan, the Jew, and the Arab. While the devout christian, if he was there at all, it was by stealth or the sufferance of the despised heretic who warred against him, and whose prophet had been of greater power in war, than the christian's God.

The prophets of the Jews were of the same character; they went on promising that the Jews should become a great nation; when they entirely failed, they accused the Jews of want of faith, and the practice of disobedience to their commands that caused them to fail and become prisoners of war, rather then victors: when the fact is apparently they had too much faith in their prophets, and fulfilled the laws so strictly that it made them a brutalized people, and an inferior nation, and prisoners of war to the nations who worshipped Gods that were nearer nature's God, and spoke more truthfully, and was more merciful to their enemies. The Gods of the Greeks were not great brags of their powers to make a great nation; yet their oracles were more truthful; it was not by the power of the infallible Gods that they were spoken; but by the priest or priestess by the power, the God of spirits that had great powers but not supreme, unless all the Gods agreed.

These gods only promised a fair amount of earthly success; but they made by the people the greatest nation of their time. But the Jews made one great God Jehovah that would overcome all nations by his favorite people; yet he made a total failure of it, and the most truthful prophecy in their history was made by the woman of Endor, when she told Saul that he would be killed and his army defeated; and she told this by the spirit of Samuel, and not by the Jewish great Jehovah. And it must be remembered that the worshippers of the great Jehovah had made laws to destroy all such prophetesses, and she would have been murdered if the law officers of this Jehovah and his people had known of her existence, and had fulfilled the edicts of the law.

The Romans had many gods like the Greeks, that may be considered the laws of nature, and their prophets, called soothsayers, had great influence over the people and government; and their prophetic sayings did not emanate from all the gods at once, but were impressed on their minds by the appearance of the entrails of animals or the flight of birds, or from some other appearance or movement that attracted their attention; and this nation was made the greatest on the earth in its time. When any one looks over the ancient history regarding prophecy, he will find the greater the pretentions of the Jehovah or gods of the power they possess over the affairs of mankind, the less the truth of the prophecy, oracle or soothsaying of the prophet. The reason is perfectly apparent; there is no such great god that rules the world and communicates with mankind only by the laws of nature. He has work to do and nothing to say to man or his spirit, or at least there has not come to the knowledge of mankind any such god.

This double-acting, man-making and damning and blessing, talking and warning and advising god has not been found in these days. The law god made man by the natural laws, and has always held them amenable to the laws of nature, and there is no talking about it. And the persons or spirits who have looked into this subject most with the greatest intelligence, are the best prophets ; and if any wish to supercede this personal intelligence and depend on a god power that is greater than man's spirit power for special prophetic information, let them go to work, as did the Jews and christians, and declare war upon the natural god and the natural man, and see how they come out. Persons who have gone deep into the powers and practices of these gods, if they are not sick of them, let them follow them until they are. If they have not found out that they are too little for a great God, and too false for a true one, and too damning for a loving one; their penetration is slow, and they should have privilege to worship them to their hearts' content, but not to deceive the nations any more by such untruthful pretentions. That is, let the truth be spoken, if it is by a Thomas Paine or a R. G. Ingersoll, and the slanders of the christians will soon cease.

The spiritualists prophesy by spirit power. There is no pretense that God is back of them, to talk through them ; yet their prophecies are of great use to the people of this age, because they are constantly saying learn the natural law, abide by the natural law, and you will be blessed in body, mind and estate ; but their God does not say so ; common sense says so ; and when people throw away their common, natural god sense for any of the other gods' sense, they soon become foolish or demented for useful purposes on earth ; they have the forms of men with lost minds.

The spiritual medium makes his prophecy by the spirit's calculation of the movements of persons as they see them. They observe their mental capacity and peculiarities and how they use them, and follow them down the stream of life, and they see the natural affinities and acquaintances, that belong to the sphere in the journey of life, and by these means calculate their future, with considerable accuracy. But it is very evident that if there is a guiding star above the mental, moral and physical life of the person that in whole or in part governs them, this plan of calculating the future of a person, must be very defective; the spirits no doubt have gone deeply into the governing powers of man, and his spirit in life and death, and among all, the astral system seems to have the most power, that has come to this age, to tell the future of persons, or nations.

The Astrologist gives the place and the power of each star or heavenly body, to influence a man's or nation's actions, and prophecy based on these heavenly movements, if he calculates correctly, will enable him to state truly future events in life in this world. But to do this may require a natural prophet who can not tell how he does it, any more than a natural born mathematician can tell how he gets the true answer to the question when in infancy. But the reasoning mathematician tells how he does it, and so it must be with the reasoning Astrological prophet. He has studied the movements of the earth, and the sun, moon, and planets, and calculated their influence on people and on particular persons, when the stars are in particular places, and then comes the prophecy; and some of these have hit it to a day, and perhaps they all will when we have the true natural prophet to tell us about it. The reason for this is that the natural prophet sees things distinctly and clearly, while the calculating one only sees his conclusions clearly. So it is with natural spirit mediums; they are the best, though others may have better worldly judgment but are not calculated for making the best of spirit judgments, and the truest prophecy.

It is from this class of part sciences, and part of man's imagination or partly understood sciences, that a God of miracles, special promises, and special commands of natural laws is made. It is easy to say God made the laws of States, and nations, when it is wholly man's work. It is easy to say; when one person raises another from the apparently dead; that it is a miracle, and the person who does it, is a God. It is easy to say, when a musical prodigy appears like Blind Tom, that it is a miracle of God. It is easy to say when a person raises a remarkable vegetable, or tree, that it is a miracle of God. It is easy to claim that a great and victorious general is a God, or that a person who prophesies correctly is a God, but it is very difficult to make intelligent people believe it, and still more difficult to prove the assertions true; so difficult in fact, that it can not be done to the satisfaction of the most intelligent people of this age; unless it is a miracle that is testified to as true, at least eighteen hundred years ago, and the person testifying was a Jew, while to-day the testimony of a Jew on such a religion would not be considered hardly up to par, by the persons who pretend those of eighteen hundred years ago were infallible, or the God back of them, that inspired them to utter the thoughts was infallible, and every utterance made under that influence was a miraculous truth. It is in this way that the God's truth and miracles of the bible are proved, and the Jews and christians are trying to make people of good common sense in this age believe these statments as truth.

There are two sciences that man can not manipulate. The god of nature made them, on the foundation for them, and there they are beyond the control of man; that is astronomy and geology. In other matters man may do something, and spirits may, that will seem to the ignorant to establish a god of miracles. But in no case can such a god seem to exist only where angels or mankind can do the work—make the pretended miracles. There are more of these miracles noted in the medical profession than any one science or part science. Persons are very sick, and suddenly and mysteriously get well. They pronounce it the special providence of God instead of the special work of an angel or man, or the workings of their own life powers under natural law ; and when the natural powers of man raise him up to life, when he has been dead to all human appearance for days, it is laid to a special providence of God instead of natural law.

The conclusion of this whole matter is, that where the god of nature rules unmistakably, there natural law rules ; and it is so acknowledged by the great body of intelligent people. But in all places and under all circumstances where men and spirits can interfere, there is a chance for the word god, the miracle god, the special providence god to show his proof of existence and the superstition of his worshippers And the less these worshippers know, the greater is the extent of their faith, and the more they believe ; and the more they know, the less is their belief in man-made gods, that must have man-made laws to punish people for non-belief, or people would not know that they ever had an existence at all. And all persons who wish to have people stop worshipping such helpless gods should join to give persons systematized knowledge on all subjects that are touched by religion.

BOOK FIFTH.

THE SCIENCES TO BE FORMED AND ADOPTED TO ENABLE THE PEOPLE TO ESTABLISH SYSTEMATIZED KNOWLEDGE AND THE SCIENTIFIC RELIGION.

CHAPTER XXI.

THE SCIENTIFIC RELIGION WHICH THE BASIS OF MORAL PRINCIPLES TEACHES.

The science of morals is based on right doing. If there is not a science of morals, then there is no moral law to guide people. The government must have just moral laws, or people can not be moral and obedient to the government. God has given men power to make moral or immoral laws, and he leaves them to do it. Knowledge is acquired slowly by experience. West the painter. Equal rights the legal moral basis. Good morals save a person. Good intentions do not pave hell, but heaven. Christians persecute those who search for moral truth. The basic principle of a moral law. Right rules should be put before every person to learn them right from wrong. The inspirations of this age are entirely one way; they agree with the sciences and demand a moral science. Some of our present laws are immoral. The Jewish law was unjust. A bad command. Just moral principles have a scientific basis under nature's law god, and not under any other god.

THE science of morals is based upon the principles that to do right is moral, and to do wrong is immoral. The person who intends to do right and does it, is moral ; and the person who intends to do wrong, and does it, is immoral. The basis of right are the natural laws by which we live and have our existence. When we live in accord with the laws of our being, so as to have good health and a harmonious working of body and mind, and do our duty to the persons that surround us, and all persons that our acts and words concern or influence, we live moral lives. When we live so as to make us unhealthy, and make an inharmonious state of body and mind, and do not do our duty to the persons surrounding us, and to those we influence by words and deeds, we live immoral lives. The natural man agrees with the natural God and his laws; and when the man knows enough to live in harmony with these laws, he will do his duty to God, man and beast.

If good moral principles have not a good scientific basis,
> They are as baseless as falsehood's venomed slur
> Which drops from the lips of the vilest slanderer;
> Or like the whims, follies and fashions of the world
> Which oppress the poor and against the good are hurled.

If the law of nature is god, then we have a moral law. If the word god, or the miracle or special providence god reigns, then there is no moral or chemical law or astronomical law. It is all delusion to say there are moral principles, and then to deny people the right to establish a system of morals upon scientific principles, is one of the incongruities of the professed morality of this age. Will any one pretend that we can have a moral system to guide people morally unless we have right law in the government that permits people to act right, and gives them equal rights to act right. It must be remembered that God makes the natural law, and man can not alter it; and man makes the moral law, and God will not interfere in it in the least.

He has commissioned man to make his moral laws and government, and if it is not well done, man is to blame for it. And when man, especially the religious man, has found that the laws he has made are not wise or just, he asks God to give him wisdom instead of going to nature's God, and learning how to do things; and then going to work to get experience, and of this experience get knowledge and wisdom, and out of these make the moral laws of justice and truth. The idea that there is a God that comes down from heaven and puts a blessing down in one place, and cursing in another, that can be shunned by prayer, is one of the falacies of the religions who make gods out of words or wood or something thicker than words and harder than wood; for words make the thinest god that ever was made. Remember that the natural god gave us a natural body and a natural mind to take care of it, and it requires a knowledge of the natural world to do this work well.

This knowledge is acquired slowly by experience; much of it can be acquired by studying the lives of others. But every person has his or her peculiar mental and physical powers, and these must be learned by experience or intuition. Not only every person has their special powers, but every age has its peculiar demands upon the persons of the age; they can not be the imitators of men and women of ages past to any great extent. There are general moral principles that apply to all ages and all persons, and there are special moral principles that apply to each age, and each person. The general moral principles can be learned by all persons who have the capacity, but the special capacity of persons to do certain kinds of work is sometimes very plain to the person, and all others who are interested, like West the painter and many persons that might be mentioned. But there are others that it requires a life time to find out what their peculiar part is; the one lives a life of harmony with himself and others; the other lives in a constant struggle and it may be in inharmony with himself and others for the want of this knowledge, or he may harmonize with others while getting it; it is to be hoped and expected that when the social science is established; people are living in accordance with its principles that the struggles of those who have great but hidden talents, that require years to develop, and turn to the greatest benefit to themselves and others, will not be obliged to suffer all the pangs of want and disappointment and contumely, and the racking tortures of mind and body which has characterized many persons who are now reckoned as the saviors of mankind in their line of study or art; because either in an association or out of it, they will find positions that will enable them to make their experiments and get their knowledge without being subjected to the intense pangs of poverty, or the insults of those who are ignorant of their greatness and noble virtues. But whatever our faculties may be, our moral duty is to develope them for the benefit of mankind to the best of our ability.

In one respect the foundation of the moral science is the same as that of the social science. All adult citizens must have the same legal rights. And the persons who oppose the equal rights' principles being adopted as the laws of their state or nation, are no more entitled to be called moral than are slave-holders, drunkards, gamblers, and persons who get the confidence of others under false pretenses and by falsehood. There is not one fair, candid reason why intelligent women should not have the same rights as intelligent men; and the hope of the world rests on these persons finally establishing a just government and peace on earth; and there is no good reason why the ignorant and vicious women should not have the same rights legally, intellectually and socially, as the ignorant, vicious men. These must always be more or less under the control or influence of the intelligent whether there is a just government or not. But all will enjoy more under the rule of equal rights than they can where that principle does not prevail, because the rule is morally and socially right. The god of spirit and nature has subjected all persons alike to the general laws of nature, and given to each and every one special faculties and duties that they must do to show their individuality. And there can be no good reason for depriving the persons of their rights, because of these specialties. Women have their special duties to perform, and the men theirs; but all must obey the general laws alike, and should have the same rights to do so.

It is curious to hear the christian preacher declaim about the importance of having good moral principles instilled into the minds of the young especially. Then to ask them if their goodness will save them? Their answer is no, it is not at all certain that it will, unless they add belief in Christ as their Savior. Belief in Christ is the first and great surety of salvation. This is the doctrine of the word god, the miracle-making god, the loving and hating god. And this is the basis of the moral conflict between the god of law and the god of words. The god of law says that the practice of good moral principles by good moral acts insures salvation in this world and the next; no matter what you believe or do not believe, or what you know or do not know. And when persons do the best moral deeds they can, according to their knowledge and belief, they are saved just in proportion to their really good moral deeds, and no more. Good intentions and good belief can only secure to persons the consciousness that they did the best they knew how to do; and where such consciousness was absolutely true of them; that is, they were not actuated by immoral prejudice or criminal superstition and ignorance, they would at once try to get the knowledge that would direct them to do morally right, and thus save themselves from the pangs of misery which persons who were guided by prejudice, and preferred to hold on to moral falsehoods, rather than learn the moral truths. Such persons must suffer the pains and penalties of their stubbornness in wrong doing, because their consciences are dishonestly wrong, and they must suffer until they are willing to make them right, and then do right; and they are saved to the extent of their righteousness, and no more.

Our information from the spirits is that some persons remain for centuries in darkness and gloom, because they prefer their superstition, darkness and gloom, to knowledge, light, and a good cheerful time. They agree with the salaried christian preacher, that hell is paved with good intentions, while the natural man believes that heaven is paved with good intentions; and he who would walk on this pavement, must get the permit by good works, and in no other way. Here is the deadly moral conflict between the natural God and man, and the promising God and the regenerated man; and this conflict can not end by any compromise, because one of these Gods, and one of these systems of morals must be wrong, and must utterly perish from the minds of intelligent moral people. And the persons who would try to patch up a peace between these contestants are engaged in a useless patch work.

The Protestants have been engaged in this work for nearly four hundred years, and the christian nations have turned into investigating and scientific nations; all of the most advanced Protestants demand proof of the christian assertions, the same as scientists demand proof of the scientific assertions; and where the proof is not verified by experiments, observations, and reason, the scientists are not slow in condemning persons as immoral who insist upon putting forth principles as true, which in their oppinion have not been well attested in this way. The Protestants demand proof of the truth and usefullness of all things, but of christianity, and many of them want that to stand upon its proved truth. They begin to see that there is no people so bad in a civilized country, as those who proclaim that belief is the most important acquisition for man to obtain to save him from pain and misery; and if belief has no more foundation in truth, than christianity, it will make the most criminal class of people among the learned professors, as christianity has done. Then it becomes immoral to be guided by belief, only when it is made subject to truth; and a person can not be considered moral who will not submit his belief to scientific tests to determine its truth.

The fact is, scientfic tests, are moral tests; and persons who will not submit their opinions to these tests, are pursuing an immoral course, as the history of christianity abundantly proves. The errors of belief are enormous as well as enormities, and it is immoral for any person to hold to them, so much as to condemn people for not agreeing with them; and more especially for them to call for laws to punish the persons who do not agree with them. The scientists do not ask for laws to punish people who will not seek the truth, while they have a thousand reasons to ask for such laws, where the believers have one, to ask for their laws. The sciences have gained their ascendency over the modern mind by the mildness of their demands, and the peaceful humane conduct of their professors, and the quiet genial gentlemanly and lady like conduct of those who are guided by the principles inculcated, and last of all by their great and intrinsic value of the truths they teach. They do not uphold any unjust or immoral act or sentiment, but they search out truth wherever it can be found, and that exposes the errors of others, especially christians in Christian and Protestant lands, and makes them violent with rage; and where the scientists have not said one word derogatory of christianity, they are hated and persecuted as the enemies of mankind.

A full code of morals can not be correctly stated to a certainty, until the moral science is fully established; but the basis and outlines may be, so people will know how to begin to make the experiments to establish it.

First. All adult citizens must have the same legal rights. There is no exception to this law, only idiots and criminals, children, and persons who have not gained a residence in the precinct where they present their votes. What other exceptions should be made, experience must determine. But the person is immoral who refuses to adopt the principle of giving all adult citizens the same rights.

Second. All children should have the same legal rights as infants, and be educated in reading, writing and arithmetic, and the basic principles of all the sciences and of all the superstitions of ancient and modern times, including astrology, mythology and theology. All should be taught as much in all these branches as they are capable of receiving, and not have their minds crowded so as to injure the health of the children; and they should be instructed in all the arts, such as drawing, painting, modeling, sculpture, and all the plays and games that keep the mind and body active, such as ledgerdemain and calisthenics and other mental and physical gymnastics, that give the mind an easy play in fun and frolic, fancy and fact, that will prepare them for the stern realities of life as it really exists. The persons who oppose the children having a fair, equal chance to learn these things are immoral, because they are unwilling the children should be taught the frauds and deceptions of the world, and in its goodness and justice. Give them all knowledge, and most of them will be just, good citizens, is the experience of mankind to this time.

Third. All persons shall have equal rights to free, orderly, decent speech. When any questions of virtue, justice, morality, rights or privileges are to be considered, or are under consideration, the persons engaged in the discussion shall have all the rights that lawyers have in the courts in prosecuting and defending their clients or claims; and the same right to make their remarks, pro and con, that parliaments and congresses have established to insure free discussion on questions that arise in those bodies. Persons who oppose these rights are immoral, notwithstanding all their pretenses and professions of morality.

Fourth. All persons should have the same right to publish their thoughts as to speak them. There must be a free press as well as free speech. They are a semi-barbarous people who deny these rights, having a great amount of chivalrous honor, but no moral honor. They can have street brawls and duels to defend their honor, but can not live in a peaceful, moral way; that is, honorable, among a quiet, civilized people. They can be boastful of their high sense of goodness, as Senator Butler, of South Carolina, did when defending Preston S. Brooks, for his assault on Senator Sumner in the senate chamber of the United States. Butler said that Senator Sumner was not accustomed to good society, when the fact was Sumner was accustomed to more refined intellectual society than Senator Butler could ever reach in America or Europe. But such is ever the defense of a wealthy, barbarous people of the brutality of its members on the unflinching, moral, intellectual persons who will defend the rights of the poor, and maintain the principle that the highest morality of any people is shown by their having the freest, orderly free speech and free press, and the lowest where people will allow the least of free speech and press, on religious and political subjects, and on any other exciting topic. Where freedom of expression is allowed, all questions are settled upon as high moral principles as the intelligence of the people will allow. Where this freedom is not allowed, all questions are settled upon as immoral principles as the ignorant and barbarous people will submit to.

Fifth. The right to do right, should not be taken from a juryman, while serving as a juror, any more than while serving in any other capacity. The law which deprives jurors of equity powers, and obliges them to decide cases according to law, instead of upon their merits as established by justice in their minds, is one of the most immoral laws, connected with present judical proceedings. It informs the common people, who make up the jurymen, that they are not good judges of what is right and wrong in the common transactions of life in society when acting as jurors. It is a curious idea that common people are supposed to know what is morally right, when not on a jury, and not to know it when acting as jurymen. There is no good moral reason why jurymen should not have all the equity powers that arbitrators have when selected to decide a case on its merits. If the intriguing law makers know that the laws which they buy through, or get through congress, or the legislatures, were met by juries, and judges with equity powers, they would spend less time to get their laws of injustice passed. Then the true merits of every law would be discussed in every trial before a jury, and there would be less talk of law, and more of justice, in our courts, and finally justice would be established by law in our courts instead of making law and justice separate institutions as they now are. This immorality is one of the relics that has been brought down from the christian dark ages, that should at once be abolished by the laws of this country.

Sixth. Church property should not be exempted from taxation. It is just as immoral and unjust to exempt church property from taxation, as it would be to exempt the associate property devoted to legal or medical purposes, and the private property and offices of priests; as it would be to exempt the private property of lawyers, and doctors, and their private offices; many of the churches are said to be the property of the priests and not of their religious associations; can any one pretend that of all the professions, the clerical which has proved the most diabolical of any of them for the last fifteen hundred years, should have exemptions and privileges which are not allowed to the best who have done more good than any others to protect people in their just rights to life, liberty, and property, and have given them the best rules, for them to practice to have the best health of body and mind, is not only ridiculous, but unjust, and immoral in the highest degree. It is about time that preachers stopped slandering lawyers and medical men, when they advance the moral and medical rules to promote the health, happiness, and virtue of the people, when we all can see, as the legal, and medical men gain power a higher civilization is established, and a longer and healthier life is enjoyed; and the proof is apparent, that if the clerical professors who go round slandering reformers, were taxed out of existence, community would be the better for it, and a great and oppressive burden would be taken from the poor industrious people of this age. It is a great immorality to let the worst institutions go untaxed, and tax the best enough more to keep up a government for the protection of people in all their rights, except in this burden.

Seventh. One of the greatest immoralities of this or any other age, is to take a text and declare it God's truth, when it is not known to be true; or has been proved by scientific observations to be false. Every priest, and every person should know there is a higher authority to-day in the world than the christian's God, or bible, and they may go to work to slander these that come with this power of proved truth ; and murder them as much as they can, still the truth is with them and will prevail; and the immoralities of the priests who utter the falsehoods will be more and more apparent to all, until all their santcity is torn from them and they stand in all the deformity of falsifiers and defamers of truth, and those who proclaim the truth. The material and spiritual scientists prove all things by the most careful processes of modern thought and investigation that is known; when a question is asked, the answer comes accompanied with the most indubitable evidence that can be obtained to prove its truth. But when the christian priests and their followers are asked to prove their statements, they refer to their book which was put together in the fourth century, and the sentences and sentiments were finished to suit the minds of some of the most infamous liars and scoundrels that ever infested the earth. This statement is made on christian and anti-christian authority ; and these writings of these men in that way are the only proofs that they can present that what they proclaim as truth is truth. And such evidence is too thin even for a mountebank in this age. None but a priest of the most solemn, pious pretentions, would think of being believed upon such pretentions; but they not only ask to be believed, but threaten horrible damnations upon persons who do not believe them. This is the greatest moral evil in existence in this age. In fact, it is the root of all the evils that arise from deception, falsehood and wordy frauds. The immorality taught by them is that the words of proved liars are to be taken for truth. If witnesses of the character of the priests of the second, third, fourth, fifth and sixth centuries were introduced into a modern court, they would be asked, do you believe it is right to deceive and lie? Yes, they would say, for the glory of God. Who are to judge what is to be the glory of God? The christian priests who utter the falsehoods? In whose hands was the bible manuscripts from the second to the fourth centuries, when the bible was put together and for a century or two afterwards? It was in the hands of these lying priests. Then the question arises, is there any truth outside of these noted liars to prove that the bible has in its present shape any other origin than from these priests and their bloody despotic assistants, like Constantine the great? None but the most flimsy statements, that would be rejected in court. Then what is the history of this book, and the clergy, and layity and all who are guided by it, or adopted it as a text book, for twelve hundred years after it was put in book form? No darker page in history can be found for cruelty and torturing abominations. How does the bible affect nations at the present time? The most barbarous people in christendom are those who receive the bible and the priests, and reject the sciences, and the scientists; and all nations are barbarous just in proportion as they adopt bible christianity, and reject protestantism and the sciences. And the most enlightened nations are those that adopt the sciences, and allow the freest discussions on what is truth, when civilly, politically, scientifically, and religiously considered. The bible christian has no better foundation for his theology, than has the author of the yellow covered novels, for the truth of his stories; that is, simply the imagination stands for their facts, and they depend on sensationalism to induce people to read and hear them. So the conclusion of this whole matter is, that the preaching of the gospel of the christians' bible, and the priests, is the most immoral business that is followed in the civilized world. It should be remembered that it is only a business.

Eighth. The State or nation should secure to all religions the same rights in every respect to its professors, to worship, or not to worship their God, or no God, and have equal rights to testify in our courts, and as citizens of the United States; experience shows that a person's religious professions do not make him or her any more truthful under oath, nor a better citizen, any oftener than it makes them worse. The lowest deceiver can pray like a saint, and lie like a spy, and profess to believe in any religion, or any God, and future rewards and punishments, for the purpose of being allowed to testify in courts of justice, and get any other rights of citizens that laws confer on religious believers, and do not confer on other citizens The christian religion is considered the best of the several religions, yet its professors were no better than barbarians for centuries; persons should not be rewarded for professing to be truly good and religious, but should be rewarded for being good whether they profess to be or not, or whether they profess any religion or not. Therefore it is immoral to give to professors of religion any rights that is not conferred on other citizens.

Ninth. It is the moral duty of the people of the State and nation to see that every child has a fair chance to get an education, and have children taught that this great blessing is secured to them by State and national laws and appropriations. They should be taught to love the nation for this great boon, as their fond mother, and they should not allow any religious denomination to step in and steal this love from them. The State and nation should take the best care that all religious denominations profess to be loyal to the nation, and teach their children to love it as their great protector and preserver in an earthly sense, or they should not be allowed any state or national funds on any pretense whatever. Such priests should not be allowed to steal the hearts of the children and people from the nation, at the nation's expense, and the people can do without the prayers and supplications of such priests, better than they can afford to pay them, for their religious ceremonies are calculated to curse the peeple rather than bless them. The State and nation will not do the moral duty incumbent upon them unless they educate their children to love them better than any religious institution in the country.

Tenth. It is the moral duty of every person that has arrived at the age of discretion, to see to it that all persons are educated to know right from wrong. If any person wishes to see the people acting under the influence of a good moral conscience, they must see that they have a good moral education. There may be various and conflicting opinions about what constitutes such an education. But there can be no doubt in the natural mind, that the person who teaches that to believe in Christ, or any thing else that religionists have taught, is a saving faith, will bring more happiness in this world, or any other, than the practice of virtue and justice, they must be mistaken. The natural laws, or the God of nature and spirit, declare emphatically that persons who act in harmony with these laws, will enjoy the greatest amount of happiness in this world, and the world to come, no matter what their belief or faith may be. Then the first education is to learn the laws of nature that confer this health and happiness, and live in accordance with their demands. This requires a knowledge of a careful digest of all the sciences of life, and living, and in addition a correct knowledge of your duty to others. Do not suppose that it is your duty to love others as you do yourself, for if you did not happen to love yourself right, you would multiply your wrongs to an amazing extent, and it is bad enough for persons to act wrong to themselves and have their wrongs stop there, instead of acting wrong under the influence of such a plea or rule to all your neighbors. But instead of putting yourself up as a standard of right, and wrong, you adopt the best rules of justice to your neighbor that you can find, and you will be sure to live better lives, than if you adopt your self love as a guide for the love you should have for your neighbor.

The rules of right and wrong established by law and adopted in courts, is vastly better. Where a wrong law exists it has all the people's knowledge and experience to go by to change it to the right, and under all these corrections the law of justice may be established to educate the consciences of the people so they will instinctively know right from wrong to a greater degree than can be attained in any other way. It should be distinctly understood that good moral laws can not be made by people who believe in a God who can make a miracle in violation of the laws of nature; because when they have made laws in accord with the the laws of nature, along comes a miracle in their estimate; and the just law made to accord with the natural law must be changed to meet the miracle law, or no law of their God, and the persons who act on the principles that their God can change the laws of nature, makes two rulers, one doing things by the fixed unchangeable laws of nature, while the other has a power to change these to help His friends, or punish His enemies, and they must make their moral laws to meet the characters of these two Gods.

The christians love the miracle God, and despise nature's law-God. The scientists love the God of nature's laws, and despise the God of miracles. The Christian, Mohammedan, and Pagan make a devil out of parts of nature, and the laws of nature, and the scientists say that the only devil that exists is their diabolical ignorance. They say all other kinds of ignorance is excusable, but for develish ignorance there is no excuse. It partakes of the nature of crime; and induces the persons who have it, to commit the most horrible deeds on record. The Protestants stand between these contending parties and are saying good God, bad God, good devil, bad devil. For the Jewish and Christian scriptures give accounts of the devil doing many honorable deeds, and of their God commanding His followers to commit the most infamous crimes. They are very useful in standing between these contending parties, and preventing the christians from committing the wholesale slaughters that they did formerly. But it is plain that they are entirely useless in trying to reconcile these parties to each other. They have different Gods, and different moral principles. A moral science can not be established under a purely Jewish or Christian rule; for their miracle God forbids it by his words, and their word-God forbids it by his pretended miracles; and the Protestants are divided, some leaning one way, some another, and some are on both sides by turns. But the inspiration of the age is entirely one way; it declares that the moral science must be established; and a scientific religion follows, and then a scientific government, all in harmony with the sciences which have been established.

There can be no compromise; the people must be guided by superstitious moral sayings, or by the principles of a moral science founded upon the inflexible laws of nature and nature's God. In the previous pages we have referred to some laws at present in force in this country that are unjust and immoral; now let us look at some that were made by the direction of the God of Israel. Look at Exodus, chapters 31st, 14th and 15th verses. There you will see that the death penalty is pronounced against any person for doing "any work" on the Sabbath day. A murderer might flee to the city of refuge, and have his life spared, but the person who did any work on the holy Sabbath day, should be put to death; there was no saving clause in the law to save his life, and many persons have been put to death; and tortured, fined, and imprisoned by Christians, as well as Jews, for violating this law of work on the holy Sabbath.

This was the religious law down to the eighteenth century among Protestants, and is the law yet in other countries. Can there be any morality among a people who will make misdemeanor worse than a crime? It was the saying among the warriors of Napoleon Bonaparte that "a blunder was worse than a crime." But these religions make a good work worse than a murder. And this arises from the influence of their first law or command, that you should love God with all your strength, and this is really the basis of the moral principles of all the ancient religions. They made a God and then went to murdering people who did not worship him to their satisfaction, knew nothing of a moral law, or morality based upon natural law. We cannot think very highly of the morality of the people who make picking up sticks on the Sabbath day a worse crime than bearing false witness against a neighbor.

The question here arises whether good moral principles, have a just scientific basis, or are they entirely baseless? These questions should be answered immediately and unequivocally, for there is every indication that there is no way to form a moral science among a people who worship a God of words, miracles, or special providences; and the reasons that a moral science has not been established, are that all religions have rejected the God of law and nature and taken to some other God that is known by them only by answering prayers, by special acts. These religionists may make what they call a moral creed, or a moral law, but there is no certainty that there is a real just moral principle in either, because their basis is a changeable law, of a changeable God, and from every fair conclusion, from all the premises, the result must be reached, that there is no basis for a moral science, only when people worship the natural God, or the law-God of nature. And all the pretentions of other religionists that have the just principles of a moral science, are as baseless as any falsehood that ever was uttered; nature's God and nature's morals are alike, and demand the same work and worship.

CHAPTER XXII.

THE SCIENCE OF ASSOCIATION.

Social science is established by just laws made by man to regulate the conduct of individuals towards each other in general society and special associations. Equal rights the basis of these laws. The most oppressed are the abandoned women. Criminals made by unjust punishments. J. H. Noyes. The murderers of witches and Quakers. Social science experiments should be given persons who worship the law god of nature. Scientists should learn how little labor will support people well. Five days of physical labor and two days mental labor per week. It is more important to lay up treasures on earth than in heaven. The hours for daily labor should be fixed. Persons in associations are expected to live the lives they pretend to. An association should be made in every state, at least one to make the experiment and publish the results.

SOCIAL science is established by a system of laws that guide people to do right to each other in association and in general society. When a person begins to write upon the principles of a science that is loudly called for by many people, but so strenuously opposed by others that the experiments can not be made to establish it, they can only state what experiments have been made and their results, and what are needed to establish the science. The object to be obtained by the social science is to establish a system of laws and rules that will enable people to live in harmony with themselves and their associates. Some people wish to be alone mostly; others want a few associates, and others want many. Some persons are capable of providing for themselves and all others that naturally depend upon them in their family relations, others can not provide for themselves under present laws; some people can do many kinds of work well, while others can hardly do any thing well under present regulations.

Some people are good to plan work for themselves and others, so that all will be profitably employed, while many people can not set themselves to work profitably, while they are very industrious and faithful when the work is laid out for them. There are other persons that are so discouraged by the present social laws, that they can not think of undergoing the hardships imposed upon them by society in a peaceful, orderly, lawful way, and turn criminals, preferring death in that way, to the slow torturing death of lawful work at starvation prices. The Jews as a people have rebelled against this hard half paid work; and have preferred the tortures of their enemies, to doing their menial service; and there is no doubt they have suffered less in christendom by torture than the poor honest hard working christians have suffered who did the hard dirty work for the governing and trading classes. The inequalities of the comforts of life in the different stations of persons in present society are so great that the least consideration of them shows the necessity of a great change in our social laws.

The first step to begin a social science experiment is to give all adult persons the same legal rights. The chemist can not make his experiments unless he gives equal freedom to the atoms of matter that he requires to move, to make the experiment such as to be useful in determining how atoms of matter unite to form the different compounds known in nature and the arts. And it is almost useless to try any experiments to establish a social science until this principle is fully adopted; but all the experiments that have been made to begin this work have been done under unjust and unequal laws. Although many associations have given their members as equal rights as the laws of the States and nation will allow.

First. There are no persons in present society, that are so low, degraded and despised as those that are called abandoned women. Their lives are short and filled with torture and shame to those who are forced into this mode of life by defamation and want, as many of them are, while yet in the walks of a virtuous life.

This shows that when the law gives the least rights and the persons have the least chance of justice in our courts, are the most despised people on earth, and suffer the most in their dens of infamy, and in the prisons of the criminals, than any other criminals in the land. But after all the real suffering of the poor virtuous needle women may be greater, who work from twelve to twenty hours a day, to eke out a miserable existence on food not much better than the bread and water that is given by prison officials to their most dangerous and stubborn criminals to induce them to do their tasks fairly.

Second. The next lowest and most degraded, are the poor virtuous females that slanderers have vilified until their neighbors will not trust them, courts will not hear their cases in a considerate manner, and are often by the courts and witnesses called the most offensive of names, and are subjected to the most indecent proposals and threatened to be subject to the most inhuman treatment, if the licentious desires of their oppressors are not complied with.

Third. The next most degraded, are men who have disgraced themselves by their low brutal acts of murder, incendiarism, or brutal attempts to commit these deeds, and it has been proved against them, and they have been sent to prison, a penitentiary, or house of correction where they have been abused instead of being humanly treated, and put to do unreasonable tasks, and being rewarded if the tasks were well done, and punished by being put upon a diet of bread and water if they refused to do their work, and displayed a determination not to try to do it. When this class of prisoners are let out of their prison, where they have been inhumanly abused instead of being made better, they are made worse by their treatment, and are made the sworn enemies of mankind in general; and the people mistrust them, and they have little show for justice, and are the most degraded men at large in the world; but their most beastly and brutal habits do not degrade them as low as that of the virtuous women with a blackened character.

Fourth. The next lowest, and most degraded of men are the drunkards, the petty thieves, and dissolute spendthrifts, gamblers, detested counterfeiters, and bogus agents, who get money under false pretences, and swindlers generally. All these stand higher than women of untainted character, because none of the men of this class are so low but they can have their political disabilities as citizens removed even if they add to all these misdemeanors and crimes that of rebel, traitor, and finally a mobocrat, whether black or white. But a woman can not have her disabilities as a citizen removed, because she is a woman. This shows just the standing of women, in the midst of the men generally, and of the judges and officers of the State and national governments. They stand just below any scoundrel, traitor or perjurer who can get his disabilities as a citizen of the United States removed.

The first demand of the social scientists is to put all the virtuous citizens in this country on an equal rights footing. Then the next thing is to have social science associations chartered, to be under the most eminent social scientists of the age. They do not want one sanctioned to try these experiments who has displayed great ignorance in this science, though he may be great in other sciences. The spiritualists have suffered greatly in this way; that is, scientists in the material sciences would be put forward to test mediums and would insist on similar conditions for their tests as are wanted in testing special points in the material sciences. But every science has its peculiar tests, and experiments and observations must be made with due regard to these matters.

Astronomical observations will not answer to establish geology, nor geological observations to establish astronomy, neither will chemical or spiritual observations and experiments answer to establish a social science; but all sciences are alike in one particular. They must be established by knowledge obtained by experiences, observations and experiments put into systematic form, so that any person competent to understand the principles of a science can easily understand its special uses, truths and principles, even if incapable of making the experiments that prove it to be a science. We want persons put at the head of social science associations who are competent and have their whole hearts devoted to the truths that have been obtained, or are to be obtained in establishing a social science.

For instance, let the legislature of the state of New York give a charter to John Humphrey Noyes and his Oneida communists to go on with their experiments, and make annual reports to the legislature of what they have done, and the results. Make laws that will put it beyond the power of their enemies to persecute them when they have lived the same virtuous, honest lives individually and collectively that they have for the last twenty years. The character of the Oneida communists for honesty and fair dealing was never excelled by any community in America, or I may say in the world. And they lived the most exemplary and virtuous lives that were ever lived by an association of people, according to their standard of virtue, which was a pure and high one. That is, they did what they agreed to do to themselves and their outside neighbors; so far as outside neighbors were concerned, their conduct was faultless; so far as the general public are informed their conduct inside the community was equally good. What inner secret history may develop can not now be told. But there is not a suspicion yet that they have been guilty or wrong any more in secret, then in public life. They have studied the laws of health so well in regard to raising children, that they have not lost a child by death who was under five years old, in ten years, and have raised about fifty children. While the death rate outside of the community, has been that two-fifths of the children die before that age; that is, twenty would naturally have died in the community, if their conditions to preserve the health of the children had not been better than the people outside the community have been.

Yet this community has been subjected to such threats and annoyances by the christian priesthood and their tools; that there is little prospect that it can be sustained; and the experiments be continued, until the best way to live to enjoy the best health, and the greatest amount of happiness is established, unless the legal power steps in and declares that scientific religionists shall have as good a chance to live according to their religion, as other religionists have. Nothing can be expected of a priesthood and their followers, that proclaims the principles that were held by the murderers of witches, and Quakers, but the destruction of social scientists by the most foul and deadly means that they have the power to use, no matter how pure and intelligent the scientists are. The christian principles are to destroy them, and now they prefer that two-fifths of the children should die before they are five years old, by their christian principles, to having all of them live by social science principles.

Such has been their history, and their present works are based on the same line of conduct. They will never be satisfied until they have out-heroded Herod and killed millions of children where he killed thousands. It is useless to expect any mercy from professional mercy preachers who have such a history as they have, and who join together to destroy the best and most intelligent citizens of the age, as they have in ages past. It is hoped that the citizens of this republic will soon become so enlightened as to put the power out of the hands of these priests, and into the hands of citizens who will mix a little of mercy and humanity with their religious sense, and who will not use all their powers to kill or destroy the best persons, that are engaged to establish peace on earth and good will among men, by the best known principles and inspirations of this age. There is one principle to note here, it is that the persons who are guided by the God of words and miracles, can not be depended upon to make the experiments to determine what principles and rules will be established to form the social science. They will be constantly looking for miracles that upset the laws of the natural God; some devout christian worshipper will pray to his God so effectively, as to induce him to change the laws of nature, and then the people would be left in a whirl of uncertainty as to what would come next.

The christians have always been in this dilemma. They could not tell who prayed aright, and whose prayers would be answered. But the persons who believe in a natural God, who made the natural man, by nature's laws, or who believes nature's laws made God and man, and rules all things by unchangeable laws, are the persons intrusted with the management of experiments to determine what are the just and true principles that made the social science, and bring it into harmony with the other sciences who have found nature's laws to be God, so far as they could discover. Never before has the God of nature, and of the natural man, had such power in the minds of any people, as now appears among all enlightened nations.

All the sciences are based upon one God, and one law; in this there is entire agreement, and that law can always be depended upon, as active, effective, and supreme; and wherever these sciences are received and understood, all other Gods pale and become thin, and cadaverous; and when the social science is fully established, with a moral science, all the ancient commanding Gods, that swear by themselves, because they can not swear by any greater, will disappear from the minds of the people, and only be remembered by the blackened pages of their history and the blacker hearts that they have given to mankind. They will be remembered long after they have ceased to have any influence among an enlightened people; even as long as there exists savage or barbarous people to be pointed at as the relics of the religious people, christian, Mohammedan or pagans who believed in a God of words, and threats. There, it will be said, is the effect of man-made Gods of unquenchable love, and implacable hate. For man makes a big man, a god or a ghost, or a word or it may be a beast, any or all are a changeable and unreliable as man. But nature points to an unchangeable law as God. This brings us to the irresistable conclusion that the basis of all sciences is unchangeable law, and if we are to have a social science it must be made upon the same principle as other sciences.

The monogamic marriage relation is one of the most important and close social arrangements in present society, and may be the only one in regard to raising families that will be required; but the laws that make the wife subject to the husband, and puts husband as her teacher, will not always stand good in the household; the wife may not require a ninny husband's instruction, and the husband may often want the instruction of an intelligent wife. This is especially needed by him in regard to the laws of the household; the present laws of the nation give him control, and often he is incapable of doing it well; and yet insists on his legal rights, and more even than the law gives him; and often the wife refuses to allow him the rights he has under the law, and from various causes like drunkeness, debauchery, idleness, want of capacity to provide for the family, and want of adaptatation to each other, and many other causes, have made it necessary for most of protestant nations to make liberal provisions for divorces to enable the unhappily married to release themselves from their unholy bonds.

The more enlightened the people, the more liberal the divorce laws, and the darker and more ignorant the mind of the people, the more illiberal the divorce laws are, and the more difficult to get divorces. Such people prefer little family hells, to having the persons divorced who make them. These unenlightened nations and religionists have made a procrustean bed for all persons that fits a few couple, but some are too short and they try to draw them out to fit the bed as the Catholics did their victims in the middle ages, and have ever since where they could, and where the victims are too long they make them a head shorter, as quickly as they can, by compelling them to live gether, to become fools, or maniacs, and raise children to be of their own type of character. Many persons prefer to have these idiotic or insane persons, and retain their old superstitious religion and inhuman laws, to adopting easy divorce laws that will raise up the wisest and most intelligent children.

The law they wish to enforce, is that those that God has united in marriage, let no man put asunder. There should be some exceptions to this rule, such as when God is in heaven, in a jealous fit, and makes a match, and the proof that He was jealous, is abundant by the jealousies of the parties that are married, man should have right to divorce them, and when he is very angry, and matches a couple in marriage, and the proof that He was angry, is that the couple quarrel a great part of their time, when they are together, man should step in and divorce them; and when He hates a couple as bad as He did Esau, and orders them married, man should step in and have the marriage annulled, because the persons that hate each other, should not be forced to live together; and the proof that God did hate them, when He made the match, should be that they hate each other. None of the Godly marriages should be considered binding only when God was truthful and loving; and the proof that he was so should be that the parties bound by the marriage bonds were truthful and loving to each other.

When social science associations are formed, the principles of the marriage and divorce laws now in existence, should be given to these associations to have their members married and divorced, as the demands of science require; that is, the State should give the officers of these associations, power to marry the members, and divorce them, so as to have everything upon a fair, open, well known plan. It may not be best for these officers to have the power to divorce persons who are married outside of the association, nor to marry them, so as to have it legal outside; some States make a legal marriage of the mere statement of the parties that they are married; and this law causes all to be legally married who declared they were before witnesses, outside of the association. But the object to be attained, is to have a community marriage for scientific purposes, and have community divorces for the same purposes.

The scientific religion demands of its worshipers a knowledge obtained by experiences, and experiments. The marriage relation is one that requires great study, accurate observations, and all the knowledge that it is possible to obtain in all the scientific ways, known to scientists, to establish the social, science on the high plain of reason, and facts, where other sciences stand. The superstitions, and guesses, of other religionists, can not answer for the scientific religionists; practical truth, equal justice, a high standard of morality, a special regard for the welfare of the most down trodden and oppressed, a plan of life that will give the most comfort, and greatest hope, to the faithful toilers in their lowly and lonely work, or in their hard oppressive associative labors; not an oppressed person is to be over-looked; not an oppressive law, or rule in society, State, or nation, that would remain uncondemned, and the reasons and experiences given for their condemnation.

The scientific religionists will not ask any special favors, but they will ask to have the same right to worship their God, that other religionists have, and if other religionists have their associative property, exempted from taxation, they will claim the same exemption for theirs. Besides the religious and marriage relations in all their bearings to be considered in social science associations, there are other matters of vast importance to be considered for the purpose of getting reliable information, to determine how to live in accordance with the laws of life, and have the needed supplies, equal to the needed demands.

It is a well established fact, that hard work and poor fare shortens the lives of people, and it may be that hard labor with good fare does in a degree shorten the lives of people; whether it does or not must be a matter for experiments and observations by social scientists. The first question of importance on this subject, is to determine how little physical and mental labor will suffice to make a good living for the members of the association, where all do their share according to their ability; the children must be raised, the sick taken care of, and the old and feeble supported. When all this is well done, under the most favorable circumstances that can be thought of; by the experiences known at the time, and the experiments have been continued for a series of years, so as to take in good and bad years for the production of growing roots and fruits from food producing plants, and trees.

The amount of labor required for the care and production of all the needs of life will be measurably determined, and the number of hours of daily work for each individual member be agreed upon. But they must also include years when people are afflicted with diseases, and the animals that produce food and raiments, for people become diseased and die. Such years may produce hardships that will be very distressing to the toilers that remain healthy and able to do their full duty. Many things would have to be neglected, and when the year of health comes, these odds and ends must be picked up and this state of things must be prepared for, and savings made to meet the necessity of hard years in good ones. But there is an idleness that leads to weakness of body and imbecility of mind.

It would be a great object to determine the true amount of labor and rest that will produce the best specimens of human beings. Some persons can do a large amount of physical labor and grow physically stronger; others will grow weaker. Some persons can do a large amount of mental labor and grow stronger mentally; others will be weakened. Some persons have little strength, but great endurance; others have great strength and little endurance. These are the exceptions to the medium capacity of the great mass of mankind. In present society the persons having exceptional powers of mind, or body, or of genius are pointed out as the model persons to be imitated in their specialty by all who wish to succeed in their line of art or business.

The business of the association will be to try all persons on the medium plane; but there are certain seasons of the year when great strength or great endurance are required to meet the emergencies, and these times naturally pick out the persons of extraordinary powers, and make them well known to the community. But the association must rely for its main support and success upon the persons who will have the constancy to do their work every day fairly, to be in their places, and faithfully do their duty. Besides these there must be some persons of more than ordinary capacity to plan the work and make the working people cheerfully labor with the confidence that it will turn out best for the association and all concerned.

There are persons that inspire others to do their full of duties, and even more, with alacrity, while others have all the other qualifications for leaders but this. It has been found in many cases that the persons who can plan well for others, and cause them to execute his wishes pleasantly, are themselves persons who have large executive abilities by their own muscular or mental powers, and can do much more than people in general can do without the assistance of others. But it may be that experience will prove that the best of those to plan are not the best to execute; and that a much better work can be done where two or more are as harmonious in their work as one person can be.

For a general rule, persons of great calculating and executive powers are not very harmonious mentally and physically with themselves or with other people. There is one principle to be adopted in a scientific association; the persons who naturally stand at the head, are the ones who have got there by their practical good judgment, proved by a number of experiments, that are entirely satisfactory to all concerned, for a series of years. If a person is divinely appointed a leader, they are divinely appointed to prove it by the satisfactory success of their management in the various departments where they have been engaged, and grow to be leaders by showing their good sense in works, but not in declaration and commands, until their correct judgment is established to the satisfaction of the members.

The rule to admit persons to become members of the association, is because they wish it after working under the regulations, a sufficient length of time, to become familiar with their demands upon them, and the persons who are members think they will be useful in their ranks. In this way all members will be selected because they are proved to be adapted to association life. In this way many persons who are poor tramps, in the present society, will become the most useful of members, and many others who have become rich by sharp hard bargains, will be found disqualified to become members because of their lack of industry in other lines of work.

To form a scientific religious association, the first step to be taken is to collect money to buy real estate where the association is to be located. The amount of real estate to be bought, should be what is thought is necessary to support at least one hundred adult persons, by their fair work of eight hours a day for five days in the week, of physical labor, and two days in the week be devoted to mental labor, one day to learn scientific religion in all its branches, which will include all knowledge that is not taught in the next mental day's work, which should be especially devoted to the study of the principles and practice of a scientific government, or governments in all their branches, from the government of children in families or associations to the government of adult people in communities or nations.

The real estate should be owned by the association, the same as a church is, or by the donors or their assignees. That is, there should be no interest rents paid to the donors or their assignees; the whole income of the estate should be devoted to the interest of the association, or to other associations. The first division would be that the workers of the association would have one-half of the products of the farm, and one-half of the profits of the manufactories, the other half should go to the real estate, to be expended in paying taxes and making permanent improvements on the real estate, and in case of a surplus, that amount shall be expended, to purchase more real estate for the association, or be given to strengthen other associations; but there never should be considered a surplus, until there is laid by at least two years provision for the support of the members of the association.

These provisions can be laid up by the members of the association, or by the income of the real estate for the use of the members in hard, unproductive years, to be sold to the association in those years at a fair average price, so as to prevent them from being obliged to pay extortionary prices to heartless speculators. When provisions are once assigned to the care of the association for this purpose, they can not be withdrawn until there is another assignment made to fill its place, whether the assignment is made by individuals or the association, or from the income of the real estate, only when the unproductive years make it necessary to prevent extortionary prices being paid to supply the needs of the association. Let all the members understand that it is just as important to prepare for a bad year as it is for a rainy day; and let all the donors understand who have given to form the association that they have no more right to call for interest or dividends than they have when they make a gift to the poor. The interest and use of their donation is for the use and benefit of the poor, faithful workers in associations; and we will see if we can not lay up treasures on earth that are of vastly more importance to the poor on earth than was ever laid up for them in heaven. And let us see if we can not lay these treasures up so deep in justice, so wisely in application, and so far-reaching in their benefits upon the poor and distressed, and so humane upon all who come within their influence, as to gradually extend over the whole earth, and give joy to all people, and pour down upon them blessings greater than they ever thought of in their philosophy or religion. Let us see if we can not abolish killing idleness and hard labor, and death-dealing luxury and poverty and want from the face of the earth.

The time to begin the hours of labor should be fixed for each division of the association. Let it be understood that each and every member should be in their places at their appointed time ready to do their duty, and then go about it with a will; and if there is a necessity for more labor to be done some years than others, it should be cheerfully done; and at some seasons the hours of physical labor may be greater than at others. It may be best to begin all associations upon the ten hour a day system, and reduce it to eight as soon as they can, and then reduce it again and again as soon as the wants are so supplied as to permit the reduction; remembering at all times when the hours of physical labor are reduced there should be an increase of the hours of mental labor; this will prevent an idleness and ignorance that is destructive of order, system, and will prevent much fault-finding and complaining and petty, ridiculous quarreling that is apt to be indulged in by the idlers and ignorant, and by all selfish people who are not fully educated and made to know that they will lose comforts by their petulent fault-finding. But the work of the association must be done, and when persons are not faithful to time and duty, it should be calmly talked over first in their division or group and have the errors corrected, if possible, there.

This will prevent the necessity of public discussion, yet let no one suppose that it will be best to hide faults and keep secret the sins of omission and commission; but rather have a clear, true, candid statement of facts, because every one in a scientific association is expected to be what they appear to be, and live the lives they profess to live, which is almost impossible in present society with its artificial shams and unjust, unequal laws and religious fanaticism, and the pretense that these are necessary to preserve virtue among the people.

In a social science association, all these falsehoods can be done away with as apears by present society regulations, except in the marriage relations; here is the fight between the secret sins of superstition and the crimes and misdemeanors which the present laws make people commit, and the scientific marriage relations which require people to abandon their secret sins, and live according to the well known laws of health and virtue. But there are many of these laws of health and virtue that are not well known, and will not be until experiments are instituted to determine the questions by a knowledge obtained by experience and reason; and there is little hope that these experiences will be allowed as long as the ministers of a superstitious and false religion have such popularity as they now possess.

The law makers in past ages, have united with the same kind of priests to torture and murder people, and we may expect them to do the same thing now to this extent, that they will continue to pass laws to disgrace the best of women and such as are calculated to kill two-fifths of their children before they are five years old. But eventually they will give way and pass laws giving social scientists the privilege of showing how this holocaust can be abated, for it is a burning crime. Under all these circumstances and discouragements, the friends of social science should unite and give of their property sufficient to make such an association in every State and Territory in this Union, and in the large States more than one, and ask of the legislatures, and of the congress of the United States in its territories, and of all the powers that have an influence, to allow them the privilege of making the necessary experiments to establish a social science, as other sciences have been established; and whether such petitions are complied with or not, proceed to form their associations, and make all preparations to proceed with experiments as far as the law will allow; and if there are laws as much against health, virtue, and humanity, as the slave laws, and slave catching laws were, still give no countenance to their being violated, more than the people of the northern States did to the violation of the slave laws, but plead for the violators of the law, the killing tendencies of it, when complied with; the same as the abolitionists did for the violators of the unjust and abominable slave laws.

Modern inventions have made such a vast differerence between this age and past ages, that they necessitate a new system of laws; a new plan of society associations. Under present laws wealth is accumulating in great amounts in a few hands, and the natural consequence is, that there are extremes of luxury and extravigance, and of poverty and want, that can be averted by scientific associations. In forming a religious social science association the members who have means to spare should be requested to give to a hospital fund for the purpose of preparing every convenience to take care of the sick, and giving the physicians and nurses as good a living as the other members of the association have; and means should also be asked for this purpose from all persons, and for the support of mediums who want rest and time to recover their energies.

CHAPTER XXIII.

THE SCIENCE OF GOVERNMENT.

The Declaration of Independence, 1776. The voice of the people the voice of God. Strange Gods. The Jews. The greatest defect in getting the voice of people is only half the people are consulted. Napoleon Bonaparte. A republican government must have a republican religion, (officers to be elected by the people.) All officers must be elected that can be consistently. United States senators corrupt the state legislatures and have become a corrupt body by their partial laws that are intended to help the rich and oppress the poor. Discredited money. Rotten borough system. The president can not do all the duties of his office. The cabinet of the president. Cabinet counsels. The cabinet officers should be elected by the people. Terms of officers to be short. Officers should have short terms and low salaries. Judges should be elected. Biennial elections. Machine politicians the worst of machinists. People should acquire knowledge. The unpardonable sin, if there is one.

ANY one who has read carefully the preceding pages will have a clear idea of what a government is that is based upon scientific principles and carried out scientifically in detail. The basis of such a government was very fairly stated when this nation declared its independence in 1776. Governments derive their just powers from the consent of the governed. This declaration made the rulers of this government responsible to the people. The voice of the people was to be the voice of God to them. They put no other god in the constitution, but recognized other gods in their laws, and in the laws of the states, and are constantly calling upon ministers and laymen who worship other gods to bless them, bless the country and the people, and give us peace and prosperity.

And this mingling of these strange gods with the voice of the people, which is the nation's God, brings great confusion in the minds of the people. They do not know whose God it is that gives them their great prosperity.

This question should be settled at once by undeniable facts. The most potent of these strange gods is brought from Italy. He seems to be a three-headed, single-bodied god of the Roman Empire, adopted in the fourth century, and ruled that people with his cursings for more than twelve hundred years; here this god and his priests had undisputed authority or triumphant control of the Italian people. They commenced with the most intelligent and powerful people on earth, and ended in being the most ignorant and debased in the civilized world. They commenced when they were the conquerors of all surrounding nations; they ended by being conquered by other nations and becoming tributaries to them. They have built up a rich church upon a poor, ignorant, debased, begging people. The mere shuttle-cocks of other nations.

Now, if the American people wish to adopt this god and his cursings and blessings, his priests are here, and you have only to say so; and the god or gods of the Romans will use you as he did the Italians. The next strange god that is presented for the adoption of the American people is the Jewish God, or the God of the people who once inhabited Judea, and made Jerusalem his capitol. This God took the Jews out of slavery to the Egyptians and landed them safely in their promised land, and allowed them a little education and but little freedom of action, and then made them the slaves of their enemies; then freed them again, then made them slaves again, and all this was done when these people were as faithful to their God as ever were human beings, according to their history. Yet he destroyed that people as a nation, and for nearly two thousand years they have been scattered among the nations of the earth, praying to their God to restore them to their loved Judea, and to a government of his own by them and for them, his own people; but he has not done it, and their history is one of sadness and sorrow, as written by themselves; and they are still worshipping their God, but not urging others to adopt him very strongly. But he was adopted as one of the Roman triune gods, and the Romanists and some Protestants are recommending him in the highest terms for adoption by the American people.

Now is it possible to conceive of any religious people being engaged in a more disgraceful work than are these Jews and christians who are endeavoring to have either, or any or all these gods put in power as the guide of the people of this country? Just compare the results of the actions of these strange gods with those of the god of the voice of the people. Look over the history of all the gods of all nations, and tell of one in all time, in all the world, that has been so good to his people, and to all other people, as this God. The voice of the people expressed in the election of all their officers of this government, would they lessen the power of this God and put a priest god in his place? The priests pretend they have a spirit god that they can not prove exists, and that they have a word of God that is a perfect guide to worldly comfort and to heavenly happiness; but it has led all the nations, who have fully adopted it, with its priests, to worldly ignorance and woe; and wherever the voice of the people was taken in any nation fairly in the election of its officers, and the priests were put in the back-ground, there was the best government and the happiest people on the earth, because every voter expresses the god within him; and a majority of these expressions comes nearer to the God that all believe in, and are willing to obey, than any priestly god that was ever imposed on a people.

But there has been one great defect in getting the

voice of the people; they have taken the voice of only one-half of the people and called it the whole. The voice of the women has not been heard by vote in these elections to such an extent as to be claimed that it was fairly heard. So only one-half of the adult citizens had a voice, and but a little over one-half of these elected the officers and made the laws; yet this little more than one-fourth that have made their voices effective, have shown that it is far more beneficial to the people than any god that was ever invented by the priests. Still the great defect of not receiving the voices of all the adult citizens of fair minds, who are as virtuous as people now are who vote, is felt to be a great wrong, and the wail of the women who are tormented, tortured and murdered by the laws and regulations that they have had no voice in making, is constantly rung in the ears of the triumphant party who make the laws; yet they heed it as little as they did the cry of the slaves before the rebellion.

But the crushing enormities of the slave holders finally were too great to escape the notice of a triumphant party, and then followed the tortures of war; oh how cruel and heart rending; the sufferings of the soldiers in the army were as great as the sufferings of slaves in bondage; and finally the voice came that the slaves were free, and then that the men were voters, and then the old vindictive slave holders and their partisans tried to get back into power by mobs, threats, and intimidation of the triumphant party, and partisans; but the voice of the God of the people comes to them and to all the world, stay your hands; and the hope is that the triumphant party will say to the mobocrats and intimidators, stop your criminal works; you have debased your humane feelings below the standard of the people of this age; your attempts to govern the people by fear and fraud must cease or you will bring upon yourselves all the torture that slaves and women have endured, and in a less degree upon all the people of this country, and you shall be classed with the women and children, and have no more right to have your voice heard than they have in this government. And if the triumphant party of this country refuse to remove the disabilities of women who have always been loyal and obedient to law, and continue to remove the disabilities of the disloyal mobocrats, the same disgrace will come upon them that has fallen upon the triumphant party that upheld slavery in this country. The voice of the humane party, small as it may be at present, will become the will of a majority of the people, and the god of this nation to correct its evils; and if the present triumphant party will not put down the great criminals and stop their monstrous public crimes, then a party will arise that will do it; and the longer it is delayed the more cruel and bloody will be the contest.

The partisans who will not give the oppressed their rights will become proud and lofty in their bearing, as the slaveholders did, and pay no heed to the cries of humanity; their love for the oppressed will be as fickle as the love of the slaveholder for his slave, and their honor be as black and foul as the honor of a professional duelist. Great evils can not be continued for a great length of time without tainting the whole people; and then when the day of reckoning does come, it must involve all the people in great distress; just as the great crimes of the christians caused the cruelties of the wars of the reformation, and more especially, just as the great crimes of Protestant and christian rulers caused the great distress to come upon all the people of Europe in the time of Napoleon Bonaparte.

But these great wars and afflictions finally purified the public morality of the people, and they have had better rulers and less public criminality since; yet there are in Europe and in this country inhuman laws and institutions that must soon be corrected, or great afflictions will fall upon the people. Human nature can only stand a certain amount of oppression before it succumbs in death or becomes hopelessly despondent, or recklessly beligerent; and these conditions beget sympathizers and friends, and the conflict begins and the oppressors of women will prepare their bastiles and Andersonvilles, as the followers of strange gods and the slaveholders did. For there is but one history to oppressors, that is they inflict the most excruciating tortures in the hope of retaining their authority; and there is but one history to the oppressed, they must suffer every kind of pain and affliction, and the most agonizing death penalties until they can triumph over their oppressors.

From this it is apparent that this government is a natural government of the people for the people; and the religion is the natural religion that avers that they are saved by virtue and justice, and in no other way. Then if you turn to other governments you find their religion coincides with their plan of government; a despotism has a despotic religion; a limited monarchy has a religion partly despotic and partly protesting against it, and a republic must have a republican religion or be destroyed. You can not have God as a king to rule the kingdom of heaven, and not have a king on earth as his vicegerent; and when the religion of a republic is established, it will have a republic in heaven to fit the one on earth. And all intelligent persons can see that the religion based on the science of spiritualism has a republican form of government in their heaven. In this way harmony is established between heaven and earth.

It should be distinctly understood that every great government has its ruling religion, and every great noted religion has been adopted by some great government. The American republic has been partly a republic and partly a despotism of the blackest dye, and the religion that has been generally adopted has been Protestantism, which is partly a despotism and partly republican in its forms on earth; but its heaven is a despotism or a kingdom with despots on their thrones. I think the most liberal

Protestants deny that they believe in this kingdom of heaven. But the most conservative hold to the most despotic of despotisms on earth and in heaven ; but no such half-way religion can stand permanently in a pure republic, and no half-way republic can be made to stand by any such religion.

The Jews tried it, the Greeks tried it, the Romans tried it, and all failed. The Americans have adopted a half-way republic and a half-way republican religion. Now the question is, will they adopt a republic in full and a republican religion in full, or go back to despotisms in government and religion? Or, in other words, shall we have an American republic with an American religion, or Asiatic despotism with an Asiatic religion? These questions must soon be answered, for the partisans on each side are straining every nerve and every power in their reach to establish their government and religion, and the battle rages with fearful ferocity at times, and victory perches upon one at one time, and upon the other at other times ; but upon the whole the cohorts of despotism are being driven from their strongholds, and the banners of an equal rights' republic are being planted firmly in all the strong places taken from the enemies of the republics of heaven and earth.

Let no one think they can be neutral in this great conflict ; they will most cordially love one side and hate the other. The motto of the despots is that they love you as they do themselves, as they have applied it for ages past in the despotisms of earth, when they have taken all the good things of life and left you the hardships and poor things of life. The motto of the republicans of heaven and earth is that we give you the same rights we claim for ourselves, no matter whether we love you or not. We do not promise to love you ; we do not ask you to love us. But we do want you to join with us and give all others the rights we claim for ourselves; that is the basis of the republic of heaven. Let us join and make it the basis of the republics of earth.

From all these premises it is seen that christianity can not be the ruling religion only under a despotic government, and spiritualism can not be the basis of a ruling religion only in an equal-rights republic. Having stated the basic principles of a just scientific republic, and the basic principles of the religion the people will adopt who form such a republic, and shown that religion is so fixed in the human head and heart that there is really no such thing as separating church and state, only in the sense that the state will give no special legal or constitutional privileges to a special church, yet in practice they will give favors and preferences to the church that is best fitted to the minds of the people. In christendom the Roman Catholics have the lawful support of some governments, the Protestants have others, and in this country there is no great amount of legal preferences, but the people are Protestant generally, and there is a great tendency to scientific Protestantism that throws out christianity entirely; yet the Protestant priesthood is the most favored, and the signs are that the people will either go back to Roman Catholicism or forward to a scientific religion ; if they go back a despotism will prevail, if they go forward a just republic will prevail.

It will not make any real difference whether the christian God or the scientific god is put in the constitution, but it will be a sign of what the people will do; if the christians prevail it will signify that tortures are to be instituted whether there is a law for them or not, and if science is to prevail humane institutions are to be established whether there is a law for them or not. The law is a sign of public sentiment; the people back of that are the sentiment.

WHO SHALL BE VOTERS.

We have determined that the voice of all the adult citizens, who are qualified by the same mental and moral principles, regardless of sex, sect or previous condition of freedom or servitude, shall have a right to a quiet peaceful vote for all the officers that are to be elected in their district, ward, town, county, state and nation; and a majority of those votes shall be a notice to statesmen of the wishes of the people, determining who the persons are that they wish for their officers; and a notice to the religious people that this is the voice of God to them; and all who wish to obey the only tangible voice of God ever heard in this world (except the law of nature) will obey it piously and religiously.

Whenever and wherever the people are not allowed to quietly and peaceably give their voice by their votes, it should be a notice that the persons who prevent this quiet voice from being expressed are the enimies of God and man, of a republic and of the people who work for republican and humane institutions. The principal argument against women voting is that they can not make good soldiers; and possibly this statement in a general sense is true, but in a great many cases it is entirely false; but suppose in a very great majority of cases it is true, then it will be taken as a sign of the peaceful intent of the people, when they give them the ballot in the election of all the officers of the government that are to be elected by votes. And the persons who oppose the equal political rights of women with men, are in favor of all the cruelties and tortures of war, whether we have war or not; for war is only another excuse to their degraded minds for practicing these cruelties. Besides the officers to be elected, there are laws to be enacted by the voters, and these must be allowed to be submitted to them in an equally quiet way; and there are constitutional provisions to be adopted or rejected by the voters, and in all cases the same quiet elections are to be held, and the same quiet small voice is to be heard to determine all matters of election of men and measures in the land or government.

WHAT OFFICERS AND MEASURES SHALL BE VOTED FOR.

The general rule regarding the election of officers is that every officer should be elected by the people, that can be done consistently with the principle that the people rule. The senators of the United States are elected by the legislatures of the several States ; and there is more proof of bare-faced bribery, corruption and fraud in their elections than in the election of any other so important a body of men. Their salaries and perquisites are large, and there is great temptation for corrupt men to buy themselves into the position, and for cliques of corrupt men to join to elect their favorite corruptionists. And as a great many of the senators are bankers, or indebted to them for their election, they have joined with monopolists and sharpers to pass laws to benefit that class of persons, and make financial regulations to oppress the poor ; or, in other words, to make the rich richer and the poor poorer.

This kind of legislation has been especially prominent in the last twenty years. Besides being a body tainted with bribery and corruption, it is a rotten borough body, some two senators representing less than two hundred thousand of people, while two others represent more than four millions. They are said to represent states or land; but it is only filthy lucre when they insist on issuing money that they will not allow the government to take for all dues in time of peace. The only excuse they ever made that was worthy of consideration for issuing a discredited currency during the war, was to enable the rich northern rebels in this and other countries to get our bonds at a great discount, and so buy them to adopt our cause cheaper than to whip them into it. But even under any circumstances, it would seem if they had the least respect for people, that they would not force the House of Representatives to adopt their views, as they did in 1862, during the war of the rebellion, and oblige them to issue this discredited currency or let the rebels conquer our armies.

When it is well understood the representatives have have a constitutional provision to originate money bills, which should give them the most weight in disagreements of this kind. But the senators are the special representatives of that part of the moneyed aristocracy, who are the greatest oppressors of the poor laboring classes; and after the war had ceased they preferred Black Fridays and the English forceing system plan to arrive at the resumption of specie payments, and making a despotic aristocracy of the rich, and wages slaves of the poor; to the French plan of taking their money for all the dues of the government, and building up a great middle class, industrious, intelligent and self-supporting.

The only hope for the continuance of this republic. Experience has proved that to prevent the great corruptions and frauds in the legislatures of the states, and in the Senate of the United States, the senators should be elected by the people of the states they represent; and to stop in some degree the rottenness of the senate, the states which are only entitled to one representative should have but one senator. The President of the United States has more duties to perform than any man can do well; and this is the ready excuse for his bad appointments and other blunders and misdeeds. It is farcical to hear politicians assert that the President of the United States should have all the appointing power he now holds; and then the next breath when they see he has made some foolish or criminal appointment, why he can not know everybody who applies for office; that is true, and he should not have power to appoint any officers that can be elected by the people, because it gives him more to do than he can do well, if he is a very competent man; and if he is incompetent, or has despotic and criminal intentions, his power for evil is great; and in the history of this country we have had such presidents, and their appointments have been a disgrace to themselves and the country.

Then there is another farcical idea: the president appoints his cabinet; he appoints a postmaster general that knows nothing of war tactics, and a secretary of war that knows nothing of postoffice management, and a secretary of the treasury that knows nothing of either war or postoffice, but is well informed in financial matters; and a secretary of the interior that knows nothing of state affairs, and a secretary of state that knows nothing of the internal affairs of the nation, and a secretary of the navy that knows nothing about state affairs; then he appoints his attorney general who is supposed to know the laws of this and other countries, and not thoroughly anything else. All these officers are appointed on the theory that they are well informed in the business they are called to preside over, and have only a smattering knowledge of the other branches, or a historical knowledge of them—no special practical information. Now, the president calls a council of his cabinet, as these secretaries and generals are called; and the president who calls them has but a general knowledge of all matters pertaining to his office, but he may have a special branch that he is well informed on practically; and besides that, he has his policy, his will—his by the eternal—his determination or lack of determination to rule his council for good or evil, as seems best to him upon subjects of which he is ignorant, or well informed.

Well, he has got his cabinet together, and they are in council; the subject of finances is to be taken up; who is supposed to know about the best mode of managing the finances of the country? in this council just one man, and the president is his sycophant or dictator. Then war measures are to be considered, and two men in the council are supposed to understand these measures, and there are five that are supposed to know but precious little on those subjects; and the president leaves it to them, or dictates, takes the responsibility, and so the council goes on; one man in each branch of the government understands the question, and the others are simply learners or lookers-on, giving their very wise counsels upon subjects of which they are gravely ignorant. And this is called a cabinet council, and the result of such councils are put into execution either by a majority of these counsellors who know but little on the subject considered, or by the president, who is generally practically ignorant, or once in seven times is well informed, and dictates six times by ignorance or prejudice to once by knowledge; or it is left to the secretary or general to carry out the provisions of the council as best he can without really having any counsel of persons who have knowledge on the subject. Was there ever a more farcical scene perpetrated in a solemn manner and with great dignity than this, that is called a cabinet council?

It may be there is not really a great expert in the council at all; but at best there are only two out of eight that can be supposed to understand the subject fully, that is the president and one of his secretaries. The president may be an expert in one of these seven branches, and his secretary on that branch may be an expert also; but in six branches of the seven there is but one man that can be supposed to understand the subject critically. Then what becomes of this dignified grand cabinet council? It is merely a jury of six or seven intelligent gentlemen listening to the reasons of an expert on the subject before them, and then they decide, as a jury does, what is right for them to do about it.

This is supposing the one-man power is not used to prevent them from deciding as in their judgment they ought to. When this dictatorial manner comes in the counsellors become the tools of the dictator, or they must resign; and when you see a president changing his cabinet frequently, you may know there is a proud dictatorial spirit in him, and that he is ruled six times by his willful, arbitrary ignorance, to once by candid knowledge.

Now the question is, how can we get clear of such farcical meetings, called executive councils? These cabinet councils have been disgraceful in the highest degree to intelligent gentlemen of knowledge on the subjects decided upon by their dictorial Presidents. And the only way to get clear of these farcical, disgraceful scenes is to have all cabinet officers selected by the people, and each of them have their cabinet councils in their special branch of the government, and each of them have the power to appoint all the officers of their department, and be as responsible for their good conduct, as the President of the United States now is, with the same advice and consent of the Senate, or in regard to the Secretary of the Treasury, with the advice and consent of the House of Representatives. If by experience it is shown that many of the offices in the departments can be filled by persons elected by the people, they should have the power to do it; in accordance with the general principle that all officers are to be elected by the people, that they can elect to the advantage of Republican institutions. These elections should take place annually, that is, the President and Secretary of the interior should be elected one year. The Postmaster General and Attorney General the next, the Secretary of War the next, and the Secretary of the Navy should be appointed by the Secretary of war, so the war department would have one responsible head, and lastly the Secretary of the Treasury. And each of these elected secretaries, and President, should have his cabinet officers that are considered experts in his branch of the government; and when he calls his cabinet together, for council, he will have persons that are informed on the subjects to be considered. The Secretary of war would consult with warriors or those educated in war tactics, and principles. And the Secretary of the Treasury would have persons about him, who were educated in financial matters, and the Postmaster General, would have his cabinet officers selected from persons who understood the management of the postal business of the country, if not of the world; and each of the heads of the departments would be accountable for his appointments, and doings, and would report to the congress of the United States, as Washington did to the continental congress, during the Revolutionary war.

This would bring about an important election every year, and prevent such a tremendous excitement, as now occurs every four years. Each of these secretaries, generals and the president should hold their offices for four years. There is great exertion among the political managers to make the terms of office longer, so as to take the power from the people, and have it in the hands of the officers; the offices that are sought with the greatest avidity, are first the Presidency for its great honors and salary, next, the judges who hold their positions during good behavior, or for life; and next to be senators, because of their long terms of office, and they can become independent of the people for some years, and if they wish, can act the tyrant over them in various small ways, that if they are continued, will amount to depriving the people of a voice in the government in a few years.

It costs the people very little to have two important elections every year, compared with the great advantages it is to them, but it may cost ambitious office seekers considerable more than it would be worth to them, to attempt to buy themselves into office for such a short time. Therefore it is important for the purity and candor of the people, and the officers, that the time to hold an office, without an election, be reasonably short, and the salaries be reasonably small, so as to be in accord with the earnings of good industrious thriving people; for large salaries are as much of a curse as long terms of office to the people, and the persons who hold the offices; for both long terms, and high salaries, or either of them, beget a pride and arrogance in the actions of the officers, that is entirely inconsistent with Republicans, and Republican institutions.

Experience has proved that the judges and justices that preside over our courts of justice should be elected by the people, directly by their votes, if we would continue Republican institutions, and a Republican government. The judges appointed by kings favor them by their decisions; the judges appointed by the slave holding power, give slave holders great advantages, by their judgments, and the judges appointed by aristocratic monopolists, see to it that their interests are secured to them. It is said to be a very bad dog that bites the hand that feeds it, and judges have not proved worse than good dogs to their masters; in short, they have the defects that belong to human nature, and their judgments are human, not always humane by any means; and for this reason the people should elect them and make it incumbent on them, to be humane, if they err in judgment in other respects.

Judges should not be elected for a term of more than ten years. The reason they have been for a longer period, or for life, was to put them above temptation; this idea has signally failed, among the United States judges, for their prejudices have been just as strong, and their rulings just as cruel as any other judges, and it has finally come to light, that the old judges are more or less imbecile, and totally unfit to judge correctly the cases that are brought before them; and in some of the States these long term, or life judges are said to almost quit all the duties of their office, except to draw their salaries. Even ten years is a very long time, except for the supreme court judges of the United States, and experience must determine the great question of the length of time that these and other judges should be elected to office; what truly Republican people want, is to establish the prin-

ciples of equality and justice to each and every
citizen.

To do this, experience has fully proved that the
people must keep the power in their own hands, and
make all office-seekers and holders bow to their will.
When this is done, inhumanity to man can have but a
short existence in the courts and penal institutions of
the country. A few judges should be elected every
year to fill the vacancies occasioned by the expiring of
the time that some judges can hold their offices, and
others that are made vacant by other causes, such as
death, resignation and impeachment. One of the
most successful tricks of the politicians that has been
practiced upon the people of any of the states of this
Union, is that of biennial elections and biennial sessions
of the legislatures on the plea of economy, when in
some states they have cost more, and in all of them so
near the same as to be of little or no advantage to the
people; but it has given shrewd politicians very much
the advantage when they have once got into office.
They can shape legislation in their interest and cause
the election of their friends to places of trust at less
expense in proportion to what it cost.

Then the money in the treasury to be invested they
can place where it will do them the most good, instead
of the people of the state. It is not only in the interest of the people to have elections of their state representatives every year, but also to have the members of
the legislature meet and exchange greetings, and give
their views on the needs and necessities of their constituents, and become accustomed to be guided by
congressional rules or legislative rules and tactics.
This meeting of members elected in their several districts or towns will not only tend to harmonize the
people of different parts of the state, but be in the interest of education generally. The call for laws, charters and resolutions will bring up discussions on the
subjects in a practical shape, and the reasons for and
against the matter under discussion will be given; and

the few who listen to these statements will carry their impressions to their constituents, and thus those matters that were considered of sufficient importance to require the sanction of law will be more talked of and better understood than by any other means.

The elections should take place in the spring and fall, and the legislatures should meet in the winter, when the mental powers are the clearest, and there is the least demand for muscular labor; and to prevent any undue legislative enactments, one-tenth part of the members of either house can object to its becoming a law until it has been sanctioned by a majority of the voters at a regular election after the enactment has been fairly considered by the people. This will tend to instruct the people still more on important state matters.

It should be the duty of the representatives and senators to see to it that their constituents are early informed about the laws and other matters left for them to accept or reject, and in this way the people will be more instructed at less expense than by any other common school system yet adopted; and it would be the best supplement to our present common school system to educate children, that can be put before the people. And besides the state laws and matters that are left to the people, the United States laws, resolutions and charters should be left to be sanctioned by the votes of a majority of the voters before it becomes a law. This would calm their bear garden, as the house is called, down to a commendable degree of common sense discussion, and make the dignified, gentlemanly trickster senators show less of solemn bombast, and cause the scheming presidents to hang less around the houses of congress to precipitate party legislation upon the country.

When they knew that their plans would be laid before an intelligent people, who will look before they leap, who will prepare an intelligent reason for their vote before they give it. Every plan should be devised to wrest the States and the nation from machine politicians, for of all the machinists ever known, these are the most useless and pernicious. It will be the greatest God send to the people of this country, when they declare they will do their own political work without any other machines than their own hands, and brains. But we will adopt all the mechanical and philosophical machinery that we can find to assist us in doing the necessary work, to support the body in comfort; and of this kind there is enough at present invented to prevent the necessity of working people being taxed with more than eight hours work, per day, for five days in the week, and give all a better chance to live in comfort, than was ever known before, with any amount of labor that working people could endure. This not only gives the people two days in the week for mental labor, one devoted to governments, and the other to religion, or to speak more definitely, one day should be devoted to the consideration of man, in all his relations, necessities, and educations, and governments, in his earthly body, and home, and the other, to the consideration of his spiritual existence, and to his devotions that are best calculated to make him happy here, and hereafter; but it allows some hours in each day to be devoted to mental labors, in the various departments of knowledge. The from two to four hours which have been devoted by the working people to hard physical labor, must not be allowed to be spent in dissipations that injure the body and mind, as much as the spare time of the laborer now is, but must be devoted to acquiring useful knowledge; and in this way the voters will be prepared to give an intelligent vote upon all questions that may be submitted to them, even if very important elections are held frequently; that is regularly twice a year; every election day should be a holiday, and if the price of liberty is eternal vigilance; let us be united and vigilant in acquiring the knowledge in every spare moment to make us wise to see the hand that would deprive us of our rights in the greatest distance, and give a warning note to all who are concerned of the approach of danger.

If the poor shall always be with us, then the trickster will always be with us, for the trickster scheming for honor and profit makes the starving poor in the midst of plenty; and the poor ignorant starvelings make it possible for the inhuman schemer to exist. Beware of a pretended benevolence, that makes a poor wretched begging people, and a rich, voluptuous, ostentatious priesthood. They support a few deserving poor, sick cripples to make a show of benevolence, but the greatest amount is expended in supporting strong healthy people in idleness, and often in crime. If they pretend that they are the followers of the historical Jesus Christ, then they should make themselves poor wanderers as He was; without a place to lay their heads. If there is any such thing as committing the unpardonable sin against the Holy Ghost, that neither God, man, or spirit can forgive, this is the one.

SALARIES OF OFFICERS.

The sentiment of high salaries to great officials and low wages to the poor is wrong. The Jews prefer martyrdom to hard, dirty work. The salaries not to exceed twelve thousand a year. The best presidents have been the weakest, and the most important reforms in England have been obtained from the weakest kings. Ex-officers and office-seekers to have poor houses in every state. Salaries of officers to be taxed. The poor workers to have good homes. Ordinary men make the best officials for the people.

There is no subject of greater importance than to affix a true standard for the pay of the officers of republican governments. There has been an opinion which exists to a certain extent to-day, that you can

not pay the greatest and most successful officials too
high a salary, and that you can not pay the common
laborer too little, if it will keep him alive. This makes
one an unfeeling despot and the other a miserable
slave. These general principles have been the guide
of people all over the world ever since the christians
became a power, until the reformation, and since then
to the greatest extent over the world; and it is one of
the hardest tasks for republicans to convince the people generally that a republican government can not
long continue with very high salaries to its officers and
very low pay to its ordinary laborers. The Protestants
have put down the slavery that pays the laborer with
the lash by stripes on his bare back, and have substituted wages' slavery. The common phrase is that the
laborer must sell his labor at the market price. It is
to be put on the market the same as wheat, oats, cattle
and horses, sheep and hogs. The popular idea is that
the common laborer must submit to take the market
price for his labor, whether it is starvation price or
not. But the official must have his large salary
whether the laborer that earns it is starved or well
kept. Commerce is king, and the supply and demand
fix the values of all things that are on the market,
unless the officials and tradesmen interfere; and as
officials do not like to be under the thumb of their
craft or of souless traders, so they have a fixed salary
or a certain fee for work done. Every way is devised
so as not to subject them to the vacillating market
prices that they subject the common laborer to.

People would not have seen the officials make the
hard times under the direction of heartless traders from
1873 to 1878, if the officials and traders had been
obliged to suffer losses as the common laborer did.
And if the hard times pinched them all alike in proportion to their means, people would not have heard
the flimsy and false excuses for the adoption of the
system of contraction that made those extremely and
most disastrously hard times, that were given.

This shows the necessity for framing laws to pay officials according to the earnings of people that labor for a living in the common industries of life, rather than to have them fashion their salaries upon the fees of professional men, or the incomes of successful traders. It should be remembered that there are two competent clerks ready for every vacancy, and these two competent persons seeking every office and as many more as you please to count, while common labor is avoided by the most people, because it gives the least hope of reward or promotion and the smallest wages. There are two principles that should be considered as important for every American citizen to adopt. The first is that fathers and mothers, and guardians of children should educate them in the best way they possibly can to prepare them to fill the highest and best paying positions in society, and in the state and nation. And the second is that all these children should seek these grand positions; it is not consistent with good republican governments to have a class set apart for hard, dirty work and small pay, and another set apart for a little clean work and great pay.

The Jews have for two thousand years preferred martyrdom to doing this hard, dirty, ill-paid work, either in a nation of their own, or among other nations. And they have undoubtedly chosen the position, where there is the least suffering. There is going around in the papers an excuse for their selecting trading to work, that in some nation, or nations, they were not allowed to own lands. That does not apply to this country; lands have been open to them to cultivate, and canals, railroads, and streets to be made, but no Jews are seen at work, in these low priced hard places, or so near to none, that it is not worth mentioning. From father to son, they are taught that the best positions in society and the State, are a learned profession, or a position as a trader; and the worst of it is, that they deal in mock auctions, as much as the Yankees do in wooden nutmegs; and all the lower grade of them engage with Yankees and others of the same class, in selling shoddy goods for the best kind. They adopt the rule of the world that there is no friendship in trade; and often there is great enmity. When bogus jewelry is palmed off for genuine gold and diamonds, or rotten, frozen meat for a good sound article, or any other of the cheats of the trades upon the people. Then again when the trade is fair in every other respect, except the price paid for an article is three or four times its cost, the people who are shaved, can not feel very friendly to the shaver. But the principle is, your eyes are your chaps, and when your eye-teeth are fairly cut, that is you have been outrageously cheated a few times, then the tricks of trade are made plain to you; and when the industrious person is hard at work, the trader and the idler are contriving how to cheat him out of his earnings, and the getting him to drink some intoxicating beverage is one of the ways to bring it about.

And then shoddy traders, and heartless bond holders who have got their bonds from thirty-five to fifty cents on the dollar, and are not content at having their bonds paid in full, in coin, with five, six, and seven per cent interest, but make the most strenuous exertion to have coin changed to gold, and receive their pay in gold coin; and they succeeded, and thus swindled the laborer; and this was done by shoddy politicians who disgraced themselves more by their back pay swindles, and their Credit Mobilier chicanery, and by admitting to the Senate and House persons who were elected by mob violence, as is clearly demonstrated by the reports of their committees; than any other Congress or Administration that ever existed in this country, except in James Buchanan's Rebel Administration and Congressmen. These stole every thing they could lay their hands on to enable them to fight the loyal people of the Union;

and the others swindled the people as much as they could, and sanctioned mob elections.

Now here are the acts of an over-paid President and Congress, and it proves what is the experience of all nations who give large salaries to their officers and rulers; and small pay to the persons who do their hard, dirty work. The principle is settled, that there must be paid more wages than is barely necessary to keep soul and body together. The intelligent American laboring people will not submit to starvation wages very quietly. And it is hoped that the shoddyites who attempt it again will have a more blackened reputation than the back-pay swindlers have.

From all these circumstances and principles, it is apparent that the highest office in the gift of the people should not have over twelve thousand dollars per year, as the pay of the person who holds it, and the use of a house, and a private purse as the President has, for incidental expenses. All the heads of departments should have the same salary and be provided with the same accommodations and private purse as the President, and other officers should be graded down until the lowest should be on a par with the pay of the common laborers; such a state of things can not be brought about only by the combinations of the common working people, so their influence will be felt for their good.

It should be remembered that the best presidents of the United States have been the weakest; and it is said the greatest reforms in England have taken place under the weakest kings. So when it is said by the advocates of high salaries that we can not get first-class men to take the offices, then we do not want them. Medium men are the best, when they have to refer all questions finally back to the people; they can not do as much harm by their want of force of character as the great executive man can by his despotism. A great many people dwell long and loud on the dignity of the common laborer, but refuse in toto to increase his wages. It is enough for him to be engaged in a noble calling ; but let a person be elected to a highly honorable office, and immediately they cry out he must have a salary sufficient to support his dignity.

This kind of logic is too thin for this age; if any one requires extra pay to keep up his dignity, it is the faithful common laborer. But he is dignified without it, so will the officer be if he faithfully attends to his duties, whether his pay is great or small. Beware of the king's counsellors and his republican prototype, who are constantly asking for increased pay to keep up the dignity of the officers, while the poor may starve, without a word from their lips to relieve their sufferings. When our centennial was being held, the foreigners came and looked on, and asked the question, where are your peasantry? Here they are. Then you have no peasantry? No, sir, not in the European sense. But the next year the order was about started in this country, and unless there is a well directed effort to prevent it, we shall have peasants here as poor and squallid as in any other country.

It is a well established fact that the greater the salaries of the officers, the greater will be the stealing appropriations and stealings without appropriations. The salaries of the officers of the government have been increasing ever since its formation. This should be stopped, and lower salaries be adopted, as above stated.

MONEY AND CURRENCY.

The government only has power to coin or make money. The senate exceeded its powers when it forced the house to accept degraded money to pay soldiers. Bonds increased in value. Mobs, tramps. The European pauper system. Money should be kept at the same price, then other articles will be governed by supply and demand in price. Do as France did, not as Germany did. National finances are learned by national experiments, not by bank financiers. England shows how a kingly aristocracy can be made. France made financial experiments to establish a republic. The objection that government should put out all the money needed is, that the officers will steal. The Rothschilds governed the war measures of Europe. The Bank of England makes merchandise of money. We should decrease the weight of the gold dollar instead of increasing the weight of the silver one to make them commercially equal. The bank has changed the interest from $2\frac{1}{2}$ to 10 per cent. since its last charter. H. H. Bryant on money. Thumb-screw finances. Paper money can save the nation in time of peace as well as in time of war.

The constitution of the United States of America gives to congress the power to coin money and issue bills of credit. Under these provisions and the pressure of the war of the rebellion when coin could not be obtained in sufficient quantities to pay the expenses of the government, large amounts of bills of credit were issued in the shape of what is called the greenback paper currency, and were received for all the dues of the government, and were at par with coin. Then came the influence of the money power of the North and Europe, which was in sympathy with the slave holders and their cotton interests, and made their power so felt upon the senators that they prevented the issue of any more greenbacks to be received for import duties. And the senate refused to let the house issue any more greenbacks that were to be taken for all dues, and under the pressure of the needs of the army and navy to put down the rebellion and to maintain the other interests of the government, the house of representatives had to succumb to the dictations of the senate; and this discredited currency was issued to pay the soldiers and sailors who were at the front shedding their blood to preserve the Union, and also to pay their friends, who were working with all their power to keep the army and navy in good condition until they wiped out the rebels and the rebellion. This was as foul a legislative despotism as was ever enacted by one of these bodies upon the other, or was ever made in this or any other country, and hardly escapes being an unconstitutional interference of the senate on the constitutional duties of the house. It certainly was a violation of its spirit. For all bills for raising revenue shall originate in the house of representatives; and this amendment to disgrace and discredit the greenback currency is a new principle to the bill, if not a new bill, and the only valid excuse I have ever heard for adopting it has been that it would turn the monied men or institutions that were luke-warm or against the continuance of our republican government to invest in the bonds of the government, because this paper currency would depreciate, so they could buy bonds at a low rate that were bearing six or seven per cent. interest. The paper currency was depreciated to thirty-five and forty cents on the dollar, and as a consequence the bonds were sold fast to such as had the means to buy them. How many rebels or half rebels invested in them I do not know; but the rebellion was crushed out. Then came the time when this degraded currency could have been received for all the dues of the government, and honored, as it was entitled to be, because of the good it had done.

It had done its full share in saving the nation; now was the time to save it from its degraded position; if it was twenty-five cents below par, then make twenty-five per cent additional tariff on imports, and the deficiency would be made good; but there was no attempt to throw off the dishonor that was cast upon it, during the war. There were no Rebels to whip, and no enemies to fear, except our own law makers, and their backers, the money monopolists and their toadies in an out of the Senate, who wished a degraded currency to be continued to enable them to obtain high interest. And they had their own way, and instead of increasing the value of the currency, they passed laws that increased the value of their bonds by making such as were issued bearing interest payable in currency, to be paid in coin, or its equivalent, by making them payable in gold, or its equivalent. That is they demonetized silver, then during all the time from the end of the war until 1877, they used every effort to contract the currency, to decrease the value of property, and increase the value of money. During that year people began to starve amidst abundance, and mobs began to cry for bread, or blood, and many lives were lost, and a large amount of property was destroyed, and the friends of the poor gained power, to stop the contraction of the currency, and succeeded in remonetizing silver.

I wish people to note that in all time befor the war, the States had chartered banks, when they were wanted, to relieve the people; but now for the first time the United States had this entire control, and it was given to a Secretary of the Treasury, who was not chosen by the people, nor responsible to them for his official acts, but to the President of the United States, and to Congress; that is, his appointment was as far removed from the people as it possibly could be, and he manifested no sympathy with them, or for them, and would heed no voice from them, until mobs made him fearful for himself and partisans.

This is the beginning of the one man power in the finances of the country; the beginning of the complete control being in the power of the Union, and the States being barred from extending financial relief to its citizens by bank charter; that is, the United States taxed such institutions out of existence. This gave the money autocrats the entire control, and the circulating medium of the country was reduced from more than fifty dollars to each person in the Union, to about thirteen dollars; when the mobs broke the contraction; but tramps had flooded the country, and the European pauper system had its beginning in this country. This plan is especially the English government plan, and has always resulted in that country in the same kind of disasters, as we had here. The French Republic has adopted the plan of keeping as full a supply of currency, as the people needed to keep all at work, and her prosperity is beyond all

precedent during hard times. But notwithstanding
these results and experiences, and the misery that
these sudden contractions of the circulating medium
always inflicts, or contraction however slow, will inflict
when it reduces the medium below the needs of the
people, to do a legitimate business. Our rulers controled by their wealthy friends, would contract the
currency with a vengeance, against the poor working
people, as great as they displayed against Rebels in
time of war; in fact the war cry is still a very potent
matter, in politics to this day; "To the victors belong
the spoils;" and now the rich had a grand victory
over the poor, and they spoiled them unmercifully.
But the time came when the poor said we may as well
be killed as starved; then came the loss of life, and the
destruction of property, and the alarm spread among
the monopolists, and they succeumed to the popular will
just as little as they could, and retain their powers,
just as the English government is in the habit of doing
when pressed in the same way.

What every honest, judicious man wants is a sufficient amount of currency and coin to enable persons
to do business on a fair legitimate basis. The amount
of money to be kept in circulation should be steady,
then the price of articles of merchandise will be regu-
lated by the supply and demand; but if the officials
have the right to contract and expand the amount of
currency as they please, and change the amount, then
money regulates the price of articles instead of demand
and supply, or there is an unfair and illegitimate basis
of trade introduced, such as belongs to shoddy traders
and shoddy politicians. Perhaps the best way to
regulate the finances will be found to be to keep about
thirty dollars out to each person in the Union, then
have three per cent. bonds to the same amount to each
person, and have it so arranged that these bonds can
be turned into currency, or used as currency; and in
a few years it could be ascertained how much currency
would be required to do the legitimate business of the

country in a legitimate way. France, according to accounts, has more than forty dollars of coin and currency in circulation to keep her industries in full operation. Americans want more, as their country is larger and her people live better and require more than any peasantry in the world.

But the scientific way to settle the question is to put out currency sufficient to set all the people at work, as France did when she was whipped by Germany, and was in great distress and laboring under a great load of debt; and the unscientific plan is to do as Germany did, demonetize silver and restrict the currency, and try to live without encouraging the industries of the country and people. There is no great financier that gained great reputation in France for taking that country through its great financial straits; they simply contrived a plan to keep the wheels of industry in motion, and specie payments were reached without a jar to the people; in fact, it made no difference to them, all their money was as good as coin all the time; but in this country sensational politicians wanted to make a reputation great as financiers, and the way for them to do it was to oppress the people by stopping their industries; and when they could not hold the people any longer, stop the oppression, encourage them to industry; and then when the people were engaged in productive business, make a great show of beginning specie payments. This was done by shoddy politicians under the influence of shoddy traders, water stock manipulators, Credit Mobilier managers and heartless bondholders, assisted by a back-pay set of congressmen.

With these persons and their sycophants our sensational treasurers have obtained a great reputation, which they could not have done unless they had first caused the European pauper labor system to be established in this country. When a person of good common sense addresses a banker or trader of some reputation for success in business, on financial matters, he is saluted by saying, you know nothing of financial matters, of banking, and the wants of trade. This may be true, but what do you know, Messrs. Banker and Trader, about the wants of the nation and the people? Where are your experiments to determine these questions among a free, intelligent, industrious, civilized people? Questions are settled by knowledge obtained by experiments, not by the dictum of the lord of a bank or of trade, or even the Lord of heaven; for the Lord of the heavens in this day says, get knowledge by experience and learn wisdom in that way, not by theory or theology, nor by command of the lords of the mannor or of the times.

England by one experiment, to prove what is wanted by a landed aristocracy, and a government aristocracy, surrounded by a trading aristocracy to be established; and the making of a hopelessly degraded national labor system, for the working people that forms a great class of pauper laborers to support these aristocracies; will give more information than all your life-time little banking and trading experiences can give, on what is wanted to establish a proud kingly or queenly aristocracy; and this experimen thas been tried in England, and they succeeded in establishing the two extremes of life in that country, the half starved poor workers, and the wealthy overfed beef eaters. And in this country little bankers and traders have been trying to establish the same things, in the same way that England has done it. But they have failed, as the northern laborers were not ready for such institutions to be fastened upon them. But England has a long line of experiments that end in the same way that the know-all bankites, and the shoddyites, and the back-payites, and waterstockites, and the Credit Mobilierites, and the great landed estateites, and the aristocratic strong governmentites, and the religiousites, who worship a God who can not take care of Himself, unless the government steps in to praise Him, and give Him subsidies, and support his priests, can refer to, to establish their claims to great consideration; and when the people of this country want a despotism in the name of a limited monarchy, the way to do it is made plain by the English experiments. And there is one experiment that England has not had for more than two hundred years; they have not had a great military commander to force these despotisms upon their country, who was at the head of the government. In this country this defect in their experiment has been supplied recently, and now whenever the people of this country want to try to make the rich richer, and the poor poorer, they will ask the British admiration societies in this country, to give us a regular English monetary experiment, with a regular English ending, and the first steps will be taken towards the consummation of their desires.

But there are other nations that have made experiments, which are worthy of consideration, by persons who wish to establish and continue a Republican government, on what relates to the financial question. France made an experiment after she became a republic, for the purpose of establishing a republic, and succeeded to the admiration of all civilized people. The fact is wonderful to relate, when we consider they had but recently been ruled by an Emperor, who had been taken prisoner by the enemy, after a short war, and part of their territory had been taken from them, and they had to pay the expenses of the war, on their own side, as well as that of the enemy, and a large amount of spoils besides; and then they had internal dissensions of a grave and expensive character. Yet with all these drawbacks, they retrieved their fortunes financially, and retained their republic

Look at this picture, then look at the English and American experiments, and see if the bankers who pretend they want a republic, and engineered our national finances, do not hang their heads in shame at their ignorance of national financiering; then they must be requested to take a back seat in national financiering, and made to feel their utter idiotic opinions in such matters. Let it be distinctly understood that the people know who makes money and what its use is; and if they want to make it, or its makers king, they will let you know, and then you little bankers and traders that silence the people by boasting of your great financial knowledge, can take the lead and make money, short and long, so as to make it take the place of demand and supply, and determine the price of articles of commerce. For national experiment after experiment have proved this.

The government has got a corner on money, and if the heartless monopolists get control of it, as they did after the war in this country, and during the war as well; but there was a little excuse for that, as noted before. Then if they pretend they want to favor the working people and republican institutions, they know it is false or they have been so long engaged in corners in wheat, stocks or other articles that they know no more of national financiers and financiering than does the corner grocery man at a scrub oak country cross-roads in the southern states; and should be put down as deluded, dangerous individuals, who are trying to establish a despotism over the people of this country, or as a people who absolutely know nothing on the subject, while boasting that they know it all.

The fact is, such people know nothing of fair, honest trade with legitimate profits. So far as experiments have been made in the civilized world, the proof is that if the currency is to be made to benefit the people generally; that is, the common working people, there must be a steady supply of a sufficient amount to allow the people to keep on with their industries; and there must be a tariff of sufficient amount on imported goods, so that the people will have their own work to do. Then if the people are industrious, as the American people are noted for being, there will be little complaint and no begging tramps, and so far as money is concerned, republican institutions are safe. But without a proper equitable supply, republican institutions are unsafe, and the true amount must be established by experiments; that is, in some way as before intimated. Prepare a plan to put out what money seems to be required, and then have government savings banks where money can be deposited at an annual interest of three per cent. or less, or have bonds at that interest; or, what is better, have both these plans before the common people, so they can put their spare money in a safe place until they want to use it. Make such plans and institutions that the sharpers that cheat and fatten on the earnings of the people shall have the fewest chances that it is possible to make, to creep into their affections and fraudulently filch their earnings from them.

In this way money will be steady, and property will be variable; money will be the standard, and property will be changeable. If money can always be obtained at three per cent., then it becomes the standard article of commerce; but if it varies from three to ten per cent, it is not, and mankind have no standard in their money, goods or chattels, or anything else in the financial line, and any one who opposes this even money plan, opposes a Republican financial system.

The limited monarchy system, or the military chieftain system, in this Republic, does not wish to have the wants of the people consulted at all. They worship gold with as little regard to its true value, as Pagans do their idols; but being limited in power, they make a currency whose interest value they change whenever they want to oppress the working people; first they may let out money and credit to a great extent on small interest; then they begin to contract and demand more interest, and soon the manufacturer fails, and the working people are thrown out of employment, and the greatest distress prevails, and the money sharks have made great fortunes, by buying goods low and selling them high. Then they commence the same tactics again, so they keep the price of money going up and down, like other merchandise, and a shoddy aristocracy is established who try to make a people believe they are doing a ligitimate business, when the fact is, they are inside the movement in the government to make money cheap, or dear, and they manage accordingly; they are simply Shylocks.

The difference between money and wheat is this: in the market wheat is quoted at so much per bushel, say, one dollar; money is quoted at such interest, say, seven per cent per anum. All merchandise is sold and delivered to the purchaser, in legitimate trade. But in regular business only the use of money is sold, the money with interest to be returned. Money is made by men, and every civilized government gets the right to make this money for its own people; and during a time of war, it is acknowledged that the government has a right to issue as much money and currency as will save the nation; but in time of peace the limited monarchist and his tribe of hangers on, will insist that money or currency should not be issued to prevent starvation mobs among the people.

The government say these wiseacres have no right to do this, and the toadies about the throne of Great Britain, and the camp followers about the government of the United States, have been enabled to bring on starvation, and enforce idleness among the people, until they could amass immense fortunes. Then they could see that the government had a right to avert the distress of people by increasing the amount of money among the people. So it is seen that the real money plan of a limited monarchy, is to have it change in interest value as frequently as they, the managers, can make money out of it, and make it merchandise instead of the standard of the value of merchandise.

The money of despotism is gold; if the people starve,

that is no concern of the despot, or the flatterers that surround him. It is not in the mind of the despot, to have a contented intelligent people surrounded with the comforts of life, but to have them his slaves; money is merchandise, and merchandise is money; interest is more like discounts, or shares on bills of credit; the despot takes the money from his subject, and then orders him killed if he makes too much fuss about it. It is a little worse than the worst phase of a limited monarchy; it is simply a military despotism carried into civil affairs. From all the considerations that have been presented, is it not plain to be seen that the true course must be to establish a currency that has a steady interest value. If we want a Republican government, look at the theories and the government experiments. I mean the English and French governments, as well as our own. Then take a common sense view of the subject.

Is the government to act like Shylock, and make corners like the modern heartless speculator? It is entrusted with the entire right and duty of making the currency of the country. Will not the people instill into it the principle that this currency shall be so managed as to benefit the whole people instead of a clique? If there is not nobility enough in our rulers to induce them to do that, then let the people hedge them around with such a force of public opinion that they will be obliged to succumb to it, and make a virtue of necessity, and never again dare to make idlers and starvation by their financial scheming.

This article would not be complete without referring to the present catch words, honest and dishonest money. This government never issued dishonest currency, unless it was done by the resolute determination of the senate of the United States, and it was continued in existence as long as they could make the people endure it. That was currency that the government would not receive for all dues. Did a majority of these proud stock-jobbing senators say when the war was over that the government and people were one, and this money should be received by the people for all dues, just as they did all the time, and by the government for all dues? No. They said to the people, you shall receive the money, but the government shall not. No majority of that body said that the government and the people were one, and sink or swim, live or die, survive or perish, they would take the money as the people did for all dues. Who will say that the credits of this country were not as good, or even better, than gold, only when the rebels under Buchanan or the senate of the United States ruled the currency of the nation? The rebels stole all the cash and credits that they could lay their hands on, and the Credit Mobilier and back-pay senators followed their example as near as they could. But the people have finally forced them to make it as good as gold, and better, and now interest is about three per cent. for the government. Let us insist that it shall be made the same for the people, and kept so. When any one says that it can not be done, say to them man makes money, and governments made by man force the people to take this money in payment of their debts.

This is wholly man's work, and the whole matter is in man's power and under his control; and if the people will elect officers who are in favor of having a law passed to have the value of money three per cent. always, it can be done as well as they could make the money to pay the expenses of the war. The only objections I have ever heard to the government putting out all the bills of credit that the people require is that dishonest, thieving officials will put out more money than they account for; that is a real objection. It is well known that persons with large salaries will steal largely, directly and indirectly, as the rebels did. The back-pay congressmen and the star postal route employes prove this; but still if the government paid out all the bills of credit the people wanted, and got two per cent. for it instead of eight or ten per cent., as bankers now get on their debts, the people would gain vastly more than the thieves would steal, or than the losses would be to the government. The experiments should be made as carefully as possible, and see if the people who work can not be protected from the wheat gamblers, the stock gamblers, and the greatest curse of all, the money gamblers.

It is said these money monopolists have power to expand and contract the currency so as to affect the values of other articles materially, and that the government is playing into their hands to enable them to do it. It was said a few years ago that the governments of Europe dare not go to war unless they could get the promise of funds from the Rothschilds; it is not said to be true now. It is about time this Union got out of the hands of private speculators in time of peace. It is a pitiable condition of things for a government like this Union, while paying millions of its debts annually, and millions upon millions more of the expenses of the government, and besides millions upon millions more as bounties and pensions, and yet have its finances so miserably managed that a few wealthy men can make a panic, or a great flush of money, when they join for the purpose, and can make merchandise of money and have it vary in price as much as wheat and cotton. Any set of officers of the government that will allow that, are very ignorant of their duties, or very dishonest. Government experiments have abundantly proved this.

When a government wishes to make the rich richer and the poor poorer, like Great Britain, they will give the money-making power into the hands of corporations and individuals, and they will make ups and downs in the price of money to enrich individual managers and speculators; but if they wish to make a good government for good working people, as the republic of France did, they will issue their money and keep up a steady supply to keep the industries going, so the people will always have a good chance to get a good living by fair, faithful work. It is the habit of the managers of the Bank of England to make merchandise of money, and increase and decrease the price of it, according to the demand.

There is a great outcry against fiat money at this time; but every government declares its legal tender money fiat money. The creditor must take it in payment of his demands, unless he makes a special contract otherwise. It does not make any difference whether the money is gold, silver or paper, or any other article. A person can not make a legal tender of gold, silver or paper unless it has the stamp of the government on it. When that stamp is on it the tender is legal, not otherwise; and the value of contracts of whatever character must be estimated by their legal money, if settled by a court of equity or law, if the special property named in the contract can not be obtained and delivered.

It is universally acknowledged that there is not gold and silver enough in the world to enable the people and governments to do the business of the world, and then it is too heavy and cumbersome for people to handle easily, so paper is substituted in the transaction of the greatest amount of business. Yet these metals, when converted into money, are the basis of this paper currency in theory; in practice, credit is two-thirds of the basis at least, and the coin metalic is one-third, or less. Now, as there is a great difference in the present value of a coined dollar in silver and one of gold, in a mercantile sense, the question arises, shall we increase the weight of the silver dollar about fifteen cents, or decrease the weight of the gold dollar fifteen cents, so as to make the metal in each of the same value? The answer to these questions will be just according to the kind of government that the individual wants who answers it. If he wants a despotism in the shape of an unlimited monarchy, or a limited one, with moneyed aristocracy to dictate its terms, they will wish to increase the weight of the silver dollar; but if they are in favor of an equal rights republic, and wish to benefit the hard working people generally, they will favor the decreasing of the weight of the gold dollar, and make its value agree with the silver dollar commercially.

It may be said this is not fair on the creditor class, the bond holders and bankers who have one dollar, owe two, and get interest on three. But there is an offset to their loss; first, all have a lighter and more convenient metalic currency, and second, inventions are constantly increasing the value of a dollar by making articles of productions cheaper, that are required to sustain life. But if the silver dollar is increased in weight, it makes a more cumbersome currency, and tends to impoverish the workers and enrich the idlers. And the question is: shall we encourage the idlers in their folly instead of the workers in their useful labors?

At present it seems Great Britain and Germany refuse to remonetize silver, because they wish to establish or continue an idle, extravagant and expensive aristocracy; while Republican France and America wish to do away with such expensive and showy lords and ladies, and to prevent the existence of a half starved, half clad working class of people who live in hovels in the shadow of the palaces of the idlers. They will unite with all nations which will join them and reduce the gold dollar to the same or less than the silver dollar; then they will put out paper money based on the credit of the nation, and the amount of gold and silver coin in their possession; and make this paper money legal tender for all the dues of the government and all that is due to individuals, States, and corporations under the government. And when the Republics and others who wish to establish the economical principles which characterize Republics that are administered in the interest of the working people, and they are united in such a currency, and are ready to settle their differences with England and

Germany, and other aristocratic nations, who are governed by tyrants and monopolists, by bullion, as they have to now, we will soon see which nations have the most contented masses of people, and where the gold will be the most abundant.

It will soon be seen that the wealth will be with the home of the free, industrious, saving people, just as it was found that the people of the northern states were by great odds more wealthy than the people of the southern states before slavery was abolished. When war prevails, there must be money enough issued to put it down, just as was done by the United States of America in the time of the war of the rebellion; and when the war is ended, there must be money enough issued by the goverment, to give the people a chance to work, as was done by France, after her war with Germany. If the French government had given its currency into the hands of pet banks and monopolists, as did the United States; they would have made idlers, and tramps, as America did. But instead of that, they kept the monetary matters in the hands of the government, and issued money, and kept their people at work; and while Germany, England, and the United States and other rich countries were suffering by a stringency in money, and while their poor industrious people in ordinary times, were suffering for want of work, for food and clothes, and were turned into beggars, and tramps, the French workers were bussy and felt none of the hard times, and they paid their debt fast enough to keep up their credit. This was one of the most creditable pieces of financiering that was ever done by any government in this world; if not decidedly the most creditable. Why do not other governments go and do like-wise?

This is a very important question, and requires a very considerate answer. First, Great Britain is a kingdom and an Empire, and requires great revenues to support a kingly and imperial family. Second, next comes the crown officers, and imperial advisers under the general name of Ministers of State, who must have names of great honor, and great salaries for little work. Then third comes the great landed proprietors, lords, and ladies, who form a nobility that surrounds and supports the crown, and its officials, to a great extent, and keeps the farmer and his laborers poor.

Then fourth comes the begging religious priesthood with their immense salaries, wrung from the work of the peasants, by law and force, by appeals to their generosity and by threatening eternal punishments to the unbelievers that only brutalized minds could make; and thousands of these salaried religious priests are giving their voice to support the crown in all its extravagance.

Then fifth comes the money power; this crowns the control and makes every manufacturer and merchant look to the Bank of England for the price of money. This bank is put into the hands of the most unscrupulous money sharpers and traders, called financiers and capitalists; and since 1844, when it was rechartered and reorganized, it has changed the interest from $2\frac{1}{2}$ to 10 per cent. to enrich the money lender and impoverish the manufacturer and merchant, and make starvation prices for the hard worked laborers of the country; and between these the grinding of the face of the poor has been unscrupulous. Such has been the work of the law-making power of England; and the house of lords and their bishops are the special champions of these laws for torturing the poor laborers, the same as the senate of the United States is in this Union; and it is the most corrupt and corrupting legislative body of the Union, and always must remain so as long as it follows the principles of the house of lords in England, and joins the land monopolists and the corporate and private bank and money monopolists and the railroad extortioners, to torture the working people by starvation wages, as they did from 1869 to 1878.

This is treated of in another place. But if any one wishes to learn how such things are done on a great scale, let them turn to the testimony before the secret committee appointed by the house of lords and commons to investigate into the causes of the financial crash in that country in 1847. See article eight of Bryant on Money, by H. H. Bryant, Boston, Mass., or refer to the evidence taken by the committee especially. The testimony of the bank officers before them, Mr. John H. Palmer, a director of the bank and made its governor, said of the contraction to keep up specie payments: "It destroys the labor of the country. In the manufacturing districts you can hardly move without hearing the universal complaint of want of employment." It has changed the price of money hundreds of times to enrich the bankers and the nobility and money lenders, and impoverish the people.

These are the financial thumb-screws instituted by church and state to punish and put down the enterprising, energetic but poor manufacturers and merchants, and to keep the poor laborers on less than half fare, and keep them ignorant and superstitious; and the laws that give the bank officers these powers should be put in the tower of London with the thumb-screws used by the church and state to punish people who thought for themselves, and published their thoughts.

These are the financial implements of torture in full use in England, and partly introduced in Germany, and that has been commenced to be introduced in America. It is the church and state thumb-screw party of financiers, and they have no more sympathy for working people than the thumb-screw priests had for unbelievers in past centuries. And there is no more reason for torturing the working people by hunger to enrich speculators and bank officers, than there was for the priests to torture them by thumb-screws in the past. It is an unreasonable, heartless set of monsters that will do such deeds of horror for mere gain or power.

What kind of a political economist is he who stops the industries of the country, to enrich a few nobles, bankers, and money lenders, while the whole people, and the country, are made poorer, by the operation? Just think of a million working people being made idlers, by a stringency in the currency, caused by the bank of England; it is a loss of a million of dollars every day to the country; this is well known to all the noted financiers of the country. When the workmen strike for higher wages, these wise financial men will exclaim, what a great loss to workmen, and the world. But when they make such a state of things to secure a thousand dollars, when the country loses by the million, they pronounce it right; and a necessary financial measure, and the idleness of the people a God-send, rather than a curse.

The fact is, the commerce of England is now in the power of the bank of England, when before the present charter, it was in the power of the legislature. It has substituted twenty-four directors, and a governor, and deputy governor, of the bank, for the executive and legislative power of England. Now let us see what these irresponsible directors have done, since they have had control. On an average they have changed the price of money about every fifty days. Just compare this with the changes in the price of money, when the government of England had control, for the one hundred and fifty-one years, before the present bank of England charter was granted; the changes occurred nearly six years apart, or only twenty-seven times in that period.

This will give the reader a very clear idea, of the class of men who were given control of the money market in England, and it may be stated that they are as good money lenders, and controllers as any country can produce. This class of citizens have the worst reputation of any intelligent well educated persons in every country, except the priests; they will torture people to get their money, almost as horribly as priests will to make them follow them, in their religious opinions. The person who said the love of money was the root of all evil, did not know every thing; the love of superstition has the greatest and worst record; and other loves that might be mentioned, come close up to the evils of the love of money.

But their reputation is bad enough to make any fair minded statesman hesitate a long time before giving them the control of the money of the nation.

It is curious to note that some American statesmen object to the government having control of the money, because they may at times issue more than is required for the use of the people. Does any such man believe that the statesman would want to change the value of the money every fifty or sixty days, have it 2 ½ per cent. one day, and 10. per cent. the next, then 5 per cent., then 8, then 4 per cent., as the managers of the bank of England have had it?

There is no doubt that there are a few wealthy senators who would gladly do it; but there is a large class of representatives who would not allow it; and while the money is in the hands of the government, where the constitution puts it, the price of money will not be allowed to vary much, now that the people are aroused to the enormity of the crime of doing it. For it is well known that to change the price of money is one of the most heinous crimes in the calendar that is not reckoned a crime by the laws of the country. The particular duty of the government is to give us money that it will take for all its dues, and then money will be as good as its bonds are, or as good as the credit of the country is.

We do not want any more of the degraded greenback currency that the senate forced upon the country in 1862, and kept in circulation until 1880—such that they force people to receive and will not take for all the dues of the government. Such a currency falls far below the credit of the government, and gives the money sharks a constant theme to harp upon about the failure and disgrace of a paper currency. Give the people of the government money that has as good credit as they make for the government, and the people will ask no better, and no fair-minded man will ask for better.

I have not mentioned the suspensions of specie payments by the Bank of England, because it is not important. The bank has not suspended since 1844, when it was re-chartered and reorganized; but to accomplish this, it has found it necessary to change the price of money every fifty or sixty days on an average. Now the question to be settled in the United States of America is, shall we have a national pet bank system to change the price of money every few days, and occasionally make it so dear as to stop commerce, manufactories, and starve the laborers into mobs, as was done in 1877, or shall we let the United States government give out its money to bridge over these stringencies, as they did in the war of the rebellion, and as England did in the great war with Napoleon Bonaparte? It is a curious kind of logic that says you can bridge over a war necessity and panic by paper money and can not do it in the time of peace when there is a financial want and panic.

The persons who will say that this nation can not do one of these wants, as well as the other, are ready to grasp the vitals of this government and for a little gain destroy it, and establish a money despotism in its place. But the nation shall live; and the people shall say so, and panics and war shall be crushed by paper as they have been, before, and the money despots shall weep and gnash their teeth in agony because they must work for a living like men of toil. They must get their living by the sweat of their own brow, as grimy working people do now.

TAXES.

Good Republican people willingly pay taxes if they are just, if not, they oppose paying them. Church property exemptions has caused great wickedness. Henry Eight of England. The Republic of France confiscated church lands. If any person's property is exempted, it should be inventors. But all property should be taxed. Extra taxes on great landed estates, and great incomes. Great estates made the Rebellion. All should pay taxes that have property, or incomes from salaries, or any other source.

TAXES are paid by an independent people willingly from their abundance, to support a government that they love and respect, or they are levied upon an unwilling people, by an unjust government that they hate because of its oppressions, and the poverty it imposes on the people; and because of the unjust manner of assessing them. And then great numbers of the people, who have large estates, oppose being taxed fairly with other property that surrounds theirs, for the purpose of keeping up a just Republican government, with the schools, courts, records, and all the necessary offices, and officers of a civilized intelligent government, for the protection of life and property, among the people.

Many very wealthy persons act as though they thought the government expenses should be paid by the poor who can not hide their property, or incomes, while they should have their property exempted from all taxation. There is a constant struggle going on in this country to have this privileged class of untaxed property-holders exempted, the same as they are in a limited monarchy, and there has been great success in having them go free.

These persons are generally very contentious, have a great many law suits, make the country great expense, and will pay as little to foot these bills as possible. These persons stand as the last relics and hulks of the despotic governments still struggling to hold to all the little despotisms that remain in the forms and practices of the governments of this Union.

These statements will serve to show the difficulties that assessors of taxes have to contend with in making up a just tax roll. Besides all the personal difficulties and the influence that these persons have upon the assessors, to prevent them from making a just assessment, there are other considerations of vast importance that make the laws unjust upon which assessments are founded.

From the beginning of despotic governments, religion was a part of the government, and the government and religion claimed alike exemptions of their property; and this exemption has continued to this day, notwithstanding there is a pretended separation of church and state in this country. If any one will examine into the history of the immense estates of the religionists of past ages in Europe, and the corruptions and crimes they committed to get property and power, and their final overthrow and the confiscation of their immense estates for the benefit of the governments, and the people, because the intelligence of the people had out grown the teachings of the priests, and rebelled against their barbarisms ; and the confiscation came with all the horrors of war with which these pious priests resisted, being deprived of their immense estates and power; and the bloody revolutions which have deprived them of these estates will again occur, unless they are taxed like any other individual and company property.

It was the church property of the Roman order confiscated by Henry the Eighth that enabled that monarch to revolutionize the religion of England. It was the confiscation of the immense church property of France that enabled that Republic to revolutionize the government of France, and finally all the governments of Europe, and bring them on to the common sense principles of modern times ; which really relegates all religious people to teaching their religion, and letting governments alone. This has not been fully accomplished, but it has laid the foundation so deep among an intelligent people that the final result must soon come to be an established fact, or the religion must harmonize with the government. And the immense estates now held in this country by the various religious orders obtained of the poor and needy, or from gifts, obtained by political chicanery many times from towns, cities, states and the nation, can not be continued untaxed without causing great excitement among intelligent people who know how unjustly much of the property was obtained, and how false the teachings are well known to be ; such as: In six days God made the heavens and earth, and all things therein, and the seventh He rested. As in Adam all die, so in Christ shall all be made alive. The stars of heaven shall fall on the earth; and such kinds of well known falsehoods and nonsense are taught to the children, and ignorant and superstitious people in a solemn voice, as though they were truths of great importance for them to learn and know. And the divines who are teaching these ancient falsehoods, instead of the modern, well known, well proved truths, request the people to exempt their gospel shops from taxes, and their superstitious and infamous followers join them in this request; such followers as join them for their trade, popularity, or loaves and fishes of any kind.

Shall they be paid for so solemnly, flippantly and many times insultingly setting aside the teachings of Geology, Astronomy, Chemistry, and Spiritualism, and their corelated material, and spiritual sciences? for the ancient and false theories and assertions is not only a crime, not to be paid for by giving them taxes to a large amount, but should have extra tax to pay if any mountebanks are to be taxed extra. For I will defy any man to point out any other class of persons called mountebank deceivers that have committed so many such great crimes, as the priests have; and nothing prevents them from doing the same now, only the intelligence of the people. It would be vastly better for all the people of this country, to tax the gospel shops of the preachers, and all their real estate, as they tax other shops and people; only if any were exempted it should be the inventors' shop; the real great, and useful personage of this day is the inventor and discoverer; persons who are peering into the secrets of nature, and making the modern inventions and discoveries that have distinguished this age, as the best the people have ever seen in this world.

But the best plan is to tax all property, except such as belongs to the public, at the same rate upon its appraised value, except large amounts of real estate owned by one man ; and great incomes which should be taxed more; and besides that, it seems from the experiments tried, that in addition to the property tax, there should be a personal tax upon every adult person who has the right to the elective franchise; and unless that personal tax is paid, the person should not have the right to cast his or her vote at the governmental elections. Let no exemptions be allowed in this particular; and the vote will represent the real supporters of the government. Tobacco and Alcoholic liquors have been taxed extra, because their use often runs into such abuse that they produce sickness, poverty, crime, and premature death. A graduated income tax should be assessed on persons who have large incomes, because they tend to make rich idlers, and an over-worked, impoverished, ignorant laboring class of people. It gives the possessors too great a power over the working people, to be permitted in a Republic, unless a tax is collected of them to be expended to support the poor in time of need. But the greatest curses to a Republic, are the great estates in land.

The land monopolists of the South caused the rebellion, and now excite mobs and murders there, to prevent citizens from voting. They have destroyed the Republic there, and will all over the Union, unless the large landed estates, North and South, are broken up. There should be a large extra tax, per acre, annually upon all the land one person owns, over five hundred acres; and when the tax is not paid, it should be sold to actual settlers, in small quantities, and thus the rebellious owners of great landed estates be sold out; and this tax should also be reserved to support the poor in time of need.

There is no class of people in the ordinary walks of life, that should be more liable to taxation, than office holders, especially those who receive a thousand dollars or more a year; not half of them lay by anything from their salaries, and when they lose their salaries, they become dependent on their friends, or the public; they have so long been living in a careless easy life, that they have become unfitted for the stern realities of life, and they naturally belong to a beggarly class that surround persons who have offices to bestow; and when they get offices, they become a useless class, only for hireling clerks. They belong to the class of shirks who naturally take all possible pains to avoid the hard work of life. They are the Jews of the community, who have not sense enough to combine to support each other in time of need. So the government should step in and take a part of their salaries to prepare homes for them, where they can earn a living, by six hours work a day, when well, and be taken care of when sick.

The Presidents' salaries have been raised from twenty-five thousand, to fifty thousand a year. This raise should be legislated in the fund for the support of the indigent in homes, by their complying with the just rules necessary to make a good home among these; the principle is a careful attention to the duties of life, in society, and faithfully performing six hours of useful labor per day. I make six hours the day's work, because clerks in the departments at Washingington D. C. have that number of hours for a day's work, and it is no more destructive to life and health, to write more hours per day, than it is to shovel dirt more; and as the workers in dirt must exist to make a nation; but a nation can exist without any persons being set apart simply to write.

Next to the great curses of a nation, of great landed estates, and great incomes to individuals; is the payment of great salaries to the officers of the government. When a nation is poor, the pay of officers is small; but as the people as a whole become rich, they increase the pay of the officers, and this increase is apt to be spent in luxury and dissipation, and the really poor are made poorer; how to stop this instead of increasing their salaries, they should appropriate to the fund for making homes for those who need them, and will do their work in homes provided for them.

COMMON SCHOOLS.

The only hope of a just government. The Revolution in England in 1648. In France 1789. Rebellion in America, 1861. The thumb screw. Bastile. Andersonville.

The only hope of ever having a highly civilized and humane society generally in a nation, with just Republican laws and institutions, is based upon the general intelligence accquired in the common schools of the country. Wherever the people generally are without this training information, they are ignorant and superstitious and base, and the governing class over them are deceitful and brutal, and barbarous. This is shown by the barbarisms enacted by the grandees of England to prevent the revolution of 1648, when the commonwealth was established under Cromwell. But is displayed to a greater degree in France in the Revolution of 1789.

Here the barbarities and brutalities of the ruling class to prevent the revolution ; and of the baseness and spite of the people and their blood thirsty demand for revenge on their brutal rulers, is displayed with the greatest plainness, and shows that the highest and lowest in the nation were governed by the most barbarous and revengeful feelings. And is manifested still more clearly by the rulers and people of the Southern States of this Union, in their Rebellion in 1861.

The brutalities of the leaders, and rulers in that Rebellion, could not have been practiced if the people generally had been educated in common schools. They could not have instituted the barbarities of Castle Thunder, and Andersonville. Wherever you find a people who burn their school houses, and strip off the clothing, and tar and feather their female school teachers ; you may expect the leaders and rulers of that people are barbarians in practice.

The only hope of ever overcoming the class of brutal rulers of the people that used the thumb screws of England, the bastile of France, and the Andersonville tortures of America, is that all the people shall have the advantages of a common school education. Then it will become impossible for such rulers to practice their barbarities for any length of time; in fact it is almost impossible for them to be elected to office at all. And by this means a humane government will be established and a humane religion.

CRIMINALS AND INSANE.

All criminals may be considered insane. The law nearly makes them so. They should be treated in the most humane manner by the most efficient plan to bring them to their senses. Pagans, Jews and Christians would clear criminals when bewitched, but when not, their punishments were senseless and cruel. Devils can not act as bad as men, because they have neither body or parts. Our criminal laws are based too much on ancient superstitions. Our physicians in insane asylums have proved in many cases inhuman, and many officials in work houses and penitentiaries are as inhuman as they can be. Whether scientific religionists will be as cruel, must be tried to be known. Governments have instituted experiments to show the best methods of reforming the criminals. The magnetic and spiritual forces must not be neglected in curing the insane.

I put these two classes of persons under one heading because in the practice of law the greatest criminals are pronounced innocent if they are insane, and kleptomania or stealing is a well known disease afflicting many persons, and it is very afflicting to the neighbors of the diseased. And the question arises, are there any criminals that are not insane? But there is another question of vastly more importance, shall all criminals be treated as insane persons? Lawyers are ready with their insane dodge, or plea of insanity, to have criminals that are really guilty of some criminal offence, let off with little or no punishment because they were out of their sane minds and in an insane condition. Whenever such a plea is made, that is an acknowledgement of the committing of the crime, and should be considered the same as a plea of guilty, and the punishment to be inflicted on the criminal, and the protection to be given to society, must be considered in the judgment just the same in one case as in the other, if a large majority of the criminals are inspired by an insane sentiment to do the evil.

It may be best to say all criminals are, and all should be treated by the proper remedial agents, and work and food that will bring them to a realizing sense of the mistake they had made, and the confinement, and their work, and their treatment, should be upon the most humane and approved plan that experience has proved to be best, to make the criminals good citizens, and bring the insane to their right mind.

It has been the practice of Jews, Pagans and

Christians when insane people, or people not insane, who did criminal or insane deeds, and said they were bewitched, to hang the witches instead of the criminals. But when the criminals did not make the plea of witchery the law officers would accuse them of being instigated by the devil to do the evil deeds, and then the insane or criminal person must be punished because the devil was wandering about the earth unseen, or in heaven fighting the hosts of God, or in hell stirring up his imps to more active work in keeping things hot; or he was out of the way some where so they could not punish him, and they had to punish the poor devil-deluded creature.

In case of witches the real criminal could be reached and punished; but when the devil instigated the crime they could not reach the criminal, but only the innocent victim of the devil, and then laws made this innocent person the victim, and so the innocent became the double victim of men and devils; and so far as modern information goes, it is proved that the men were the most cruel and infamous. For the devil is proved to be a creature of the imagination, and although the mind of man has made him as bad as it could, he does not lack in any criminal desires, designs, or interests; but as he has neither body, mind nor existence, only in the imagination of people, and consequently could not torture and murder criminals as men could, people can make a devil as bad as they are, but they can not make him act as bad, because he is like the christian's God, without body or parts.

All our criminal laws came through religious governments, and were based upon superstitions that prevailed among the people; and although the old superstitious forms are not now used, still the evils of their estimate of crime, and criminals, and the way to reform criminals in our jails and prisons, are too much in force at present; and now is the time to eliminate from our laws, or criminals, and insane people, every vestige of the religious superstitions both in the crimes they commit, and the way to use them to correct their criminal or insane actions in life.

The conduct of a great many of our most honored and eminent physicians at the head of insane asylums, have been proved the most inhuman of wretches in their treatment of the insane under their charge. They have proved as bad in a small way, as the christian priests have on a large scale; human nature with similar sentiments is the same. The reports of committees of the various state legislatures prove these statements to be true; and then the conduct of penitentiary officials and house of corrections, have proved them to be of the same heartless stamp; whether people who adopt the scientific religion will be as inhuman as the superstitious, is a question to be settled by experience; but there is one thing certain, they can not behave worse, because worse conduct can not be done; savages do not excell them in savage tortures.

When we examine into the minds of people, and determine what is the basis of them, we can not only find out what makes the peculiar phases of insanity and crime in certain individuals, but what makes the most highly educated and honored individuals inhuman wretches. Every person has in his head the organs of acquisitiveness, combativeness, and destructiveness, or in other words of savagery, and if these are allowed to take the control of individuals it makes them savages when engaged in peaceful pursuits, but the greatest commanders in time of war; and this class of persons will always be in high and responsible positions in peace and war, as long as a church militant and state militant exist; and a church militant will exist, as long as the states exempt their property from taxation, and as long as our peaceful assemblies are allowed to be opened by the prayers and supplications of the priests of the church militant, or while these priests have any commanding influence over the people.

In all persons' heads there are organs of benevolence and justice, or in other words of humanity, and when people get on the humane plain of life, these organs will come to the front, and persons acting under their influence will receive the highest honors; but as long as savage acts and habits receive the greatest honors and endowments, we may expect people will educate themselves to get those honors, and we must find such persons at the head of our insane and criminal institutions, and have such reports of the enormities of their deeds as we have had. The humane hope that soon the time will come, when the people generally will be on the side of humanity, and the savagery of war will not be a necessity, at least in our humane institutions.

The criminals and the patients have the same faculties as have their physicians and overseers; and humane treatment to be restored to a sound mind, or to a just appreciation of the rights of others will be just as necessary as a humane public sentiment is to have the most intelligent and humane persons appointed to have charge of them. As long as these persons receive their appointments because of their religious sentiments and praying habits, instead of their real worth in filling the office, there will be little progress in the humanitarian practices in these institutions. But amidst all the wilderness of religious fanaticism, governments have here and there appointed persons to put in practice the best principles to make our worst criminals the best of citizens, and some of the most hopelessly insane to become sane and useful citizens.

The first and great idea is that the persons be employed to do some useful work. There are a great many people in the world who have the insane notion that the world owes them a living, whether they earn it or not. This idea is legitimate from the theories and practices of religions and governments, who give great rewards for little labor, and little rewards for long and hard toil. When these practices are enacted before the people daily, it makes the criminal out of the resolute, to resist being killed by hard work, while others are luxuriating in ease and plenty, on their toil. Then again they see so much rascality and abuse of power among the idlers that they think it is a greater sin to toil patiently for their support, as well as their own, than it is to be robbers and steal from them, instead of supporting them.

When such persons are imprisoned for their criminal deeds, the first thing to be done is to make them willing to do their share of work, as society is now constituted. The state, nation and society have imposed great wrongs upon this class, the working people, by making their hours of work longer than is necessary. It is well known that more work can be done now in six hours than could be done in ten hours fifty years ago. The president of the United States will not discharge an official who will not enforce the eight hour law upon workmen, but the man who refuses to work ten hours per day will be summarily discharged by the official.

It does not require more than half the hours of labor to get a living now, that it did fifty years ago, but the masters of the laborers still wish to enforce the same amount upon them; and this great wrong makes criminals of the working people, who say they will not stand it; and some are lucky to act as their masters have, and steal their way up to an independent idleness by law; but the great majority fail and get into prison. Now to reform them is the great talk, and the reformation consists in making them willing to do their share of the work that is assigned to workers generally. The idea is that we wish to enforce upon them the habits of industry, which they will not enforce on themselves. This idea has been entertained by benevolent, practical men, and governments have given them power over penal institutions, and their success in making good citizens out of the

damp muggy atmosphere. The old Capitol with its beautiful buildings, might do very well for a winter congress of the delegates of nations to agree upon what should be international laws, and to settle national disputes, and they could stay as much longer as they thought they could enjoy the Malaria of the place. It is possible that there may be found as wild and desolate a country somewhere within a hundred or two miles of the center of the continent as was Washington when that was selected to become the Capitol, and more romantic; and have greatly the advantage of it in every other respect that can be thought important in this matter.

RAILROADS AND THEIR MANAGEMENT.

Railroad kings have been made lately as fast as little kings of states were formerly. They mark the modern from ancient times. They show what the new earth must be. And ancients had no just idea of the power of Angels, or their spirit-Gods. Men do the works that they supposed their Gods must do. The Railroads were built by means given by the people generally, and by appropriations of congress and of states, but they have got into the spoilers' hands, and they oppressed the working people until mobs stopped them; and these magnates have caused the most bloody riots of poor people in this country. Railroads should be taxed to make homes for their workmen. Railroad corporations have no souls to damn, nor bodies to be kicked.

TELEGRAPH CORPORATIONS

Should be subject to the same kind of laws.

MINERS AND MANUFACTURERS.

Giving to the poor is not as good as giving work at fair wages. The giving should be made by taxes, on just principles. Common schools are supported by a common tax. Rebels to Republicanism are found where the school is not. The working poor want attention as much as the poor children.

Railroads have become immense institutions in this

country; and in fact in all civilized countries in the world, they have become of great importance; within the last fifty years, railroad kings and magnates have been made as fast as they made little government kings and magnates in other countries before that time. The great uses of these roads can hardly be estimated, it is a modern invention that improves the condition of high, low, rich, and poor, especially those who wish to travel on land. But this is not all, every convenience of life that comes from a distance, is brought to our doors in better condition than was ever done before by land conveyance.

This invention alone is sufficient to separate the old times from the new. It is the special mark that all can see, that makes a new earth, and a new heaven as well; for it makes the earth more blessed, and the heavens appear more bright; and when we add all the other inventions of this age, and the past, and all the comforts that follow from them to mankind, it is easy to understand that another God is ruling the minds of man, and that it is the true God that is good to his creatures, and gives them all more knowledge of the secret forces of nature by which the heavens and earth are ruled; and man can find more happiness than was ever obtained before; and shows distinctly how a heaven can be established on earth, if we obey the true God of law, whom we have obeyed to get these inventions into practical use in the world.

When we look over the old chronicles and prophets prophesying that there would be a new heaven, we find they knew absolutely nothing of the physical heaven and earth, or the spirits of heaven. They did not think that the new earth would be made by man, by his knowledge of the laws of nature that surrounded them. They expected that the God that made the heavens and earth in six days, had left the earth and would come down out of the heavens in gorgeous trappings and in great glory accompanied by all his holy angels. They did not suspect that the angels of God were the laws that ruled the heaven and earth, and were unseen, and known only by their effects on the heavens and earth, and the people and creations of earth. The angels which they saw and felt and thought under their God were all powerful, when really known men are found to have no power over these laws only as these laws give them power; nature's laws made the angels and Gods of the ancients, but they did not make them bigger and more powerful than themselves to govern them, but they made them subject to their power ; and never was the true God worshipped in so true a way before as he was in the studying of these laws and turning of their powers to benefit mankind ; and yet the ancient religious worshippers, or the modern worshippers, according to the ancient religion, will call it devil worship or no worship at all, because there was no formal prayer or wordy worship that the old religionists considered so essential in worshipping their God. But the God of the modern inspiration of the inventor and of modern thought does not need any such formal worship.

In this connection comes the conflict. The ancient religions gave all the benefits of the work and inventions to their gods, or to the priests, or to a lucky family ; but the modern religions give all these benefits to the poor workers and their assistants who work for the poor and down-trodden sufferers of humanity. The theory of the christians is that the rich should give all they have to the poor. This so overdoes the matter that persons of common sense treat it as a joke, or as a senseless, glittering generality. So in practice we find the christian clutching all he can get, and asking for more. The railroads were built principally by the people of the country by taking stock, giving farm mortgages, or from getting appropriations of land ; and then again generally when the managers had obtained all they could get in that way, the roads were mortgaged, and in a short time after the roads were finished the mortgages were foreclosed and all the stock holders and farm mortgagers in this way lost their property in the roads; and they became profitable to the owners; and then the officers increased the stock by a money-making management called watering the stock; they have amassed immense fortunes just as honestly as mock auction, Indian agents, and shoddy dealers have amassed theirs; and in this way we have the railroad kings and magnates who have great power over large numbers of working men, that they pay less than living prices for their work. All this has been done before, and is the common practice among the rich who have power over the poor in christian lands, and is said to be worse in other lands; and this would have gone in their case as well as in others, only these magnates carried the matter so far that their workmen began to suffer for bread; and then the cry arose, bread or blood; and thousands upon thousands of dollars worth of property was destroyed, and these magnates with the millions upon millions of wealth in their hands have laid upon them the disgrace of causing the first bloody, destructive riots of poor people, to any great extent, in this country, that commenced the tramp system on an extensive scale, and shows how anxious they are to introduce the pauper labor system of Europe into this country.

When a person takes into consideration many of the cheats and swindles of the railroad magnates in getting the ownership of the roads and then their heartless management after they have got them, on the laborers, giving them pauper labor wages, and then making them labor more hours than men can stand it to work, and then finally paying no regard to humane calls until mobs were commenced; they would not even pay them the meager sums that they had agreed to, until forced by fear. That is, they would not pay them only after long delay, and at irregular intervals of time. When all their infamous deeds are considered from the time they commenced to get possession of the roads and all their fixtures until they caused the mobs and the great destruction of property and lives, any one can see that there is a demand for laws to be made to force them to pay a tax to put by for a time of need, so that laborers shall be well used, and fairly paid; and if they are not, the State or United States should have this reserve fund on hand to help them through, and also have some power to look into the management of the officials who caused the distress.

If corporations have no bodies to be kicked nor souls to be damned, as asserted in old laws, the officers may have; but it would be hard to find some of their souls, and even their bodies disappear when some of their rascalities are exposed. From every consideration of their history and the history of human nature, and the necessity to protect the weak against the abuses of the strong, and the rich from starving the poor, the State or Nation should not only lay up a fund for the laborer in time of need, but these railroad corporations especially should build homes for the old and worn out workers in their employ, and for the injured who are disabled so as to prevent them from doing their duty.

It should be remembered that these roads are built in all sections of the Union. They extend from ocean to ocean, across the continent, and from the gulf of Mexico to the northern limits of the Union; and all these extended lines are fast getting into few hands; and they control an immense power, and they have proved unscrupulous in the use of it; and now is the time to prepare men's minds for the changes in the laws which the new earth demands. If the faithful laborers are allowed to be oppressed, as the laborers of Europe have been, the greatest curse that can come upon a country will be visited on this—the destruction of a contented, laboring class of people. But if it ever does come here, it will be greatly the blame of the laborers themselves, as they form a great majority of the voting population; and when the elective franchise is extended to women the same as to men, it will show that the laborers are determined never to have the pauper labor system inaugurated in this land.

In some kinds of business the well paid and well housed laborers of this country come in competition with the poorly paid and poorly housed laborers of other countries. But in railroads there is no such competition; it is wholly a matter in the hands of the government and the people; and if these laborers are left to be oppressed by soulless corporations, it will be evident that persons have wormed, or bought, or got themselves into power, that have no sense of justice or sympathy with the faithful laborers of the country. The hours of labor should be fixed by law, and their wages be sufficient to enable them to live in accord with American working people generally.

TELEGRAPH COMPANIES

Should be subject to the same kind of laws as the railroad companies—they are co-extensive and wholly on the American soil, that this government has to deal with; and there must at all times be persons that can be employed only occasionally, and are very much needed in case of emergency where operators fail in cases of sickness or other disability, or a great press of business. This occurs in all business, and it is not a good plan to have these persons be obliged to go to the poor-house, to be called from there when they are wanted. But prepare some home for them, when they are not wanted, and have some work for them there that will earn them a living, so that at all times they feel that they have a respectable standing in the society of laborers.

MINERS AND MANUFACTURERS

Should be protected from foreign competition in some degree, and then the laborers should be protected from oppression the same as those of the railroad and telegraph workers are. The greatest sufferers at the present time are the sewing women. These are condemned to starvation prices, and then cheated out of these to a great extent; and as they are not voters, not the least government protection is extended to them, or if done at all it is in the most stingy and grudging manner, after great pressure is brought to bear upon them by benevolent individuals or society.

The way to heaven is not so much gained by individual gifts to the poor, as it is by making laws to tax all upon just principles to support the poor, or give them work to enable them to support themselves. This puts the rich under obligation to do their duty to the poor, whether they love to do it or whether they prefer to go to hell rather than give a proper amount to the poor faithful workers, when they know the way to heaven is by means of these gifts. The idea of the old religions of making people do right by their fear of hell or love of heaven, is proved useless or worse than that. It causes the rich to pretend to do their full share in support of the needy, when their gifts are really to the shiftless and useless persons whom they encourage in laziness, while they are engaged in cheating and oppressing the prudent industrious laborers to the greatest extent that they have power to bring upon them.

The new religion, the one of science, will not depend on the private benevolence of people, but upon a law of justice as made known by experience. The religious idea, that private benevolence will answer the purpose of the public necessity, has proved a total failure, regarding the supplying of the needs of the poor faithful workers, as seen in the case of the railroad officials in this country whose hearts only mobs could touch, and the merchants and traders regarding the condition of sewing women in the cities. The fact is, if the wish is to have a united people in heart, soul and mind, there must be a uniting in financial interests, there should be no occasion for the truly benevolent to say, that the stingy will do nothing; they may cheat the tax collector and then they will be classed among the criminals, when it is found out; but every one is bound to pay his true share according to his means and income; and when a tramp comes along begging, there is a place for him to be sent where he will be well taken care of, and not abused and overworked, but still put to do duties that he is able to do; and his fare will be good if he is faithful according to his ability, and the fare will be spare and common when he is not faithful to do such useful labor as is wanted to be done.

It took a great many years to get a majority of the people to believe it best to have common schools supported by a general tax on the property of state, towns, and districts. But that tax and these schools have done more to make the people of this country one people, than any other plan that has been adopted; and where this system is well and fairly carried out, and the children have generally been educated a little in the common branches, there is no sectionalism or a rebellious people against Republican institutions; and where this principle is not fairly adopted, there are rebels and will continue to be, until the tax to support common schools is fairly collected and applied to the education of all the children honestly and fairly. This has been the result of the common school system; now we wish to extend this system to education of the poor begging crowd. Have a general tax system that all who have property to be taxed will pay their proportion, and have the United States have an income tax on large incomes, and a land tax on great landed estates, to be applied to making homes for the homeless, and work for the unimployed begging poor; and we will see if mobs must be inaugurated before the needs of the working people are considered; and then we will see another thing, that is, when the rich see they can not oppress the poor, and the poor see they are cared for by the government so they can not be inhumanly oppressed, then it will be found we are one people united in the great work of human redemption of the rich from their inhumanity to man, that makes countless thousands mourn; and of the poor from a heartless task master, and starvation and sufferings of every description that arise from poverty,

This can only be brought about by a system that will not really oppress any; but will be good to all. Then it will be found the government has as much to do to take care of the ignorant, and poor men and women, as it has with the poor children's education; and individuals have their personal duties to do; but in their public benevolence, they are not called upon to give to support more than they are called upon to give to support the public schools; every person who has the good of the people at heart, can not help doing something to see that the officials do their duty, and take a general interest in seeing that the humane intentions of the law be fully complied with, and enforced.

In this way there will be no necessity for the benevolence of the catholic church, which is rich and makes a poor begging people, and yet it steals the hearts of many people by its pretended benevolence and little gifts; and if it was not for its large numbers of voluptuous and expensive priests, it might do great good, and prevent many crimes; but under the influence of these priests, it costs more than it is worth; and the same thing applies to life insurance companies; their Presidents and other officers and agents, are paid so much and swindle the insured so many times, that it is found they take more bread from needy families, than they help by the death of the head of the family. The government should take all these wants into consideration, and not have any necessity for such societies and companies. We never had good common schools until the government made them. We never had so good money, as government money, and we shall never have the poor well provided for, until the government makes the provision for them.

The soul-saving religions have proved entire failures, in the business of body-saving, although they make great pretentions in that line, and ask the government to leave these affairs, as well as schools, in their hands. The Protestants do not ask this as much as other religionists do, and if they did they would have more sense, and more modern knowledge to enable them to fulfill its duties better; it is a modern phase of all ancient religions, and approaching the scientific religion in a slight degree; there is a dogmatic vicious, biblical end of it, that is as worthless as any of the ancient fanatical religions; and the worshippers insist upon the children's reading, and learning, and being guided by their biblical falsehoods; and there is another that rejects these falsehoods, and only insists upon the truth being taught wherever found.

But this one principle should be considered, that any society or church, that claims to do what the government ought to do in any benevolent work, will attempt to steal from the government the hearts of the people, and say to them, we have better principles than the government, and can do better for you. This should never be truly said, by any society, regarding the care of the bodies or minds of any class of persons in this nation. While there should be freedom for all societies, and persons, to do all the good they can, and set the best examples they can, before all the people, it should be the duty of the government officials to learn all they are able to, about the systems and works of these private enterprises, and adopt the best for all the people, that is known. But one thing is to be considered as settled, that in selecting the best way to accomplish any good, they must be guided by experiments, and experiences, and not by theory. This is the scientific way of establishing the sciences that have blessed the world more than all other ways, that have ever been done, or known in the world. It is said, experience is a dear school, but fools will learn by no other. But it may be truthfully said of them, that if none but fools learn by experience, they have done the world more good than all the wise persons the world has ever heard of; and it becomes the duty of the government officials to take lessons from the fools, who can learn by experience.

CHAPTER XXIV.

THE RELIGIOUS TEACHINGS OF ALL THE SCIENCES, AND PART SCIENCES.

The general religious opinion is, that law rules under God. The scientific opinion is that law rules God. The word-God gets his support from the half sciences, and fiction. Nature's God made man to make his governments, and will not make them for him. All the God religions have the same fashion of taking, all a person has to live on, and praying for them. God's people are the wickedest people on earth. Prayer the lazy man's work. The path of knowledge, is the path towards the true God. Intollerance is handed down from the dark ages. Thomas Paine. The question of spiritualists. Why has there been so much opposition to the people getting knowledge? Ask the Philosophers. Ask the Chemists. Ask the Astronomers. Ask the Geologists. Ask the Palaentologist. Ask the Botanist. Ask the Zoologist and other like scientists. Ask the Agriculturists. Ask the Inventor. Ask the Psychologist. Ask the Medical Professors. Spiritualists have looked over all the sciences, and conclude they all show that law reigns, and not God. The moral and social sciences must be established. Religion must be finished up by superstition, as christianity, was, or by science, as the scientific religion must be.

HAVING given a short statement of the most important sciences, and part sciences, it will be best to determine what religion they teach, and whether they teach the same kind of religion, or different kinds; we have seen that every material and spiritual science teaches that the law of God rules; that there are no accidents in nature, nor works done that are in consistent with natural and spiritual law. Then the question naturally arises, how a religion has maintained its position so long that declared special providences, miracles, and special destructions as part of God's work in nature; and more especially in spiritual affairs.

In the first place, all religions have an idea or principle that law rules, or at least that the Gods rule in a general way by law. But they have the command of the law, and do command it on special occasions so as to stop the movements of the earth, or sun, and do great favors to some persons, and great injury to others; that he causes one man to walk on the water contrary to the laws of gravitation, and some persons escape from punishment, or death, by the special interposition of their God, that broke the law of nature, or spirit, or both; and then after suspending the power of the law for a time, permitting it or empowering it to proceed on in its regular movements, as though nothing had been done to stop its power and action.

In this way they give their God power over the law, and He changes it to suit himself and His special friends. For it seems that He makes some persons that He hates, and others that He loves like Jacob and Esau, and alters the laws of nature and spirit, to bless those He loves, and to curse those He hates. But all the well established sciences deny to any power, any control over natural and spiritual law. The utmost any God or man can do, is to counteract one law by another. That is, spirits can cause a man to walk on water, or float one in the air, by laws that people do not understand. And people can make man or iron float on water or in the air, by laws that they do understand. But every well informed person knows these things can not be done by man at all times and in all places, unless they can have the conditions and implements required to make them float, and the same requirements are made by spirits; That is, they must have the conditions, and the implements they require, or they can not cause these things to be done; and it is just as much of a miracle for man to raise weights by a balloon, as it is for spirits to raise them by their appliances; and ignorant people will regard the one as the work of the God or Gods as much as the other.

When the ignorant writers of the Bible of the Jews wrote that the sun stood still, and the day was lengthened to enable them to kill their enemies, they spoke of a matter that neither God or man can do, unless they destroy the means of reckoning time and begin an eternity. The law of regular order and exact succession of time in the movements of the sun and earth, make our time and distinguish it from eternity. It may be in the spirit land they have not yet discovered revolutions of spirit planets, so as to make a spiritual time. One thing is certain, many spirits make mistakes in reckoning our time; and say it is difficult to keep the run of earth time. This may be only spirits who pay very little attention to such matters, and are, as a consequence, easily confused about time on earth; and yet they may be well informed about spirit time.

But the claims of the word religions of people are not so well made by disputing the well established principles of science, or when pitted against the well established sciences, as they are when claiming their miraculous powers among the half sciences, or pretended sciences, like medicine, alchemy, astrology and physiology and anthropology; and the pretense that their god has declared what the laws of government shall be; and that he makes the government instead of the people; and that he declares what is just and right instead of leaving these things for people to find out by experience. This is the center point of the conflict between the ancient religions and the modern scientific religion. Did God give to mankind sufficient intelligence for them to make their laws and governments, or must God be called upon to make them for man? If God has given the people sufficient intelligence, it is the greatest curse that can be inflicted upon them to teach that God will do it for them.

Having touched upon the difference in the basic principles of the religions of the past, of words and grace, and the religion of nature and truth, we will look at the different religions of the past to find out whether there was a radical difference between them in principles, and to try to find out what they fought for, and why the people manifested so much malignity towards each other when they, in the name of their religion, fought their battles and tortured their prisoners. It should be remembered that all religious people declare that persons should be virtuous and moral ; but their religious worship twists virtue and morality from its natural standards to the artificial ones that their God represents and their priests demand.

To be truly virtuous among the worshippers of the sun, a person must worship according as the priests of the God of the sun dictate. This not only saves their spirits after death from torments in hades, but their bodies from pain here; and they must pay the priests largely for their influence in making the sun god propitious to them; or they would not be considered either virtuous or moral. This payment would make all peaceful and lovely, and these worshippers would not only be sure of heaven, but of happiness on earth also. These promises would remain good until another set of priests set up another worship of the sun, and these would send the old worshippers to hades and make war upon them and torture their prisoners in an unmerciful manner if they would not fall down and worship them. The star worshippers set up the stars as gods to be worshipped, and the priests of the stella worshippers promised happiness here and hereafter to all who paid them well and worshipped faithfully and were ready to fight for the cause. The priests of the fire worshippers demanded the same praying, fighting and paying devotions as the other. The priests of the worshippers of beasts make the same demands, and a person is not either virtuous or moral in their dominions who do not worship the beasts they worship as their priests direct, and support them by gifts. The priests of the people who make gods out of reptiles claim of their worshippers all the devotions of their whole might and strength to their gods, or they are immoral and unjust to their gods. The priests of the gods of idols make the same demands upon their worshippers; that they shall expend all their might, mind and money to the support of their religion, and by such means they will become moral and virtuous, and be saved; and the different kinds of priests order their followers to fight and torture other idol worshippers, and compel them to worship and pay their money into the treasury of their idols and the priests who worship before them. The worshippers of the various spirit gods have the same invariable plan of salvation. They must support their special priests, as well as worship their special gods, to be able to save their souls from utter despair.

It will be observed in the history of religions that it makes no difference whether the worshippers pay their devotions to the same God, or to another; they fight each other with the same beastly fury, and torture their victims with the same merciless vengeance, when they do not worship as the victorious priests dictate, whether they worship the sun, moon, stars, beasts, idols, man or spirit Gods; they must bow to the popular successful victorious priests, or be punished unmercifully. Each of them have established a church militant, or fighting church, and it has been the business of the victorious priests, to put down all opposition, no matter whether they bow to the same God as the victors or not. For proof of this, any person has only to refer to the wars of Pagans, Mohammedans, and Christians. Priests like kings maintain their places by stealing and murder, when driven to the last resort, but the priests are the most cruel, wicked, and inhuman.

The first that is noticed of the spiritual religions that become of great national importance, may be said to be Brahmanism, introduced on the banks of the Ganges in India, by an Indian legislator named Menon; he was succeeded by the Judean legislator named Moses, and he was succeeded by Zoroaster, who moralized among the Medes and Bractians or the Egyptian systems, and may be said to give them their spiritual meaning. From these persons, or their followers, may be said to arise all the spiritual religions; but the dates of their origin, if not entirely fictitious, are at least very uncertain. All these religionists had a spirit God and devil, and they spiritualized the sun, moon, stars, and the world, and all the productions of the world; and introduced a double meaning to their religious writings, and sayings, that is, a material meaning, and a spiritual meaning.

These foundations for spiritual religions spread in the east of Asia under the name of Budhism. In western Asia, and Africa, especially in Egypt, as the mystical systems of the Medes, Persians, and Egyptians. The Mosaic, or Judean system, hardly made a mark on the ages previous to the advent of Christianity. The principles of their spirit God, were to horrible to make much of a nation, until the people of western Asia, Africa, and Europe were so ignorant and base as to inaugurate the dark ages, could such spiritual doctrines form the religion of a great nation. The Greek religion was one of any number of Gods, and Godesses, but they stuck to their mediums; they did not kill them as Saul the first king of the Jews ordered should be done in that little nation. But they consulted their mediums, who became renowned through the oracles of Delphos, not the oracles from God, for the most wicked priests that ever cursed the world, pretended to get their communications from the true God.

People may look the world over, and they will not find in history so brutal and dangerous a name given as attaches in principles, orders and practice to the name of a talking god. He ruthlessly orders the torture and murder of innocent men, women and children, and not satisfied with that he consigns them to eternal torments afterwards. This is the lovely god of the morality-loving priests of the Jewish and Christian people. As these religionists have different gods and different plans of worship, how can they be called one? This is plain when we consider all of them are guess gods, whether spiritual or material, and every one of them is different from the laws of nature, or nature's god. All their plans of salvation are against the principles that people are saved by knowing and doing what is right, mentally, morally, physically and spiritually.

All must believe some dogma, such as their god saves by burnt offerings, by the worship of idols or of beasts; by the worship of a man or of a book; by trusting in God instead of in his own powers, which the true God has given him for his consolation and guide. The question arises in principle, whether a person believes that the blood of a man will save him, or the water from a stone idol. In either case the person or worshipper is depending upon an outside power that is entirely powerless to save them; or if persons say that the proof is that faith in the blood of Jesus has cured many people, so the proof is that faith in the power of idols has cured thousands more; and the proof is as reliable in one case as it is in the other.

These religions are all alike in that they demand that people shall be satisfied with faith, and not seek knowledge to prove that their faith is well founded. They are all alike in demanding sacrificial offerings as the price of salvation. Blood offerings, burnt offerings, fruit offerings, or it may be to crucify the flesh in some way, as thrusting a hook through their flesh and hanging swinging by a rope attached to the hook; or they will force themselves to stand upon a pillar, exposing them to all the inclemency of the weather, and in many other ways. The way to heaven and to please their God and his favor is gained in some other way, besides doing right to themselves and other people.

Then, besides these by-ways that all religionists have to induce their God to pardon their sins and assign them a place of glory and happiness in heaven, they approach him with prayer to induce him to grant them success according to their wishes ; so prayer becomes the lazy, faithful religious man's work. The most ignorant and lazy write their prayers and put them on wind mills for the wind to work them up into the mind of God and make him answer the prayers and bless the writers.

The next most lazy prayers are those that make long prayers at stated times by their own breath to induce their God to do their work for them so they can live in idleness and luxury without doing any hard, useful labor. The persons who make these prayers are the most ignorant and superstitious in Pagan, Mohamedan and Christian lands. But there is another class of persons who pray in public that they may be seen and heard of men. They may be superstitious and believe that God answers their prayers ; but of one thing they are certain, that if many men hear their prayers and see their pious ways, there will be some of them that will give them gifts, whether God does or not; and by these public prayers they may deceive many and get their money for their breath instead of being obliged to sing a song or furnish a mess of pottage for it.

Some people are willing to give the Jews the greatest advantages in the race of life, because they furnished the world with some excellent music; but the general opinion is that he that sells his property for a song sells out mighty cheap; but he that sells out for a prayer to God sells out a mighty sight cheaper. The true Christian is expected to sacrifice his property to pay for such prayers, and for sermons that are more senseless, because they teach that there is a God outside of the natural world that is an enemy of the natural man. This falsehood is worse than praying to an imaginary god.

The scientific religion is opposed to all these forms of religion that have so long swayed humanity. The scientific religion has a natural God who is not influenced by prayers, supplications, sacrifices, mutilations or mortifications of the flesh, or any other worship that man can institute; and it has a natural man and a natural spirit that is influenced by prayers and requests to help the afflicted, and frequently answers them in such a mysterious way that the ignorant and superstitious suppose it is their God that answers them; and this may be true if they make a god out of man or his spirit. The great object of the scientific religionists is to get into harmony with our spirit friends of the great angelic hosts of heaven.

The spirit's advice in general terms is, to keep strictly to the laws of humanity. Be true to your own faculties, and just to other people's. It must be remembered that the natural God gave you your powers, to be used for your good, and the good of your neighbors; and the orders or requests of our Angel friends is, that you use them for such purposes. Then the inhabitants of earth and heaven will work in harmony, and the people of the two worlds will be governed by one law, of one God; and the sciences will be known to be the saviors of the world. The sacrificial religionists, who had control of most of the people of the earth, did not like the Poet Pope's saying; "all partial evil is universal good". They had built a little heaven, with the spirits of a few people in it; and a big hell, with the spirits of vast crowds of people in it; so he should have writen to suit them; "All partial good, is universal evil".

About all the religions have it, that their God cursed man, and the world, for man's wickedness; so few could be saved, and these few would be saved by God's miraculous goodness, and powers. The greatest miracles, are these of curing the sick, or raising the dead. There is no doubt but some persons are endowed with life-giving powers, so they can lay their hands on the sick, and they will recover; and they may put their hands on the apparent dead, and they will rise up, as though they had been dead; but the real facts are, they were not dead, and there was no God power required to raise them; it was only the magnetism of man, and spirits, that was required to do the deed.

From every point of view, all the sciences agree on the principle that law is God, unchangeable; and when we draw reasonable conclusions from the teachings of half developed sciences, they agree with the well established sciences, and scientific conclusions. There is not any difference; their teachings all proclaim one God, one law, and one religion; and the religion is, that the natural God is the true God, and the natural man is His greatest production; and that every man becomes more and more natural, as he becomes better, and better informed; and when he has acquired the greatest information of the laws that govern the universe that he can, he will become one with the laws of nature; and will be the greatest wonder of all the creations in space. Then it will be known, that the way to knowledge is the way to heaven, and peace, and joy, while on earth, or in spirit life; and to be natural is to be God-like, in knowledge; and to be ignorant, and to be guided by faith, is to be beast like. Then it will be known that the path of knowledge is the path of wisdom, and of triumphant peace.

The religious intolerance handed down to us from the ancients, is the foundation for all the intolerance of this age. This is kept alive by christian priests doing as near like their ancient prototypes as they can; they proclaim the same doctrines and laws, and support their claims by the same kind of specious theological logic; and when that fails to convert people to their belief, or to silence the reasoning person from showing the fallacy of their logic, and the falsehood of their belief, they pray to their God for assistance, and he tells them through their word of God, to kill the unbelieving set, especially those who have familiar spirits ; and if the present civilization prevents that, then they appeal to the government officials to punish them ; and if the government officials will not do it, they then commence to make up mouths and faces at the anti-Bible believers, and lie about them to the best of their ability, as they do now about Thomas Paine, and all the great and good infidels of past ages, and the spiritualists of this age; so some of the most unjust laws are continued ; and the priests are trying to get power to repeat the abominations of their priestly predecessors, and show distinctly they have been inspired by the same murderous spirit, and are covered by the same mantle, which made them the worst persons of any learned order that ever inhabited the earth.

Spiritualism has come to put before the people this query, to all the learned professions—to the professors in each of the sciences, and to the common-sense people of all lands—this being the last science that people have allowed to be formed. The spiritualists will very naturally ask the best informed in all classes of society, what the reasons are, in their opinion, that so much and such deadly opposition to the people getting knowledge has been manifested since the christians got command of the Roman Empire. The enquiry might properly go back of that date, but from that time to the present will be sufficient to give the reader a proper idea of what this opposition arose from.

First. Ask the philosophers and learned persons that lived in the fourth and fifth centuries of the christian era, why were the teachers of philosophy maltreated and murdered in those centuries? Simply because they taught the people in all the knowledge of the age; the religious, political and common-sense philosophy of the times. Who did these barbarous deeds?

The priests of the christian religion in person, or by heading mobs. One of the most cowardly and dastardly deeds ever done by beastly, brutal men, was committed by the christian priests on the person of the most eminent female philosopher of that age, in Alexandria, Egypt—Hypatia, the daughter of Theon, the mathematician. What was the character of the priests and of those who were over them in authority? The whole lot were the lowest and most beastly and brutal of the learned that was known in that time; and it was this class of persons that edited the christian bible and put its principles into practice under christian commands and laws.

Second. We will ask the chemists what treatment they have received from the christians and their priestly leaders; and the answer comes, the priests have acted like barbarians towards us, for centuries. Beginning in the thirteenth century they imprisoned, persecuted, tortured and burned chemists for ages. We will begin with the learned Roger Bacon, who was a priest as well as a chemist, but he was imprisoned by the priests in authority and narrowly escaped being burned, being recorded a magician and heretic. But the degradation of christian priests is shown by their judging chemists worthy of the flames after they were dead. But this is not as cruel and brutal as it was to burn them to death. What did chemists do to bring these awful judgments and punishments upon them, from these priests? Nothing but teach the people chemistry or give them knowledge. We did not meddle with their religious dogmas in any other way; and lately they have said that their religion did not teach the sciences, which is true. But they killed our scientists for teaching our science, just the same, and they proclaimed it anti-christian; and if it is, then the christian religion is deadly opposed to it, and will not permit it to be taught if they can prevent it. What kind of a God does chemistry teach that exists in the earth? None, unless the law of nature is God. We find this law pervades and rules all matter and all the forces of nature, so far as we can discover.

Third. We will ask the Astronomers, what kind of treatment they have received from the christian priests, beginning with Bruno in the sixteenth and the beginning of the seventeenth century. They burned him, simply, because he was a Philosophical Astronomer, because he would not lie, and recant; but stood up manfully to the well known Astronomical truths; and they tortured him, and burned him to death without pity or remorse. But rejoiced that there was one less magician, and heretic in this world; and the priesthood has continued the same kind of hostility to Astronomers ever since, only where public opinion obliged them to acknowledge the truths of Astronomy; and adopt some humane principles towards them. Can you inform us what has caused the priests generally to be so brutal towards Astronomers? We think it arises from their education. They are taught that the natural man is an enemy of God, and they treat him as an enemy of theirs in war against them, and they formed the church militant to meet these enemies by the well established military law, that they must deceive the enemies by lies, and frauds, of every kind; spies must be sent into their camp, to deceive and lie to them, and then return to their friends and give them true information regarding the enemies' strength and position; and then when they are brutal men, and can get their enemies in their power by force, or stratagem, they are known to have less mercy, and more brutality, than any other class of persons in the learned professions, even including other kinds of military men. But when we compare them with the lawyers, and the doctors of medicine, they seem like persons banded together, to commit outrages on society generally; while the lawyers demand that all sides of a question shall be heard, that justice may be done; and the doctors demand the right to allay human suffering; and these lawyers and doctors have not gone in great bodies to demand laws, that they might murder people who did not agree with them. But the priests have, and have executed such laws in the most savage manner, so that no learned people in the world have been as bad as they have. It will not do for Astronomers to say the priests are naturally worse than other people, but their doctrines, and the manner of teaching them, must be the cause. What is the kind of God that Astronomy teaches that exists? None, unless the laws of nature are called God. We have never found a God of words in heaven, or on earth. All heavenly bodies are moved under the laws of order, and we can rely on them in making all our prophecies and calculations.

Fourth. We will ask the geologists, how have you been treated by the christian priests? Our science was not known in the middle ages, when these priests had such entire control, and murdered people with impunity. But the venom that they have shown against us for showing by the rocks the great age of the world, has been such as astonishes ordinarily good and intelligent people. When we showed by the rocks that the laws of order and progression have prevailed, and that the earth has been millions upon millions of years in coming to its present state of productions for the home of man; we have put our facts down, and they have attempted to confute them by their theologies and inspirations in the most crude and ungentlemanly manner; but finding our facts would stand, they finally concluded to change the meaning of their biblical inspirations and their theological dogmas, while manifesting a constant grumbling, grudging madness, because it shows their God of words is not reliable, and entirely different from our God of law, order and progression; and shows that their God is their guess, and their interpretation of His word is their guessing at what it means. This shows that their guess God is fallible; and their guessing at the meaning of His word, and changing their minds about their meaning every time that our undeniable facts make it important for them to do to retain any semblance of truth in their theology, makes it appear ridiculous, and is followed by denunciations of geologists, in such violent terms, that it shows that all they want is man's laws, and an ignorant and degraded people to back them, and they would at once put us on their torturing rack, as they did the philosophers, chemists and astronomers, when they had the power. And some christian geologists have made themselves insane by trying to make their word God agree with the God of nature's laws. If the miracles which they ascribe to their word God were done, or can be done, then time may end at any moment. If He made the world by His word, He can stop it by his word, as He is said to have done the sun, at any moment. If He can change the movements of the sun or earth so as to make one minute's difference in time, our earth time is destroyed that instant, and the laws of nature are overpowered, and the word law is almighty, and four miles of granite rocks in thickness were made in a minute, and the sixteen miles of other rocks and soil on them, with all their little animals and fish, and the great monsters that are found petrified, or their shape preserved in the rocky layers, could be made in another moment And the boy who said that a three-year-old colt could not be made in three minutes, would be wholly mistaken, because the word God could destroy time and let on eternity, and the colt would be made in no time. Well, what kind of a God have you geologists discovered? None but law, order and progression. We have not been able to find any power back of them that was able to rule them. But they rule all things. That is, nature's laws are omnipotent and omnipresent so far as we have been able to discover.

Fifth. Let us consult the Palaentologist or the science of animal fossils, found in the rocks, and earth, to learn from them ; what they think of the candor and truth of the Jewish and Christian records, and of the priests who sanction, and sanctify them. How have the priests used you? Their conduct has been abusive, and dictatorial; not a step in our science has been taken, to find out about the age of fossilized animals, and man especially, that they have not found fault with as a desecration, when it is seemed to militate against their inspired word of God; and soon finding they could not deny the facts, of the great length of time that these fossils have existed, they threatened the damnation of their God, and that He would punish us eternally, in His fiery hell. Then they scolded, jabbered, and found fault with us, for our unholy work; and finally altered the meaning of their scriptures, to meet the facts of our science, as well as they could; still grumbling about the people obtaining this knowledge; in fact we think they have acted as bad as the people would let them. They never seemed to have the least consciousness of right and wrong, only as they got it from their understanding of their scriptures; and as their opinions changed, their conduct changed; but one thing all the orthodox christians held to, that the unbeliever will be damned; this they assert positively, as their scriptures do. Under all these circumstances, and after full examination of all the facts, theories, and scriptures, ancient, and modern, what kind of a God seems to have ruled in the science of the fossils of the earth? The God of law. If there can be a God of words in the universe, in the science of Palaentology, he is subject, and always has been, to the law of order, and progression. For proof of this, look to the progressive order of fossilized remains, in the various strata of rocks, and alluvial soils of the earth.

Sixth. The Botanists come next ·in regular order, who have two kinds of botany. The fossil branch, and the science arising from classifying present plants on earth. This science did not come into existence, until the priests had been obliged to stop their wholesale tortures, and murders, by the people; but they have displayed the same surly insolence against botanists, as against other scientists. Why was this done? It is impossible for us to divine, unless it was, we found the God of law to be omnipotent, and did not find the God of words at all. It is curious to see them flare up with their old word-god like anger, if His existence and power is questioned. But we can not find anything to comfort them; the god of law prevails, and none other, that we can find.

Seventh. We will put together the sciences of Zoolology, or animals, ornothology, or birds, entomology, or insects, and consult the scientists about how the christian priests and their most devoted followers have treated them. They have treated us in the most harsh and ungentlemanly manner, at all times, when they suspected we were teaching doctrines that militated against their word-god, or his bible doctrines. Well, what kind of a God have you found, in your sciences? A law-God; or a law without a God; law is all powerful. All animals, birds, and insects, are made by a law, each after their kind, and all is order; neither a miracle, or an outlaw, has been found in nature, in either of these sciences.

Eighth. Now let us ask the Agriculturists, including the Hortuculturists and all other scientists that are engaged in producing more and better qualities of food, for man or beast, and improving useful animals, and destroying those that are injurious to mankind. What kind of a God do you depend upon, to make these improvements, and changes? And the answer is, they depend upon the law of nature; the God of law; we place no reliance upon a God of miracles, but we search for information of the law, and how experience proves it has given the best products. But can you not get as good results from prayer to the God of words and promises? no, we are not certain of any crop from prayer to Him; those that depend upon such a plan, are the greatest kind

of failures; so the law of nature is your dependence
whether there is a god back of it or not. As far as
we can learn, law rules over all the powers of the
world of agricultural productions.

Ninth. This brings us to ask the inventor, and
discoverer of the useful inventions and devices, such
as the telegraph, photographer, or sun painter, and the
phonographer, or the sounds of the letters, to make
all words, so that every one will pronounce them at
sight, in the way the writer intended. What is the
kind of god you rely upon to make your inventions
of use to mankind? We rely upon the unvarying
law of nature as God, or no God. So far as we have
learned, law is God, and there is no other.

Tenth. Next comes the sciences of Mesmerism,
Psychology, Psychometry, Phrenology, and all the
mental sciences of modern life. How have the christian priests conducted themselves toward these scientists? Just as bad as they could; just as violent and
denunciary as the people would allow; say the discoverers; they have put their theology against our facts,
but our facts, and system of facts, which show the
Phsychological effects of one person upon another,
stand so firm in the public mind, that theology has to
take a back seat. This magnetic power, as it is called,
of one person over another, is now almost universally
acknowledged to be true. Then the power of a min-
eral, rock, or hair, or other substance, to impress its
history on the mind of the sensitive, is well known;
so Psychometry is a well established science, though
not so generally known.

Then Phrenology comes and establishes the fact,
that the brain is the seat of the mind, and in the base
of the brain, are the baser passions, and in the front
is intellect; and to the back part is given love of children and family, and in the top is unfeeling dignity
and pride; and these parts are divided into many
special organs, that when large and active, give special
faculties, like music, love, or hate, benevolence, or

stinginess. And it is found that the good faculties can be educated to have a commanding influence on the character of ordinary persons, and the baser organs can be educated to have a commanding influence on ordinary people, and make of the naturally base, the most despicable characters that the world has ever seen. What do you think makes the true history of the christian priests, that give them such a monstrous character for the most atrocious wrong, and cruelties, and unmerciful inhumane tortures? We see that it must come from their education. The baser organs are stimulated to the highest degree, to imitate a God who will torture people eternally, for their mistakes of belief. They are taught that the natural man is constantly at war with God, and consequently always the enemies of the converted priests, and their tools; and as they have no peace between them, but always war, they can not be friends at any time. Other people and nations will have peace occasionally: sometimes real, at others only patched up to give them a chance to prepare for war. But these priests are always on the war path, with the natural man, and they are taught in their theological schools all the arts, artifices, frauds, and deceptions that warriors are taught in their schools to practice against their enemies, in time of war; and now they may seem to be quiet; but priests are as slyly on the war path, as are the warrior savages of the forests, when pretending peace, but really seeking to know the weak points in their enemy's camp; to attack them unawares.

From every point of view, if there are any schools that should be suppressed, the Theological institutions are the ones; where are taught all the horrible doctrines of the Roman Catholics, and orthodoxy. They are corrupting the youth of our country, more than any other institutions of learning in the land, because they educate their youths to be constantly on the war tactics; and send them forth to teach, and deceive the people by pretending to be for peace, when their whole scheme is to make war upon the natural man, and make him obey them, or have him murdered.

If the priests and their supporters deny these statements and conclusions, show them the history of the Christian priesthood, and ask them to match its abominations and atrocities by the acts of any other of the learned professions in christendom ; show such great combinations by them to commit such great cruelties and wrongs, and for no good purpose whatever to mankind in general. What is the character of the god that you find in investigating these sciences? Law is God, or we have not found any God at all. What! no word god, no spirit god? Not any; all are under law. The mind, body and spirit of man are under law, so far as we have been able to discover.

Eleventh. Next we will take the testimony of the medical professors of the science of medicine in all its branches. What has been established in your profession regarding the organism of mankind and the means that give them good health, and the causes and cure of their diseases? There is a law that if complied with produces healthy children, and another that produces unhealthy and deformed children. There is a law that if complied with will make a healthy people, and another that will produce a sickly, diseased people. Or, more properly speaking, there are many laws that are combined together, that if people comply with in their living, they will be healthy and strong. But if they do not comply with them they will be subject to the laws that produce diseases and weakness.

That is, healthy conditions give the people good health ; unhealthy conditions make them sickly. But will not prayers, supplications, and making sacrificial offerings to the god of words make the unhealthy conditions healthy? We have not found these ceremonies of any value for such a purpose after a vast number of observations. The miasm from decaying vegetables and animals produce different diseases. Some will produce intermittent fever, or fever and ague;

some remittent fever, others typhus fever. Each disease is known by the symptoms that are manifested; each follows its own special laws, and the medicine to cure people of each disease acts so as to give the patient's powers of life a chance to make a healthy action and overcome the disease.

The rule is to overcome the force of the disease by the force of the medicine. Each acts upon the patient by its peculiar laws of action; the disease to cause distress and death of the body; the medicine, by its peculiar medicinal effect, to procure relief and good health. Does prayer and supplications to the god of command and promises, cure the sick and make them well? We have no well authenticated cases of such a cure. But magnetism is a great curative agent; and we think the community very fortunate who have a well educated, sympathetic magnetic physician among them who is devoted to his profession. This health-giving magnetism goes with his medicines, and may be much more beneficial to the patient than the medicine.

This is one of the most pleasant, safe and efficient agents in the hands of the profession, or of ignorant persons, that is known; and all persons who have these powers in themselves, or by the influence of spirits, should be encouraged to acquire a knowledge of the science of medicine, especially that part of it which relates to the Psychologic department, and they will soon know, and other persons will soon learn, that God does not turn aside the machinery of His government, to cure diseases, or raise the dead bodies to life, as the ignorant and superstitious firmly believe; but cure comes from magnetic man by the help of angels, who are always around us, to do us good if they can.

These persons who heal by the laying on of hands, and by magnetic remedies, should be especially encouraged and protected, by law, if any special laws are required, by any persons who practice medicine. But giving special privileges to the learned, or unlearned physicians, must be considered of doubtful efficiency, in any case they are apt to make humbugs and quacks in the profession, and the people need protection from these, whether learned or not; when people are relieved by the magnetic influence, they are apt to say God did it ; especially if done by a priest. This was the case among all enlightened people, before the magnetic and spiritual powers of man were known; in the way that magnetic and spiritual sciences were established so as to give the people correct knowledge on these subjects.

Well, have you found any God to show himself clearly in the science? Not a word-god, not a threatening God, not a promising or commanding God, and no God, unless law is God. There is a law of healthy growth, and a law of healthy decay; there is a law of unhealthy growth, and decay. There is a law that governs each disease, so that it is known from others. There is a law, that determines the adaptation of medicines to cure certain diseases, and be hurtful in others. There is a law that shows the good effects of good food, and healthy surroundings, and a law that will show the bad effects of poor food and unhealthy surroundings. There is a law that will show the good influence of good habits, and the unhealthy influence of bad habits on the mind or body.

Spiritualists have looked over all the sciences, and of modern thought, and inspirations, and all tell one story ; that law is God, the same as has been shown in the sciences mentioned, and the priests have been the deadly enemies of these inspirations, and of the proof that sustains them, and of the persons who learn and publish the proof. The priests have made a God out of a guess, or a belief, and made a heaven and hell in the same way; then they guessed how God made the heavens and earth, and beast and man, and did not guess right in any instance; and the first glimpses of the sciences showed their errors, and they were mad, and at once, and all the time since, have shown that their brains were like their guessing, too thin for this age.

They hated the industrious truth loving people, as bad as they said their devil hated virtue, and justice. And their influence was dominant, until spiritualism was established, which proved that christians were not spiritual, in their belief, only so far as spiritual manifestations go to prove in their opinion, that the men were Gods, or semi-Gods that made the manifestations, or through whom the spirits made them; and spiritualism has proved that this reasoning is not true.

All the sciences prove that the priests and their palls have had no good foundation for either their belief or persecutions, so far as they go; but we have two sciences yet to form to cut them completely from the sympathies of modern thought and intelligent, truthful society. These are the social and moral sciences. The priests are exerting themselves to their utmost to prevent these sciences from being established. If they can prevent these sciences from being known by the people, they will be able to stop our scientific civilization where it now stands, and begin to turn the tide to priestly tortures and the dark ages.

A scientific religion, based upon the science of spiritualism, can not be fully known until the social and moral sciences are fully known and established. Then a scientific government can be formed. Then the sciences will have their special, separate principles, that will distinguish them from each other, and all will be locked together by the general principle that must allow experiments and observations to be made; and these must be reasoned upon and made into systems before they can be called sciences; and all persons who have no faith in the efficacy of scientific, experimental and reasonable conclusions, will oppose the knowledge being obtained by experiences, and be joined by all those who conceive it to be to their interest to have ignorance and superstition prevail on these subjects. At present the spiritualists are divided and the christians are divided. All the priests who wish to continue their sensational talk wish the superstitions to prevail.

Spiritualism is only the foundation of religions. They are finished up by a superstitious, social and moral sentiment, or by a scientific, social and moral system. The religion of the spiritualists must be in accord with all the sciences, whilst the christian religion is in accord with all the most deplorable superstitions. This brings us to consider the social and moral sciences, and how they will differ from the superstitious, moral and social sentiments as now practiced in enlightened countries.

CHAPTER XXV.

CONCLUSION.

THE scientists worship truth instead of the God of truth. They are always searching for truth in all the works of nature. They worship nature's laws instead of the god of nature's law, because they know something of these laws certainly, and nothing certain of any god that has any management of them. They worship justice, and not the god of justice, and this makes them call for the laws of justice to establish a government upon just principles. They worship the law of right and righteousness, instead of the god of right, because their law god has given them power to learn right from wrong, and not the power to consult with God and have him tell them what is right by word or any other way, only by experience and reason. They worship the law of mercy, but not the god of mercy; and the question may be properly asked, why do you worship these laws and principles and not the god that stands for them? The reason is that the laws and principles never give orders for murderous and unjust punishment for breaking these laws; while the god that people cause to stand for these principles does order the most cruel and unjust punishments; such as he that breaks the Sabbath day shall not live.

These principles never tell us that we shall be punished in hell eternally for our wickedness on earth; but the god does tell that such outrages will be committed by him. These laws and principles never tell us that if we believe in Christ and worship him, we shall be saved from hell torments and enjoy the blessings of heaven. But the god does. Any god that speaks, makes assertions that the natural laws do not justify, and the priests and the god they represent want people to take their dictum for truth, law, love and justice, instead of proving them true ; and besides this, these dictators will say all manner of evil of the people who are governed by the proved principles of justice and truth.

It is this God worship that makes the church militant, and this church requires the same kind of frauds, lying, and deceptions to be successful, as military chieftains have to practice to be successful; and neither the priests nor the successful warriors can hear the counsels of scientists, or of eminent statesmen, who wish to establish truth or a just government. Alexander the Great could not bear to have independent statesmen in council. Julius Cæsar, put down the free discussion of statesmen in council in his day of triumph. Oliver Cromwell silenced the English Parliament in a summary manner. Bonaparte could not bear to have a statesman live that had an opinion of his own, in his empire.

The reason for such conduct of great military commanders, is that they are taught to lie, steal, deceive and kill their enemies; and to have their friends obey orders, stand and be killed, or rush into the jaws of death. They must give up life, liberty, property and the pursuit of happiness, to give victory to the commander; and when the victory is won, this commander demands all the benefits that are gained by the victory. He has been a dictator in battle, and in war, and he demands it in time of peace.

The education of statesmen, is entirely different; they are instructed in the best principles to guide them in establishing laws that will give people the best protection to life, liberty. and the pursuit of happiness; and in this country, when General Andrew

Jackson was elected President, he assumed dictatorial powers as far as he could. He took the responsibility by the "eternal," as his phrase was; and the slanders that were heaped upon Henry Clay, and Daniel Webster, by him and his partisans, can hardly be stated at this time; and these were the greatest statesmen of that age, and as great as ever existed in any age. He not only overcome these, but others of great experience and power, such as J. Q. Adams.

When General Grant was elected President, he was only noted for his military success. He was entirely without experience, as a statesman, and there is every probability that he had less information about what was right and wrong, in the laws of a peaceful and just government, than any man ever elected to so high an office in a civilized government. But instead of agreeing with the most pure, renowned and best informed statesmen, like Senator Sumner, and Schurz; he made political war upon them and all other statesmen who had an opinion of their own that differed from his. The result was that he made some of the worst appointments of persons to office that were ever made; and the actions and appointments of Jackson and Grant were as near like Bonaparte, Cromwell and Cæsar, as they could be in this country.

But people would not permit them to assume imperial powers; and their administrations were the most despotic and infamous that have ever been visited upon the American people. The end was, in each case, the people chose statesmen to succeed these military heroes, and gave them directions to agree with the wisest and best statesmen, or at least to use them decently; for they were educated to plead for the laws of truth and justice, and the government that will give the people the most real security in their pursuit of happiness.

The priests are educated to deceive the people, the same as military men are, only military men declare the necessity of their frauds and deceptions boldly, squarely and fairly, while the priests declare their lies the truth of their god, and their frauds and deceptions are necessary to save the greatest number of mankind; so the bare-faced falsehoods of the priests are without any excuse, while the military men have a good excuse when fighting enemies; and the priests are as much worse than military men as rulers of nations, as their falsehoods are more inexcusable; and this is one important reason why the laws and rulings of governments become such important religious questions.

One of the amusing incidents in the religious scenes of the present is to hear people talk against the Jews of the present time, and denounce them as vile cheats, while they read as truth that Moses, David and Solomon were the meekest, purest, wisest persons that ever lived; yet they can not find among the Jews of the present day persons that are as despotic, licentious, foolish and mean as these men were according to their history. Judge Hilton may exclude from his hotel all the well dressed Jews that apply to him, but he will not exclude one that is as bad in their acts as these ancient Jews were; which I learn that he teaches as the models of good, God-fearing men, the best that God ever made on earth; when the facts are that Moses was not as good and humane a man as William the Conquerer of England; and Henry the Eighth of England was a better defender of the faith and a better man than David; and Charles the Second or George the Third of England were wiser men than Solomon; not so despotic, and did not rend their kingdom so disastrously.

The reason was, society would not permit it; and present society will not allow the Jews of the present day to act as bad as did their two great kings of ancient times.

But it must not be understood that the Jews, who are guided by the laws of Moses, are living in this age; they have adopted the barbarisms of twenty-five hundred years ago, and live as near to them as their surroundings will permit. The Russian Jews now coming to this country, not only are living as near old

Mosaic law as they can, but bring Russian barbarisms and ignorance with them besides. They take Solomon as their pattern of wisdom, who was a despotic, lecherous spendthrift, who fooled away the people's money in the most scandalous and criminal way. They take David as their pattern of purity, who was a licentious, treacherous, blood-thirsty, criminal deceiver; and Moses was the meekest man when he pretended to get his laws and commands from the God of heaven and earth.

These pretentions are very great for the meekest man that ever lived. The greatest pretender to divine favors that ever lived, never exceeded him in boasting of his familiarity with God, and getting orders and instructions about what laws and commands he should proclaim; and many of these were the most infamous that man could proclaim. Any one can see that if a people come among us with such base examples of purity, wisdom and meekness as their guide, and teaching these things to their children, with the addition that they should have an eye for an eye; that is, a system of revengeful punishments instead of merciful ones, what a great task it must be to bring them up to a civilization with the humane sentiments which characterize the best people of this age. The sentiment of the times is for humane laws, institutions, and punishments.

From all these statements, and the principles of the christian Roman Catholic religion, and the Bible that they appeal to, to prove the divinity of their principles; any one can see what a load the free-thinking protestants and reformers have to bear before they can establish a humane religion that is consistent with the best feelings of the best people of this age—not bear and forbear, but remove this ignorance and superstition from this large class who oppose the truth, and just laws and principles, with all their power and vengeance. They want to perpetuate revengeful punishments, instead of humane, reformatory ones. When the christians first made their creeds to be their principles, and their idea of what they meant when they put the bible together, they made these damnatory creeds that are a disgrace to the gods and men who made them, and to the bible that contains sentiments to uphold such horrible doctrines.

The natural man can think a good thought and do a good deed; there are none so wicked that they cannot think and do good. There is no one thing that shows the deceptions that priests put on mankind more than the pretence that the bible is guide to a correct chronology of ancient times. They agree with the bible record from Adam to the flood of Noah's time. From that time, the marginal notes of the bible differ from the bible more than 150 years, to the time when the Israelites left Egypt under Moses. The character of the priests who publish these marginal notes, for truth and veracity, can be truly estimated by comparing the bible, which they declare God's truth, with their works. They pay no more regard to biblical statements than they do to scientific truth, when they think they can gain a point by denying a fair statement.

Now the question is, how shall the persons proceed who wish to establish the true, just, scientific religion? Let us look the ground over. In the first place, have we knowledge enough to make the religion of knowledge? We have all that the sciences teach, besides much that is not yet classified into scientific systems. In the previous pages I have given many references to such knowledge. My idea has been to give as much of it as I could on all the subjects where superstition was worked into the religious systems. Who will prefer the ancient inspirations to the modern? Which is the best, the inspirations of the legends, or of the sciences—the God of words or the God of law?

The wonders that have been discovered by material scientists, are greater than the ignorant, superstitious bible writers ever thought of. Their knowledge has turned what the ignorant called curses, into blessings; a cursed world into a blessed one, and a cursed body into a blessed one, that bears a mind of wonderfully blessed powers. Then when we add the still more wonderful blessings that spiritualism and the co-related mental and magnetic sciences, we find the power for good so great and the power for evil so small, that it seems like blasphemy to say that the world was ever cursed by any god who had any power, sense or knowledge of the world, or of human beings that are dwelling upon it.

When scientists have decided that the world and the people of it were never cursed by any God or any people that knew anything about the matter, then they decided that there must be a change of worship from a cursing God to a law God—from a swearing God to one that would not swear; from a jealous God to one that never was jealous; from a God that judged the people, to one that gave power to the people to judge themselves. After surveying this whole field, the conclusion was reached that the worship which consisted of prayer, and beseeching God to pardon our sins and keep us from misery, and other forms and ceremonies, that priests have set up as necessary to appease an angry God; are entirely useless; and worse than that, because they lead persons away from the true way, that the god of nature points out that will save them.

This salvation must come by their correct judgment; this will bring us to the conclusion that all education, whether religious or secular, should be directed to give persons the best judgment in all the affairs of life. The first and most acceptable worship of the god of law, is to educate ourselves and others in such a way, that it will give each, and all the knowledge to judge correctly of all matters that concern people on earth or in heaven. This is the first and great command of the scientific religion; and the second is very much like it, that is, we should study to learn what kind of education will give that knowledge.

In this way we reverse the plan of the ancient religionists, who said: judge not lest you be judged. We say judge and be judged. Form your judgments as the scientists do, by searching into the truths of nature, or as a court of justice does, by taking all the evidence and facts in the case, and form your judgments by reasonable deductions from the facts and evidence; consider you are arbiters in all matters; and make up your judgments from all the knowledge you can obtain, when the judgment is required. But temper all judgments with mercy, because more knowledge may induce you to amend or reverse your past judgments. On these principles all just laws and practices are based by the scientific religionists, and with these begin the true worship of the true God.

If persons will look over the history of religious people, they will see that the persons who are searching for religious truth are merciful, humane people. But when they pretend they have found this truth, they become unmerciful, intolerant, and barbarous. The scientists never pretended they had found all of God's truth that may become known to mankind, and consequently they never killed people. Those that worship truth and justice are always searching to find out the truth of every principle that attracts their attention. This demands teachers who demonstrate the truths they teach instead of preachers who give dogmatic discourses on subjects that they will not try to prove true, nor permit others to have a fair opportunity to determine their truth. So far as the material scientists worship, it consists of acquiring knowledge and perfecting their judgments so as to make the best possible use of their information to benefit themselves and the rest of mankind. Their entire devotions consists in getting such kinds of knowledge for the most benevolent purposes.

When we turn from these scientists to the mental and spiritual ones, we begin the verbal worship; we pray to the spirits who answer our prayers; we assemble in circles to make conditions that will enable the angels of heaven to come and counsel with us, and by that means we unite all the wisdom and knowledge of heaven and earth to enable us to form correct judgments of our duties in life; these counsels should be held sacred, never to be relinquished, because by them we gain the highest wisdom in establishing the best laws and institutions to guide people in society, and nations the best rules for people to govern themselves by, that can be made. Let all who love justice, truth, and mercy, join together and stand by them wherever found.

Let there be no turning to the right or left, but let the laws of truth, justice and mercy, be their guide in society and government, and let each one be guided by pure motives in what concerns them personally; and correct their judgment to the best of their ability about all the duties of life, to themselves as well as to others; and wherever there can be gathered a number of persons who will be guided by such righteous principles, who are not depressed by fear, nor too much elated by hope, so as to injure their judgments, they will form a band that shall be a power in the land; and when many of these bands are formed in this country or any country.

They will have all the peaceful powers of the angels of heaven united with that of all the good justice-loving people of the earth to help them to establish a just government, which will permit them to be guided by the religion of truth. It has been my purpose in writing this book to put before the reader a sufficient number of facts and principles to enable persons to judge where the great questions are that are in dispute, and how easy it is for persons to be mistaken by inspirations, and how difficult it is to get the experiences and make the experiments that establish the truth. And when we see these bands of spirits and people gathering together all over the land to establish the laws of righteousness and truth, we shall know that the great day of judgment is near, which will determine whether the wicked, ignorant and superstitious shall have rule over the people, or the persons of knowledge, wisdom and justice shall be the chosen rulers. I hope to live on earth to see this great battle fought, and see the triumph of the purest angels of heaven and best people of the earth.

Before this year is past I hope to see and hear of the gathering of many of these bands, composed of those who stand by truth and justice wherever found—firmly, unflinchingly, yet modestly and mercifully. Because it will be a great change to turn preachers of gospel into teachers of truth, and political laws into just laws, and politicians into patriots for justice, and a church militant into a church that is triumphant in its truth and peace. When we see great numbers of people that gather in their several localities to find out exactly what justice and truth is in all the affairs of mankind, and who are determined when they find what is right to stand up for it manfully and reasonably on all occasions, at all times, then we shall know that the trial between truth and justice on one side and falsehood and wrong on the other is fairly commenced.

In this trial let no one contend rashly for an unproved principle, but stand firmly for all that is proved true; and the army of scientific reformers and justice-loving people will always be right, and by the power of right they shall be triumphant, and make a peace on earth among all the people like that of heaven among all the purest angels of heaven; and the good of earth will be separated from the evil, because the good choose the just reasonable principles, and the evil the unjust unreasonable principle, and the law god of justice will be with the just, and they shall make a government of justice and a religion of truth that shall be a blessing to all the people of the earth.

INDEX.

A

AGES, 10.
Alexander the Great, 237.
Arabia, 39.
Arabs, 38.
Agassiz, 116.
Attraction, 115.
Atoms, 102.
Astronomy, 384, 81, 86.
Agriculture, 388, 240.
Augustian Age, 242.
Astrology, 254.
Adult Citizens, 265.
A Sixth Sense, 84.
Asteroids, 24.
Andersonville, 247.
Agrarians, 240, 245.

B

Bible, 5, 192.
Bruno Giordano, 30.
Botany, 387, 118.
Berries, 215.
Biennial Elections, 248.
Butler, Senator, 267.
Buchanan, Prof. J. R., 235.
Bonaparte, Napoleon, 340, 299.
Bastile, 317, 390.
Buchanan, President, 317.
Bank of England, 336.
Bonds, increased value, 321.
Bryant, H. H., 357.
Bacon, 243.
Blind Tom, 257.
Brahmanism, 377.
Bacon, Roger, 161, 382.
Books, 1, 86, 135, 198, 259.

C

Confucius, 68.
Chineso Gods, 68.
Christians, 70.
Crenoid, 129.
Chemistry, 385, 101, 116.
Coal fields, 97.
Clairvoyance, 188.
Clairaudience, 188.
Christs, modern, 234, 197.
Cæsar, 240.
Crooks & Wallis, 187.
Chronology, 53.
Currency, 339, 319.
Corner on money, 327.
Common Schools, 369, 368, 346.
Cromwell, 316.
Criminals and Insane, 317.
Capitol, shall it be removed, 354.

D

Delaware, 30.
David, 138.

Diseases, laws of, 219.
Dyspepsia, 232.
Davis, A. J., 231.
Delphos, Oracles of, 377.
Davenport Brothers, 185.

E

Earth, 171, 25, 32.
Eye for an Eye, 192.
Egypt, 68.
Empire, Roman, 29.
Electricity, 113.
Ezra, 75.
English Judges, 181.
Echo, 205.
Elections, 312, 248.
England, Henry VIII, 342.
Exodus, 275.

F

Faith, 222.
Facts proved, 173.
Franklin, Benjamin, 114
Fire, 108.
Fish, 97.
Finney, Selden J., 179.
Fletcher, Mrs., 182.
Fifth century, 183.
Free speech, 266.
Force, 1.
French republic, 322.
Fiat money, 333.
Farm mortgages, 364.

G

Gardening, 215.
Germans, scientists, 179, 180.
Government, science of, 246.
Ghost, Holy, 240.
God making, 59.
Geology, 385, 95.
Genesis, 531, 59.
Greeks, 68.
Garfield, President, 358.
Grant, U. S., 398.

H

Hare, Professor, 116.
Hydrogen, 104.
Horticulture, 215.
Hipocrates, 217.
Hnry 1. of England ; Henry 11. of England, 243.
Herschal, J. F. W., 26.
Horse fossil, 35.
Hydesville, N. Y., 154.
Hours of labor, 342, 351.
Home D. D., 186, 185.
Hilton, Judge, 380.

I

Inspitations, 76, 39, 1.
Isaiah, 138.
Infidelity, 84.
Inventions, 389, 294.
Infallible, 84, 287.
Ingersoll, R. G., 30, 84, 255.
Incomes, 316.
Intolerant religions, 381.

J

Josh, 68.
Jews, 316, 238, 36.
Jupiter, 24.
John King, of En land, 243.
Judges, 310.
Jackson, Andrew, 398.

K

Knowledge, 250.
Know all bankers, 325.

L

Lion, 225.
Liver, 232.
Lycurgus, 237.
Landed estates, 315.
Log Cabin Capitol, 390.

M

Matter, 1.
Motion, 1.
Middle Ages, 31.
Moses, 377, 183, 74, 34.
Mormons, 192, 20.
Mathematics, 138, 145.
Magnetism, 392, 145.
Mesmerism, 389, 145.
Mammals, 97.
Marsupals, 97.
Monkeys, 97.
Man fossilized, 35, 97.
Mars, 25.
Mercury, 26.
Mumler, Wm. H., 184.
Mosheim, 166.
Mysteries of nature, 191.
Mahomedans, 242, 194.
Music, 198.
Medicine, science of, 217.
Medical men, 391, 218.
Medical schools, 217.
Magnetism, 223, 218.
Man-made laws, 241.
Miller excitement, 252.
Moral science, 262.
Marriage; 283, 254.
Mobocrats, 298.
Moon, 25, 27.
Money, 350, 319.

Miners, 361.
Manufactures, 361.

N

Neptune, 25.
Noyes, J. H., 281.

O

Oneida Community, 281.
Oxygen, 104.

P

Pagans, 69.
Paine, Thomas, 255, 30.
Pathology, 231.
Palmer, John H., 337.
Periods, 77, 84.
Plants fossilized, 118.
Phrenology, 389, 144, 135.
Psychology, 145.
Psychometry, 145.
Pitman, Ben, 204.
Phonography, 202.
Photography, 204.
Puppets, 204.
Physiology, 228.
Phillip, King of Macedon, 237.
Protestants, 254.
Presidents, 308, 305.
Postmaster General, 308.
Planets, 22.
Prison Discipline, 353.
Preachers, 103.
Parliament House, 360.
Philosophers, 382.
Paleontologists, 134, 386.

Q

Quakers, 282, 192.

R

Rothchilds, 332.
Religion, 72, 391, 376.
Railroads, 361.
Religious teaching of the sciences, 372.
Roman Catholics 390, 285, 400, 199.
Right, Triumphant, 405.

S

Spirit, 186, 185, 184, 180, 1, 376, 178, 176, 175, 189.
Shakespeare, 243, 6.
Smith, Joseph, 234, 20.
Sea Lions, 126.
Solomon, 138.
Soul of things, 128.
Silurian Age, 129.

Sun, 11.
Saturn, 24.
Sprague, Archie W., 179.
Spiritualism, 280, 173, 153.
Soldiers, Swiss, 189.
Soldiers, German, 189.
Substances disappear, 191.
Self love, 193.
Servants, man and maid, 211.
Sacrificial offerings, 213.
Stomach, 232.
Sympathetic nerves, 232.
Spleen, 232.
Socrates, 234.
Solon, 243, 246.
Saracen, 253.
Sabbath, 275, 241.
Science of religion, 270.
Science of association, 277.
Space, 2.
Sahara desert, 36.
Slaveholders, 295.
Secretary of War, 308; Secretary of Navy, 308; Secretary of Treasury, 308; Secretary of State, 394.
Salaries of officers, 314.
Shoddy, 317.
Star worshippers, 375.
Slade, Wm., 380.
Sumner, Senator, 398; Schurz, 398.
Salvation, 102.
Scientists, 442.

T

Time, 40, 1.
Trilobite, 129.

Telegraphing, 361, 206.
Trees, 215.
Theology, 59.
Taxes, 311, 311.
Thumb screws, 347.
Teachers, 403.

U

Uranus, 24.

V

Venus, 26.
Vital forces, 224.
Viper, 225.
Voters, 302.

W

Wallis, 187.
Watt, 207.
Witches, Salem, 174, 182.
Women, 245, 298.
Who shall be voted for, 301.
Worship, Truth, 196.

Z

Zoology, 384, 126.
Zeuloden, 131.
Zoroaster, 377.

www.ingramcontent.com/pod-product-compliance
Lightning Source LLC
Chambersburg PA
CBHW030556300426
44111CB00009B/1006